Hold on to
Your Veil,
Fatima!

Hold on to Your Veil, *Fatima!*

And Other Snapshots of Life in Contemporary Egypt

Sanna Negus

with a foreword by
Lawrence Wright

Garnet
PUBLISHING

HOLD ON TO YOUR VEIL, FATIMA!
And Other Snapshots of Life in Contemporary Egypt

Published by
Garnet Publishing Limited
8 Southern Court
South Street
Reading
RG1 4QS
UK

www.garnetpublishing.co.uk

First Edition

ISBN-13: 978-1-85964-238-2

British Library Cataloguing-in-Publication Data
A catalogue record for this book is available from the British Library

Typeset by Samantha Barden
Jacket design by David Rose
Cover photograph reproduced courtesy of istockphoto.com/
Ricardo De Mattos

Printed and bound in Lebanon by International Press:
interpress@int-press.com

Contents

— —

Foreword

Lawrence Wright

— —

Shortly after he got out of prison in 2002, Saad Eddin Ibrahim, the esteemed sociologist at the American University in Cairo, observed that Egypt has always been suspended between two opposing forces. "We say in this country that we look either to the sea or the sand," Ibrahim told me. The sea opens toward Europe and its traditions of democratic pluralism, secularism, openness, and Mediterranean sensuality; the sand leads toward the Arab traditions of tribalism, piety, the stoicism of the desert. For more than half a century, since the Islamists burned down the restaurants, cinemas, and nightclubs in cosmopolitan Cairo in 1952, Egypt has been turning its gaze toward the sand.

The fact that Egyptians have turned away from the liberalism and secularlism they once enjoyed has influenced Muslims everywhere. Egypt is the idea factory among Arab nations. The revolution led by Gamal Abdel Nasser in 1952 spread Egyptian versions of socialism and Nasser's romantic notions of Arab unity throughout the region, where they still resonate. The powerful television, cinema, and music industries based in Cairo have long been significant carriers of Egyptian ideals of fashion, values, and social attitudes. Egyptian politics, although intellectually impoverished, influence other political actors in the region, who seek to imitate the appearance of democracy within an autocratic system. Al Azhar, the thousand-year-old Islamic university in Old Cairo, is the closest approximation Sunni Muslims have to a Vatican; meanwhile, telegenic Egyptian clerics shape the minds and the morals of millions from Morocco to the Persian Gulf. Some ideas travel easier than others. When Anwar el-Sadat went to Jerusalem in 1977 and proclaimed in the Knesset, "We accept to live with you in a lasting and just peace," most Arab countries rejected the opportunity to open a new dialogue in the Middle East. On the other hand, the idea of politically active Islam – Islamism – first associated with the Muslim Brotherhood, was also born in Egypt and has now carried through the Muslim population all over the world. One only wishes that the Egyptian sense of humor was similarly contagious.

When I lived in Egypt, in 1969 to 1971, teaching at the American University in Cairo, the country was undergoing the Islamist uprising that would one day lead to al-Qaeda. Nasser, who had imprisoned and executed many of the leaders of the Muslim Brothers, died of a heart attack in September, 1970. Egypt at that time was a very religious country, but ostentatious displays of piety were rare. Nasser himself was an observant Muslim but a conspicuously secular leader. The fact that his successor, Sadat, carried the dark callous on his forehead – called the *zabiba*, or raisin – from countless hours of pressing his head into the prayer mat was actually embarrassing to many Cairenes. Now in Egypt, as in many

Muslim countries, the *zabiba* is a mark of honor. In those days, one seldom saw educated, middle-class Egyptian women dressed in black robes and hijabs – it was mostly a phenomenon of the villages. Nowadays, even at the American University, uncovered women have become increasingly rare. One of the many cruel ironies of Egyptian history is that the pious Sadat freed the members of the Muslim Brotherhood that Nasser had imprisoned, only to be murdered by their progeny after he signed the peace treaty with Israel.

The precursor to al-Qaeda was the Egyptian terrorist organization, al-Jihad, which was led by Ayman al-Zawahiri, an Egyptian doctor. Zawahiri grew up in Maadi, which was the center of sophisticated, Eurocentric Cairo, and yet Zawahiri started an undercover cell to overthrow the Egyptian government in 1966, when he was fifteen years old. Zawahiri and his organization would later form the core of the terrorist group started by Osama bin Laden. It was the Egyptians who had the brains, the experience, and the determination; one can argue that all bin Laden added was money and mystique. To this day, al-Qaeda is largely an Egyptian organization.

When I returned to Egypt shortly after 9/11 to study Zawahiri and al-Qaeda, few Westerners in the country were familiar with the organization or the thinking behind it. Among those few was Sanna Negus, who had been studying political Islam and radical Egyptian organizations well before that tragic event. A fluent Arabic speaker, well traveled in the Arab world, Negus is one of the most informed and well-connected reporters in the region. Now she has used her experience and her impressive storehouse of knowledge to write the book that has long been missing in the library of Western perception. Negus sees Egypt with a rounded understanding that goes past the stereotypes and introduces us to a culture rarely seen. She writes authoritatively about the unempowered Egyptians

– women, gays, Copts – who rarely play a part in contemporary narratives. One has the refreshing sense, after reading this book, that Negus has turned the country inside-out, making the repressed visible. Her knowing, amused eye sees Egypt in a fresh manner, free of the encrusted wisdom about Islam, radicalism, and misogyny that have become so yawningly familiar. She introduces us to a society that is still very much in turmoil, but also still spinning off ideas that will gain influence far beyond Egypt's dusty borders.

1

Islam is the solution?

—‑—

Mahdi's phone rang. We were just finishing filming my
TV debut, a story about veiling. The interview with
a veiled mother and unveiled daughter was drawing to a
close, and everyone seemed happy with it. As a finale, we
filmed the family photo album in the brown shades of a
Cairene living-room, lit by pale fluorescent lamps.

"Come to the office quickly, there's been a major accident
in New York!" a nervous voice shouted into cameraman
Mahdi's phone. We hurriedly packed away our cameras
and said our goodbyes to the mother and daughter. More
information on the accident became available while we were
on our way to the office: two airplanes had crashed into the
World Trade Center towers. All of a sudden, Muslim women's
veiling options, and with it my TV debut, seemed like the
least important things in the world.

We drove as fast as we could through the Cairo afternoon traffic jam, to the Video Cairo camera crew office, located next to the Egyptian TV building, beside the Nile. At the office, TV screens were showing for the first time the now-familiar images: the blazing twin towers; smoke, ash, panic. To my surprise, the soundman and a few other members of the office staff cheered – finally someone had taught the Americans a lesson! At this stage, the magnitude of the tragedy was not yet apparent – but looking at the pictures, I prayed for the sake of Egyptians and Arabs that the attackers weren't from the Middle-East. Fat chance.

Very soon it became evident that one of the perpetrators was an Egyptian, 33-year-old Muhammad Atta who had studied in Germany. In a widely published passport picture, square-faced Atta looks straight at the camera, piercingly serious, with a hint of scorn. This man, whom his university friends and tutors remember as a serious, conscientious student, allegedly steered the plane which hit the World Trade Center's north tower, between the 94th and 99th floors.[1]

Journalists from all over the world, especially from the United States, started flocking to Cairo. Fixers and translators worked around the clock, earning stacks of dollars but at the same time complaining about how distorted the stories were, written by journalists with little understanding of the region. Suddenly, in the eyes of America, Egypt had become the haven of terrorism, producer of the fanatic Attas.

We Cairenes didn't recognize this picture. So what if an individual was involved in a horrible act of terror? Could he tarnish the image of a peace-loving people, an image so carefully crafted by a country so dependent on tourism? Egyptians were as bemused as foreigners about the involve-ment of a countryman in this act of terror. But Egyptians wouldn't be Egyptians unless they turned tragedy into comedy.

According to a joke which rapidly made the rounds in Cairo, the perpetrators couldn't have been from the Arab world because the timing was planned to the second. There is no way Arabs – who have a nonchalant attitude towards time – could have done it!

Muhammad Atta's father was hurled into a media frenzy. Reporters from the far side of the world needed a story, but Atta senior stuck with his version of events: his son was innocent. The father held a 'press conference', which was little more than a monologue – and certainly not a question and answer session. His voice became louder, and his face redder as he defended his son: he asserted that he received a phone call from his son on 9/11, after the attacks had taken place. Footage from airport security cameras didn't convince him either: his son wasn't as broad-shouldered or big-nosed. Annoyed journalists looked in vain for answers.

In the streets of Cairo reactions were mixed. Once the magnitude of the destruction became evident, many expressed sympathy for the victims: an American friend told me that out of compassion, a taxi-driver even refused to take any payment for a journey. But almost immediately the conspiracy theories so loved by Egyptians started to circulate. According to one persistent rumour, 4000 Jews had been warned beforehand and so didn't show up for work on that faithful day. Mossad and the CIA were the real perpetrators, not Bin Laden, many believed. On the contrary, Bin Laden was seen as a kind of resistance hero, who was admired either openly or in secret.

The Egyptian press, however, stayed silent on the fact that an Egyptian seemed to have taken part in this horrific action. Their own years of violence were still fresh in the minds of many Egyptians: in the clashes of radical Islamists against state security forces. Between 1992 and 1997 about 1200 Egyptians were killed.

Egypt can be considered as the birthplace of modern Islamism. The ideological roots of Islamism or political Islam stretch back to the establishment of the Muslim Brotherhood organization in the 1920s. This group, which fought against colonialism and supported an Islamic revival, paved the way for the more radical groups of today. The ideology became radicalized in the 1960s and '70s when young fanatics in the Middle East harnessed a distorted interpretation of Islam to the widespread fight against governments. Despite the terror attacks of the 1990s, the strategic fight has ceased in Egypt, although international Islamist terrorists represent a continuation of the same extremist ideology.

Hasan al-Banna, the founder of the Muslim Brotherhood, has been described as a charismatic leader, who ran his organization with an authoritarian grip. Preaching the strict moral code he had adopted as young boy (an unfaltering belief in the omnipotence of God), while at the same time cherishing good physical health, were the guiding principles that shaped al-Banna's life. He called believers to salvation, while the Brotherhood's military wing launched attacks on the British occupier. To this day, al-Banna's thoughts form the ideological foundation of the Muslim Brotherhood.

Al-Banna's activities were informed by movements within Egyptian society as a whole. Throughout al-Banna's life, Egypt was (directly or indirectly) occupied by the British. In 1882, they had captured Egypt and made it into a 'Protectorate': the King and the Parliament were the nominal rulers, but real power lay in British hands.

A nationalist awakening in the early 20th century led to mass demonstrations initiated by the *Wafd* (Delegation)

Party, demanding independence. This demand was realized only partially: in 1922 the Protectorate was abolished, and Egypt declared formally independent. However, the British ensured that neither the Egyptian monarch, King Fuad, nor the parliament acted against the interest of their former colonizer. In addition, the British Army maintained an obviously visible presence.

Egyptian society was undergoing a transformation brought about by modernization, industrialization and the rise of capitalism. The population was increasing fast, and rural to urban migration increased steadily. Conditions in working-class quarters of cities were often appalling, and poor sanitation led to frequent epidemics. The global depression of the 1930s only made the circumstances of the poorest worse.

By contrast, Europeans in Egypt enjoyed an easy life. French cafés and cinemas were visible reminders of the foreign presence. The Egyptian elite adopted not only European customs, but also thinking and beliefs. They spoke French and English with better fluency than Arabic, and dressed according to European fashion. Many Egyptian secularists believed that West was better than East.[2]

Hasan al-Banna was born into this transitional period, in the city of Mahmudiyya in the Nile Delta. Even as a young boy he showed signs of religiosity, and his childhood games gave clues to his future calling: he arranged the neighbourhood boys into 'believers' and 'non-believers' and acted out wars in this vein. As an adult, al-Banna was serious, deliberate and even though he might laugh with others, he would never make a joke himself.

One of the strongest influences on young al-Banna's ideology was Sufism, the mystic element of Islam. Al-Azhar university in Cairo, the highest authority of Sunni Islamic learning, actively doesn't recognize Sufism on the grounds that it is mixed with folk traditions (such as visiting tombs and celebrating saints' birthdays). Al-Banna was a member of a Sufi group that emphasized the importance of *shari'a* (Islamic law) and following the rituals described in the holy scriptures: the Qur'an, the Sunna (i.e. Muslim law based on the Prophet's words and actions), and the *hadith* (the traditions).

Although religion was al-Banna's calling, he didn't choose to study at the distinguished Islamic al-Azhar university (where most Sunni Islamic scholars study). Instead, he graduated as an Arabic teacher from the new Dar al-Ulum university, described as a combination of modern education and Islamic learning.[3] Al-Banna thus combined successfully the roles of a teacher and a preacher.

On moving to Cairo, al-Banna saw for the first time the Westernization of Egyptian society, which he equated to atheism and immorality. He became convinced that Egyptians were no longer following true Islam. In his eyes, the entire society was polluted by vices: alcohol, half-naked women, theatres and dance salons. In 1924, during this formative period in al-Banna's life, Kemal Atatürk abolished the Islamic caliphate. The discussion over the future of the *umma*, the Islamic community, was heated but attempts to restore the caliphate derailed.

In 1927, al-Banna was appointed to a teaching position in Isma'iliya, a town on the Suez Canal. The British Suez Canal Company, which managed the canal, had its headquarters there, and the town also hosted a British barracks, making foreigners were clearly evident on the streets of Isma'iliya. Al-Banna observed how foreigners lived a life of luxury thanks to the canal profits, while Egyptians were starving. In the midst of this self-evident inequality, al-Banna became convinced of his mission in life: corruption of Egyptian society must come to an end.

Al-Banna started to preach in coffee shops and to give private lectures. His message was simple: only a return to true Islam could heal the feeling of alienation, because Islam is comprehensive. Like many Muslim reformers, al-Banna emphasized the importance of identity: Muslims had in Islam their own perfect set of values, which needed to be restored to the place it deserved.

His unfaltering willpower and teacher's patience started to bear fruit, and he gained more and more followers. He first termed his organization as 'The Muslim Brotherhood' (*al-Ikhwun al-Muslimun*) in 1928; al-Banna was only 22 years old at the time, but already an old-timer in organizational life.[4]

In the beginning, the Muslim Brotherhood's goal was twofold: the advancement of true Islam – as defined by al-Banna – and fighting against foreign occupation. The Brotherhood's message was in tune with the times and soon it spread to other northern Egyptian towns, and its headquarters were moved to Cairo. Although the Brotherhood grew continually, it wasn't an open-to-all organization; rather, its members were admitted through a gradual process. The same policy applies today.

Naturally, al-Banna was the leader of the organization, and was referred to as the General Guide (*al-murshid al-'amm*). The name refers to a guide under God's command, who guides others to God. The members had to take an oath of loyalty to the Guide, in which they promised to obey him absolutely and under all circumstances. Swearing an oath (*bay'a*) derives from the early Islamic era – followers of the Prophet pledged allegiance to him – but also from Sufism: a Sufi initiate takes an oath to his teacher. This swearing of allegiance points to al-Banna's appreciation of strict rules, and the distinct roles of the ruler and the ruled. It also hints at authoritarianism – the Leader's actions were not to be questioned.

A young man (who preferred to stay anonymous) who was involved in Brotherhood activities during the 1990s told me about his experience of the importance of discipline and rules:

> I joined the Brotherhood when I was in high school. I had been living the Persian Gulf, so I didn't know many people and it was very difficult to make friends. I didn't join for political reasons – it was mostly the desire to become more religious, and also to be encouraged to be more observant.
>
> Then I met an older Brother, who took me to a mosque to meet others. I had always liked the company of older boys, and this was like another world. They painted a picture of living happily, and of entry to Paradise – of course I couldn't say no to something like that!
>
> Each Brother had a 'sponsor Brother' (*al-akh al-mas'ul*), once he became a full member (*al-akh al-amil*). The 'sponsor Brother' acted as a go-between if the senior Brothers wanted to talk to me. This same categorization is still in use: you get to become a full member if the 'sponsor Brother' thinks that you are mature enough. The 'sponsor Brother' is never questioned; everything is disciplined but no one abuses the loyalty (*bay'a*). I believed in all the discipline, and that you didn't question the leaders.
>
> Their way of bonding is to have as much collective activity as possible, to fill the day of the young Brother to an extent that would make any life outside the Brothers unimaginable. It's a gradual process of organizing your day: meet every morning at 5 am in the mosque for prayers … then you had something every day, one or two meetings… And the more meetings you had, the more self-important you felt. An empty day would make you feel almost envious, that you hadn't made it yet to an adequate rank within the organization.
>
> You also feel it's a religious duty to initiate things, and that's the thing that is completely absent from any other political organization, or even from professional life. You feel that if you do not initiate activities, then other members who do, are sort of

better Muslims, they get more scores – this becomes a mentality of keeping scores for the next life. Of course there are all sorts of human tensions, and envy and competition, but for the younger generations who are carrying the movement, they don't have these things because they know that their reward is in the next life and there's no access to the scores, so you can't know how well you're faring!

As the Brotherhood's membership grew, its activities started more and more to resemble those of a political party rather than an Islamic charity. Its programme, and particularly its criticism of the government, was attractive to those elements of the populace which most suffered from the economic depression: civil servants, students, the urban working class and farmers.

The starting point of al-Banna's ideology was the omnipotence of Islam: it covers all aspects of life, in this world and in the thereafter. Muslims should therefore return to the origins of Islam – Qur'an, Sunna and teachings of forefathers (*salaf*) – and not follow Islamic jurists' interpretations (*taqlid*). At the same time, he encouraged independent reasoning (*ijtihad*) so that Muslims could respond to the demands of modern times.

Like many modernists before him, al-Banna believed that a return to Islam would not only strengthen the nation's self-esteem, but also its political power vis-à-vis the West. His ideal societal model was Muhammad's Medina community, which would become a reality if believers went through a thorough internal revival. However, for many, their faith lay dormant, and so the Brotherhood had to awaken it with the call (*da'wa*) to Islam.

The Brotherhood's ultimate goal was to establish an Islamic state, or societal system. Its constitution would be the *shari'a,* it would have one creed, and centralized governance. The Brotherhood slogan puts it this way:

> God is our objective, the Qur'an is our constitution, the Prophet
> is our leader, Struggle is our way and death for the sake of God is
> the highest of our aspirations.[5]

In other words, the possibility of using violence to establish
an Islamic state hadn't been ruled out – a means hinted at
in the existence of the secret apparatus. Al-Banna's primary
objective, however, was to liberate Egypt from its occupiers, and
to establish an independent state. Unlike secular nationalists,
al-Banna considered the wider Islamic community, the *umma*,
to be more important than identity based on nationality.
Al-Banna saw the Brotherhood as the vanguard of Islam, with
himself as its leader, ready for martyrdom. The details and
practicalities of an Islamic state were of secondary importance
to him – they would take shape on their own once the state
was established. This obscurantism remains a problem that
the Brotherhood suffers from to this day.

In al-Banna's vision, the political structure of an Islamic
state comprises three elements: the Qur'an (as the basis of
the constitution); a parliament (formed by a single party,
functioning by consultation, *shura*), and a ruler (who must
abide by Islam and will of the people, and can be ousted
by majority vote). Decision-making would be based on a
simple majority vote, which the minority would agree with in
the end. But as a precaution, discussion of philosophy and
hypothetic questions should be avoided.[6]

This model is authoritarian in style, where opposition is
not allowed to function fully. Al-Banna naively assumed that
the *umma* would agree on basic issues. He also sketched an
informer system, whereby citizens would keep an eye on each
other. To him private and public were inseparable.

Al-Banna was happily married and had five daughters
and a son. Advancement of women's position wasn't exactly

top of the Brotherhood's agenda – neither is it today. Al-Banna addressed the subject in a small pamphlet – *al-Mar'a al-Muslima* (The Muslim Woman), which is a rather provocative piece of work, in which al-Banna quotes various conservative *hadith*s which mostly portray women as seductresses who must be veiled and banished from the streets.

Puzzled by this booklet, I went to ask Hasan al-Banna's youngest brother, the last of the siblings still alive, what his take on it was. Gamal al-Banna is in his 80s, a former workers' union activist, and an author, with greenish eyes and an infectious laugh. Like many elderly Egyptian men, he favours dark safari suits and thick-rimmed glasses.

Big brother Hasan was 14 years older than Gamal, and their relationship was "dialectic, but warm", as Gamal puts it. The younger brother has become a vocal critic of today's Brotherhood, charging it with stagnation and failing to respond to modern day demands, instead still following the teachings of its former leader literally.

When I arrived, Gamal al-Banna was sitting at his desk, surrounded by bookshelves stacked from floor to ceiling. He proffered foil–wrapped chocolate bonbons and gently stroked a white cat, which purred in his lap. He, too, has written a book called 'The Muslim Woman', but in which he puts forward altogether different ideas from those of his brother, for example that veiling is not a religious obligation per se. He was amused at the memory of his brother's booklet and thought it best to defend him.

> Hasan's eldest child was a girl – Wafaa' – and the father would have wanted her to attend university and get a degree. But other Brothers were against this idea and so Wafaa' had to settle for vocational training. My brother's family matters were openly discussed in the Brotherhood.[7]

Many Islamists – and conservative Muslims in general – see women's role as being tied to biology. The basic assumption is that all women want to, and can, have children. Al-Banna wanted to restrict women's educational pursuits, and their work outside the home. Yet in reality, the 1924 constitution gave women the right to study at universities, while in the countryside and in manual labour, men and women have been working side by side for centuries.[8] At the end of the day, his conservative ideas on the position of women didn't much differ from the mainstream opinions of the day. But it was his thoughts on struggle, *jihad*, that sets him apart from the traditional interpretation.

The term *jihad* (struggle) has a dual connotation in traditional Islamic theology: both an inner striving against evil thoughts (greater *jihad*), and an external struggle in defence of Islam (lesser *jihad*). In al-Banna's view, the inner *jihad* is the basis for all action, and the armed struggle is the last resort to defend Islam. During this period, all of Egyptian society was in turmoil, and al-Banna's foremost reference was anti-British activity. He drew support for his view from the Qur'an:

> Warfare is ordained for you, though it is hateful unto you; but it may happen that ye hate a thing which is good for you, and it may happen that ye love a thing which is bad for you. Allah knoweth, ye know not. (2:216)[9]

For al-Banna, armed struggle was both an individual and communal obligation. He didn't rule out offensive warfare – thus differing from the Islamic canon – but he also didn't specify the circumstances for it. He quoted often a *hadith*, which remains the basis for Brotherhood's attitude towards *jihad* to this day: "One of the loftiest forms of *jihad* is to utter a word of truth in the presence of a tyrannical ruler."[10]

During the period when al-Banna was formulating his ideas, the global economic depression, mounting lack of trust in the government, and the privations of war had brought Egypt to the brink of chaos. The Anglo-Egyptian Treaty of 1936 gave independence to Egypt in principle, but the British Army tenaciously remained. The Brotherhood refused to accept the Treaty and declared *jihad* against the British. And al-Banna really meant it – in probably the same year, the Brotherhood established a secret, armed special unit.[11]

At the time, Egypt had several paramilitary groups, but the Brotherhood's 'Boy Scouts' were the largest and most powerful of them. The fighters of the secret force, the *mujahidun*, were recruited from the Brotherhood's scout-like youth division, the Rovers, which instilled discipline, military spirit and solidarity. This emphasis on cultivating good physical health and the idea of training camps were adopted from European scout organizations.[12]

The secret group's role was initially to defend the Brotherhood (and Islam). It amassed weapons via army contacts – among them the future Free Officers Gamal Abdel Nasser and Anwar Sadat. When the domestic scene got more restless, the group conducted revenge attacks on the police. The government had finally woken up to the Brotherhood's political power: by the 1940s it had over 300 branches, and more than a million members (Egypt's population at the time was less than 20 million). The Brotherhood had infiltrated the professional associations, and ran its own factories, companies, schools and hospitals. It was particularly active in the social sector, long neglected by the government. The Brotherhood had become a state within state.[13]

When the state of Israel was declared in 1948, the Brotherhood's best fighters fought side-by-side with their Palestinian co-religionists. That year was particularly grim for the Brotherhood: Prime Minister Nuqrashi declared a state of emergency, and ordered the Brotherhood to disband. Three weeks later, Nuqrashi was shot dead – by a Brother who is presumed to have acted without al-Banna's authorization. The Supreme Guide had previously expressed concern over losing control of the secret force. Al-Banna proclaimed his innocence of the murder, but he was arrested briefly. On his release on 12th February 1949, an officer of the Special Police Force shot him dead – with the blessing of the new Prime Minister.[14]

Hasan al-Banna's thought made an impression on another Islamist thinker, Sayyid Qutb (1906–66), who is often considered to be the father of radical Islamism. His drastically different theses – of the un-Islamic nature of all society, and of *jihad* – forced the Muslim Brotherhood underground, and gave an impetus to newer, more radical groups.

Like al-Banna, Qutb graduated as a teacher from Dar al-Ulum and quickly worked his way to employment as an inspector at the Ministry of Education. Similar to his mentor, the young country boy found city-life confusing, and started to unravel his thoughts by writing poems, essays and even love stories. Later, he was to renounce these works as un-Islamic.

In the 1930s and '40s, Qutb participated in the literary discussion about Egyptian identity under foreign occupation, and made his mark as a literary critic. But he soon started to use more Islamic arguments and references, particularly when criticizing the moral decay of his fellow citizens.

But it was only after a study trip to the United States in 1948 that Qutb became convinced of the moral and cultural superiority of Islam. To him, the United States – which openly supported the newly-established state of Israel – could best be described in terms of materialism, racism and sexual promiscuity. When he returned home in 1951, he found kindred spirits in the Brotherhood, which Qutb considered to be the best weapon against Western cultural imperialism.[15]

After the death of Hasan al-Banna, the Brotherhood had been torn by inner disputes. The new General Guide, Judge Hasan al-Hudaybi, gave the movement a dignified image, but he didn't enjoy the support of the ranks. He condemned attacks by the secret force, unintentionally making it even more independent. Quiet and introverted, Qutb was designated as the director of the Section for the Propagation of Call and Publishing. He was to fill the ideological vacuum left by al-Banna's death.[16]

In the meantime, co-operation between the Brotherhood and the Free Officers continued. The Brotherhood believed that the Officers had both a similar social programme (based on Islam), and a will to oust the occupiers (and the monarchy). For their part, the Free Officers were impressed by the attacks launched by the *mujahidun*, and the Brotherhood's internal discipline. Both sides were to be disappointed in their expectations.

The Brotherhood was very active in the preparations for the Revolution. The secret force was to protect foreign interests and strategic communication centres. It was also supposed to garner popular support – should it not arise spontaneously – and oversee security if the police refused to co-operate with the army. As it turned out, none of these measures were needed, because the Revolution took place with negligible resistance.[17]

It wasn't long before the Brotherhood became disillusioned with the new regime's reforms. They didn't apply Islamic legislation, but rather seemed to support secularism and socialism. The Brotherhood started to spread anti-government propaganda and the government counter-attacked with their own Islamic campaign. The incipient power-struggle charged the atmosphere.

While President Nasser was giving a speech in Alexandria in 1954, someone from the crowd shot at him. Once more the attacker was a member of the secret apparatus, who according to the Brotherhood again didn't have organizational approval for the deed. However, this act gave Nasser a perfect excuse to settle the score with the group. The Brotherhood was abolished, its assets were confiscated and its high ranking members were put behind bars. Qutb was accused of plotting a revolution, and given a 15-year hard labour sentence. Prison practically annihilated the organisation, while confessions under torture crushed the core group's morale.[18] Except Sayyid Qutb's.

Utterly disappointed by Nasser's empty promises, Qutb became embittered. He had suffered from bad health all his life, but in prison his condition deteriorated to such an extent that he served most of his sentence in the prison hospital. All this added to the introverted man's depression and isolation from the rest of the world. He purged his bitterness by writing. He wrote an extensive Qur'anic commentary in prison, as well as his most controversial book, *Ma'alim fi al-Tariq* (Milestones), which radical Islamists adopted as a guide. His sisters smuggled the texts out of the prison and gave them to the Brothers.

Qutb's thoughts on an Islamic state were similar to al-Banna's, yet even more obscure. To Qutb, Islam was all-encompassing, so practical details were of less importance. Like al-Banna, Qutb believed in reform of the individual, and the importance of Islam's original sources. But Qutb differed radically from other thinkers on his views of Egyptian society. In his view, the whole society had side-stepped from the sphere of Islam, to the extent that it lived in *jahiliyya* (pagan ignorance). Qutb was the first to use this word to describe modern societies – Muslims had generally used it when referring to pre-Islamic era.

Because Qutb (like al-Banna) was a self-taught religious thinker, he could more easily criticize the theologians of al-Azhar, and think more independently (he emphasized the importance of independent reasoning, *ijtihad*). On the other hand, this led to his thoughts shifting further away from commonly accepted positions – his personal experiences had clearly affected his judgemental thinking.

Towards the end of his life, his world-view became completely binary: only two kinds of societies existed – Islamic, or ignorant (*jahili*, thus un-Islamic.) In his mind, even Islamic societies just pretended to be Islamic, because they didn't give the highest authority to God, but rather supported un-Islamic rulers, like Nasser. Qutb suggested that a vanguard was needed to awaken the dormant faith of individual Muslims. They needed to keep themselves separate from others, but at the same time they should learn the habits and values of the *jahiliyya*, in order to overcome it. His ideal society was the Medina of Muhammad, which lived surrounded by *jahiliyya*, but proved to be victorious in the end.

To Qutb, the ideal Islamic society wasn't confined to a certain place, but rather a Muslim's home was wherever *shari'a* was properly applied. Qutb identified with his religion, not his nationality, regarding himself as a member of the *umma*, within the realm of Islam. A Muslim's only relatives should be those who believed in God – family, tribe or nation came second.[19]

Intimately connected to the idea of an un-Islamic society, was the notion of fighting against it – *jihad*. Qutb's interpretation of struggle was the most controversial of his theories. According to him, *jihad* was justified against un-Islamic (*jahili*) rulers. Although he didn't mention Nasser by name, it was obvious that Qutb considered Nasser's regime to be un-Islamic. To Qutb, *jihad* was a tool of Islamic revolution.

According to Qutb, the revolution was to be led by a vanguard, which would correct the beliefs of the age of ignorance by preaching and persuading. It could also use force and struggle (*jihad*) when destroying pagan institutions and authorities which forbade Muslims to renew their faith. If anyone was to obstruct people in their belief, they had to be fought until they admitted defeat – or died. This clearly referred to Nasser, who had jailed Islamist dissidents.

To Qutb *jihad* wasn't just defensive warfare, and he selected Qur'anic verses to support his thesis:

> Tell those who disbelieve that if they cease (from persecution of believers) that which is past will be forgiven them; but if they return (thereto) then the example of the men of old hath already gone (before them, for a warning). And fight them until persecution is no more, and religion is all for Allah. But if they cease, then lo! Allah is Seer of what they do. And if they turn away, then know that Allah is your Befriender – a Transcendent Patron, a Transcendent Helper! (8:38–40)

For Qutb, these verses encapsulated the essence of *jihad:* to establish God's authority on earth. To him, those who fought against tyrants were on a higher morale plane due to their faith. The struggle may lead to death, but to a *mujahid*, a martyr's death was the way to Paradise, while tyrants burned in the fires of Hell. In the end, the Believer would receive the highest of rewards: the pleasure of God.[20]

In 1964 Qutb was released from Liman Tora prison. He held small gatherings with his supporters until mass arrests of Brotherhood members began anew in summer 1965. The Muslim Brotherhood was accused of plotting an extensive conspiracy against the state; Qutb was charged with terrorist activities and encouraging sedition – the principal evidence against him was *Ma'alim fi al-Tariq*.[21]

General Fuad Allam, a former chief of the Egyptian Intelligence's Interrogations was present during Qutb's interrogation. Allam, who is in his 70s, has become a kind of semi-official expert on Islamism, because he took part in all the major Islamist grillings.

I met Allam at his home, a heavily guarded villa in the middle-class Muhandisin neighbourhood of Cairo. Genial as an uncle, it is hard to picture Allam as the head of such a notorious unit. We sat in his reception room, decorated in the Louis XV style, much loved by the Egyptians: golden, curvy chair backs, colourful carpets and an Indian horoscope tapestry on the wall, crystal ashtrays on side tables. His male servant left a tray by the door with *karkadeh*, a wine-coloured hibiscus drink.

Although Allam attended Qutb's interrogation only very briefly, the outwardly fragile radical thinker left an impression on him:

> He spoke very calmly, steadily, like I am now. He was truly impressive. Even if you knew nothing about his background, or that he had a religious background, he would have made an impression on you.

Allam was of the opinion that it was specifically Qutb's illness that had affected the radicalism of his message.

> He was very disturbed mentally. He was also physically ill; at that time, there wasn't a proper cure for tuberculosis. He was someone who knew he was dying. And being in prison added to the feeling of being smothered slowly. I believe that a combination of his illness and the atmosphere in prison created in him a disturbed mental state, and confused his thoughts. Above all, it made him jealous of other people. That's Sayyid Qutb.

Qutb denied the charges, but not what he had written. He was sentenced to death, and hanged in 1966. Many youngsters, inspired by Qutb's texts, revere him as a martyr.

Several of the younger generation Islamists imprisoned in the 1960s and '70s shared their cells with older Brothers, who didn't accept Qutb's philosophy and denied violence. These youngsters were disappointed by this pessimism, and found in Qutb's action-oriented message an escape from frustration. They read the Qur'an selectively, and (in particular members of smaller radical groups) were quite ignorant of the principles of Islam. For many of these groups, the real objective was a revolution through armed struggle.

Radicalization received another boost in the humiliating defeat of the 1967 Six Day War. In the early 1960s, some Arab countries had misgivings that Israel was developing a nuclear weapon. Egypt and Syria signed a defence agreement, which in turn made Israel nervous. There were incidents on the Syrian–Israeli border. Israel threatened to occupy Damascus, and overthrow the Syrian government for its support for Palestinian fighters. The situation grew tenser when Soviet intelligence sources told Nasser (untruthfully) that Israel had increased its troops on the Syrian border. Israel provoked war, because it knew it was stronger militarily than the Arab states.

Nasser responded to the Israeli threats by demanding that UN observers withdraw from the Sinai. Egypt concentrated troops in the Sinai and signed a defence pact with Jordan as well. Nasser believed that if Israel attacked, other Arab countries would send troops to Egypt's aid. Right until the end, Nasser believed that war could be avoided, and that Israel wouldn't attack. Green conscripts were sent to the frontline. The final straw was the Egyptian blockade of the Straits of Tiran, which Israel took as a declaration of war.

Israel attacked on 5th June and practically destroyed Egypt's air force in a matter of hours. Israel advanced with ease across the Sinai, all the way to Suez. Egypt lost 12,000 men and the Sinai Peninsula; Jordan lost the West Bank, and Syria lost the Golan Heights. The capture of East Jerusalem affected all Muslims, as Jerusalem is the third holiest city in Islam, after Mecca and Medina. Egypt, Nasser and the whole Arab world were shocked by the crushing defeat. Nasser offered to resign on 9th June. The masses gathered on the streets in support, and so the president withdrew his resignation.[22]

But Nasser's prestige had suffered a telling blow. No longer did the nation buy the mantra of Arab socialism and secular ideology; many ascribed the defeat to the abandonment of Islam. The religious stream gained strength: mosque attendance went up; religious literature was printed in greater quantities; and more and more women took the Islamic veil. Migrant workers, returning from the Persian Gulf oil countries, brought back the influence of Wahhabism, a more conservative school of Islamic thinking, which interprets Islam in a more literal way than the school prevalent in Egypt.

Another sign of growing religiosity was the boom in mosque building. While in 1970, the whole of Egypt had 20,000 private mosques, by 1981 the number had risen to 46,000, and (according to some estimates) to 150,000 by 1991. The mosques were funded by the voluntary Islamic *zakat* tax, and by contributions from the Gulf countries. The building boom was further encouraged by a law which allowed mosques to be built tax-free.[23]

At precisely the same time, unemployment was on the rise and recent graduates were no longer guaranteed jobs by the state. Young engineers and lawyers couldn't find employment to match their skills, and so had to seek work as mechanics, waiters and taxi drivers. This 'lumpen intelligentsia' came to realize that education was no longer a foolproof way to a better standard of living. These people formed the backbone of the Muslim Brotherhood's support.[24]

In Nasser's Egypt, political participation was strictly limited: the only legal party was the Socialist Arab Union, led by the president. Nasser had failed to accomodate the religious and political opposition, because he was too afraid to test his real popularity by allowing a multi-party system. Qutb's revolutionary message filled this ideological vacuum, which had been left in part by the clampdown on the Muslim Brotherhood. Young, action-oriented Islamists distanced themselves from the Brotherhood, which was becoming a moderate reformist movement. Some of these young radicals took Qutb's theories on *jahilyya* and *jihad* to the extreme, often with destructive results.

After Nasser's death in 1970, the vice-president – Anwar Sadat – took the helm. Almost immediately, he released hundreds of Brothers because he saw them as a counter-weight to the Left and to Nasserists, who criticized the new president's anti-Soviet policy. Sadat didn't fill Nasser's boots well: he was neither particularly charismatic nor popular, so he opted to play political games. He changed the political field a bit – the only legal party was reformulated into Left, Centre and Right.

Simultaneously, he encouraged Islamist infiltration of student unions and professional organizations. He liked to portray himself as the Believer President, praying in front of TV cameras. Egyptian citizens just didn't buy his piety. Before his death, a 'raisin' (the aubergine-coloured callous marking frequent praying) had appeared on his forehead. In Cairo after his assassination, the joke was that the street sweepers cleaning the reviewing stand had found his 'raisin' on the floor.[25]

But Sadat also supported religiosity more widely – after all, he had sworn an oath to Hasan al-Banna of the

Brotherhood.[26] In 1971, the constitution was altered so that the *shari'a* became one of the sources of legislation (in practice, this referred to family law). The Muslim Brotherhood was allowed to function relatively freely, and it even got permission to publish its newspaper, *al-Da'wa,* which had been banned for more than 20 years. The hope of obtaining legal status motivated the Brotherhood to support the government.[27]

Compared to the charismatic Nasser, Sadat was considered lightweight as a statesman. But he made returning the Sinai to Egypt his mission. He first approached the Americans, so that they would pressure Israel to withdraw. Sadat's aim was to end the stalemate, using international attention to push Israel to withdraw to the 1967 borders. When talks led nowhere, Sadat started toying with the idea of a partial re-invasion of the Sinai. Syria and Jordan joined in the plan of attacking Israel.

Egypt and Syria attacked simultaneously on October 6th as Muslims were observing Ramadan and Jews Yom Kippur. The attack took Israel completely by surprise; it hadn't considered Egypt's military build-up to be serious. Israel didn't think an Arab surprise attack would be possible – its intelligence failed. Egypt successfully crossed Suez and the Bar Lev line – this in itself was a victory for the Egyptians.

Although Israel was eventually able to win the war militarily, in the Arab World this was seen as a symbolic victory, and proof that the Arabs were catching up with Israel in the arms race. In terms of losses of men and equipment to both sides, the end of the war was closer to a draw than had been the result in 1967. Other Arab countries had supported the war effort with an oil embargo, and they were revelling in their new-found power.[28]

Sadat had used a lot of Islamic symbolism and rhetoric during the war, bestowing upon it a morally sanctified label. The use of religious symbols continued to grow, and Sadat supported this trend. As a result of the war, Sadat experienced increased international recognition as a noteworthy head of state, but at home the flush of victory turned sour very quickly: the Sinai remained under Israeli occupation and many regarded his religiosity as superficial.

Throughout this period, small groups of loose affiliates split off from the Muslim Brotherhood. They were termed *anqud* (cluster of grapes), from the idea that removal of one bunch didn't hurt the whole vine. These small groups were very transient – many broke apart, or merged with another whenever the police got wind of them.[29] Whatever the internal dynamic, external support for these groups was always marginal.

First to study Islamist groups' support in the 1970s, sociologist Saad Eddin Ibrahim discovered that most members of radical groups were recruited at universities or among recent graduates. Three recruitment channels emerged: family ties, friendships, and mosques. Rank and file members were younger (17–26 years) than their leaders, and the majority were from the countryside (particularly from Upper Egypt) and provincial towns. They tended to be better educated than their middle-class parents, often having chosen to study engineering, medicine or pharmacy – subjects for which entry requirements were the toughest. In other words, they were the extraordinarily talented sons of ordinary families.

What made these men join radical movements? Ibrahim suggested that it was an identity crisis: young country boys encountered Western influence in Cairo for the first time in their lives – just as Hasan al-Banna and Sayyid Qutb had experienced it. In the 1970s, Egyptian society was again in turmoil: migration to cities was on the rise, but the state was unable to offer economic or political opportunities to young graduates. At the same time, American influence on Egypt, and the financial prosperity of those who had benefited from the Open Door policy (few, and far between) – became glaringly obvious. Opportunities for immediate employment and prospects for the future looked very bleak for most Egyptian youths.[30]

In comparison, radical Islam offered a culturally acceptable (albeit distorted) way out of despair and social inequality. Through Islam, and by destroying 'Pagan' (i.e. Western) structures, these youngsters believed they could not only have a positive effect on their own fortunes, but also heal the rest of Egyptian society. Scholar Nazih Ayubi put it this way:

> The Islamic militants are not rebellious because they are opposed to development (or even, to an extent, to modernisation), but rather because they desired it so strongly and yet could not get it. [...] The Islamists are not angry because the aeroplane has replaced the camel; they are angry because they could not get on the aeroplane.[31]

Later on, they did indeed get on those aeroplanes. The first evidence of the existence of armed Islamist groups became apparent in 1974, with the 'Technical Military Academy' case. Basing its ideology on Qutb's thinking, the Islamic Liberation Party believed in direct action (preferably a coup d'état), followed by an Islamic transformation of society. The plan was to break into the Technical Military Academy in Cairo and steal weapons and ammunition. They intended to continue to the ruling party headquarters where Sadat was giving a speech, and assassinate him. The plan failed and 30 soldiers were killed in the action.[32] Although the group was broken up and jailed, there was more to come.

Agronomist Shukri Mustafa was one of the Islamists released by Sadat. He had participated in Muslim Brotherhood activities, and while in prison he read Qutb's radical thesis and embraced it. After completing his prison sentence, he began to preach in his hometown Asyut, in southern, Upper Egypt, where many of the Islamist groups stemmed from. Charismatic, fiery-eyed Mustafa quickly gained followers and he started to call his movement the Society of Muslims.

Mustafa was an authoritarian leader, and unusually for Islamist movements, within his group he was revered as the *Mahdi*, a messianic figure. Yet he didn't know the Qur'an very well, and read it selectively: only the *suras* supporting his narrow vision were deemed correct.

He wanted to destroy what he considered an un-Islamic state and erect a new, Islamic society in its place. Armed *jihad* (struggle) would serve as a revolutionary tool. For Mustafa, those who heard his *da'wa* (call) but failed to embrace it, deserved to die. In this, he was an early proponent of 'takfirism', denouncing someone as infidel. Taking the possessions of non-believers was also deemed lawful – many Islamist groups regarded it as legitimate to rob Coptic Christians' shops because they didn't convert to Islam. Like many cult leaders, Mustafa's theories weren't well developed, and he didn't have a plan as to how the group would function in the unlikely event that it gained power.

Mustafa took Qutb's idea of isolation from the rest of *jahili* ('ignorant') society literally. For Mustafa, isolation meant a physical move away from the un-Islamic society: *hijra* (this term usually refers to the Prophet Muhammad's flight from Mecca to Medina in AD 622, which marks the beginning of the Muslim (Hijri) dating system. Some of the group's members fled to mountain caves near Asyut. By establishing their own 'orthodox' Islamic society there, the group could denounce others as infidels (*takfir*).[33]

The Islamic Society recruited both men and women, whom Mustafa married to each other. The couples lived in furnished flats in working-class quarters of Cairo, and they didn't consider *jahili* marriages legal. Often the men of the group worked temporarily in the Persian Gulf oil states and sent their salaries back to the group. Upon return, they were 'rewarded' with a wife. Group members were not allowed to be state employees or to join the army. This policy was based on the requirement for 'isolation': the group maintained internal purity, and wasn't financially dependent on the state it viewed as un-Islamic.

The group made the headlines in 1976 when its internal disputes broke out into violence requiring police intervention. Several members were arrested, although Mustafa himself managed to avoid prison. The Egyptian press described the members as 'fanatic militants' and labelled the group *al-Takfir wa al-Hijra* (Excommunication and Flight).

Mustafa continued to demand the release of the detained group members, but when nothing happened, the group kidnapped the former Minister for Religious Affairs. They also demanded a ransom and an apology for slandering the group. When their demands weren't met, the minister was killed. In the trial after the mass arrests, it became apparent that the group had managed to recruit between 3000 and 5000 members around the country. Mustafa and four other leaders were sentenced to death.[34]

Fuad Allam was again present at the interrogation. I asked him what Shukri Mustafa was like as a person:

Crazy. But one has to take into consideration the circumstances: he used to live in the streets and mosques, because his father had remarried and the new wife kicked him out. He was a poor student at the agricultural faculty. When he was arrested, he had a large number of followers and he believed himself to be a prophet.

At this time, many Islamic groups (*al-gama'at al-islamiyya*) enjoyed broad support on university campuses, and soon they dominated the most important student organizations. Sadat himself encouraged these groups, which organized religious conferences, distributed subsidized religious materials and even arranged special transportation for female students.[35]

In the mid-1970s, the Religious Committee (*al-Gama'a al-Diniyya*) functioned as an official part of the Student Union. It then changed its name to *al-Gama'a al-Islamiyya* (Islamic Group), and subsequently became a proscribed organization. In the south it was in the hands of the radical Islamists, but in Cairo it was mostly manned by members of the Muslim Brotherhood.

I visited the Muslim Brotherhood headquarters to meet a member of its so-called younger generation, 'Isam al-Ariyan. A former Deputy Secretary-General of the Egyptian Doctor's Union, he was once the youngest member of the Egyptian Parliament. It was a hot day in May 2001, but wearing long sleeves seemed like the minimum requirement for entering that bastion of conservatism. Because I am not a Muslim (and I wasn't going to a mosque), I didn't think it was necessary to wear a veil, although many colleagues have done so.

The headquarters are located in an ordinary block of flats on the Nile island of Manyal, in the same street where several secular NGOs are also based. The Brotherhood flat was like one big prayer-room: the floor was carpeted wall-to-wall in Islamic green, and shoes are taken off and put in a rack as soon as one steps inside. My Sudanese snake-skin loafers stood out, because they were the only women's shoes in the whole rack: the Muslim Brotherhood is a man's world, and not a single woman could be seen.

'Isam al-Ariyan is a short, bespectacled, serious man, who had just spent five years behind bars, for 'reviving the activities of an illegal organization'. Brotherhood members don't usually like to shake hands with women; al-Ariyan took my hand, but unwillingly, limply and averted his gaze – these are signs of piety. But al-Ariyan took pleasure in talking about both past and present. This is how he talked about his student days:

> All the activists belonged either to al-Gama'a al-Diniyya or to al-Gama'a al-Islamiyya. But there was a huge difference between Cairo and Asyut, in the use of violence and how to approach 'encouraging good and forbidding of evil' [armed resistance or not]. By 1980, a visible difference could be noticed. In Cairo the majority were Muslim Brothers, whereas in the south they used force and violence. At that time al-Gama'a al-Islamiyya was open for everyone and could be found in all campuses.

Some, such as the members of *al-Jihad* organization, considered *al-Gama'a al-Islamiyya* to be too moderate. *Al-Jihad* didn't operate in universities, but had been an underground organization since its inception. The ideologue of *al-Jihad*, electrical engineer Abd al-Salam Faraj, had written a small book, *Hidden Imperative* (*al-Farida al-Gha'iba*) which was heavily influenced by Qutb. In it, Faraj wrote that the group's goal was the establishment of an Islamic state in the place of *jahiliyya*, through struggle, *jihad*. He understood the struggle only as armed and considered it the duty of all Muslims. Like Mustafa, he read the Qur'an very selectively, choosing only passages which supported his vision:

> Then, when the sacred months have passed, slay the idolaters wherever ye find them, and take them (captive), and besiege them, and prepare for them each ambush.

But, Faraj doesn't quote the complete *ayat* (verse), which ends:[36]

> But if they repent and establish worship and pay the poor-due,
> then leave their way free. Lo! Allah is Forgiving, Merciful (9:5).

In his book, Faraj quotes the Islamist favourite, Ibn Taymiyya, a 14th-century AD theologian who issued a *fatwa* (a religious scholar's formal opinion, legitimizing *jihad* against a ruler who didn't rule in accordance with Islamic law. Again, Faraj selected Qur'anic verses which supported his view:

> Lo! those who disbelieve in Allah and His messengers, and seek to
> make distinction between Allah and His messengers, and say: We
> believe in some and disbelieve in others, and seek to choose a way
> in between; Such are disbelievers in truth; and for disbelievers
> We prepare a shameful doom. (4:150–151)

According to Faraj, this verse described Egypt: the ruler could be fought against because *shari'a* was not applied. While *al-Jihad*'s primary target was domestic, it also had a global vision, of expanding the Islamic state.[37]

Sadat's surprise visit to Jerusalem in 1977 and the subsequent Camp David peace agreement with Israel in 1979 angered Egyptians (see Chapter 8). Islamist students organized mass demonstrations in Alexandria and Asyut, and the previously cordial relations between Sadat and the Muslim Brotherhood soured. The Iranian Islamic revolution in 1979 further encouraged the Islamists in their demands. Yet Sadat even invited the unpopular Shah and his wife to Egypt.

These events, coupled with the Open Door economic policy, which benefited very few, undermined Sadat's popularity even more. Although Egypt's GDP grew approximately 9% annually in the decade 1974–84, only a few reaped the rewards. According to some estimates, until the late 1980s Egypt's private sector was in the hands of 18 families (of which 8 were actually members of the Muslim Brotherhood). Sadat got a foretaste of the mass's power in 1977 when he ended bread subsidies: Egyptians flooded onto the streets to demonstrate and protest. The resulting death toll was 171, and many more injured. Overnight, the subsidies were re-instated.[38]

The Iranian revolution of 1979 also gave hope to Islamists outside Egypt. That year, an armed group stormed the Grand Mosque in Mecca, the holiest city for Muslims, accusing the House of Sa'ud of immorality, and of being unable to protect Muslims from outside influence.[39] At home, Sadat decided to forbid all political activities on Egyptian campuses, and security guards appeared in universities. Protective checks were stepped up, and Islamist students' names were erased from electoral rolls.[40]

The President forbade the establishment of political parties based on religion (this edict remains in force), but he included the main leaders of the Brotherhood in the Centre Party (part of the former Arab Socialist Union). Brotherhood members had served as Members of Parliament since 1976, and the Brotherhood's political influence grew as it expanded its branches all over Egypt. Because the Brotherhood hoped to gain legal status, it went along with Sadat's policy, and criticized both the Communists and the more radical Islamists, although (officially) it too was still an illegal organization.

The honeymoon ended with the Camp David peace agreement. For many Muslims, including the Brotherhood, this peace meant recognition of the state of Israel; in other words, the triumph of an outside force in the lands of Islam. The sheikhs of al-Azhar told the people and the opposition that peace with Israel was in the interests of Egypt: if the ruler saw that peace with an enemy was for the benefit of Muslims, he had the authority to pursue it. Independent religious organizations were banned from then on.

Yet the opposition, and particularly the Islamists, continued their mounting vocal criticism of the head of state. A month before his assassination, Sadat ordered the arrest of more than 1500 politicians, authors, journalists, Muslim and Christian religious authorities – including the leadership of the Brotherhood. He also enacted a new law requiring all private religious societies to register with the Ministry of Religious Affairs, which also applied to the 40,000 private mosques. Sadat's measure was to ensure government control – or at least that was the aim.

Sadat had not anticipated that the radical Islamist groupings had already infiltrated the security apparatus. Radicals and soldiers (Faraj and Lieutenant Abbud Abd al-Latif al-Zumur) from Southern Egypt formed the leadership of *al-Jihad*. Their spiritual guide was a Professor of Theology in the University of Asyut, a blind sheikh called 'Umar 'Abd al-Rahman. He 'legalized' the group's activities by issuing *fatwa*s. In 1980 he issued a *fatwa* declaring Sadat to be an infidel. A year later *al-Jihad* started to fight – justified by the *fatwa* – against the ruler they deemed un-Islamic.

Fuad Allam had first met 'Abd al-Rahman at the end of 1960s, when the Sheikh was involved in shady activities in the Fayum oasis. Allam's picture of the radical preacher is frightening:

> 'Umar 'Abd al-Rahman was truly evil. He is one of the most evil people that I have met in my whole life. He was cunning, mean and very intelligent although he was blind. He remembered my voice after 12 years.

Lieutenant Khalid al-Islambuli, who was also from Upper Egypt, met Faraj in Cairo. He absorbed Faraj's teachings, but only became truly convinced of 'Sadat's un-Islamic nature' when his brother was detained in a mass arrest of Islamists in

Asyut. He was thirsty for revenge and had uttered to his mother that "every tyrant has his end".[41]

Al-Jihad decided to take advantage of al-Islambuli's army connections. At a parade commemorating the 1973 war al-Islambuli was commanding an armoured truck, which was to drive past the dais where Sadat was reviewing the parade. Suddenly, al-Islambuli and three other *al-Jihad* members opened fire on the auditorium. Al-Islambuli shouted: "I am Khalid al-Islambuli, I have killed Pharaoh and I do not fear death."[42]

The bullets killed not only Sadat – who wasn't wearing a bullet-proof vest that day – but seven other senior officials. Soon after the incident, riots occurred in Asyut, but the spontaneous revolution in the aftermath of Sadat's murder – the hope of *al-Jihad* – never materialized. Yet on the other hand, people didn't publicly mourn the unpopular president either. In the subsequent trial, al-Islambuli stated his motive for the deed: *shari'a* wasn't the basis for legislation, the peace treaty with Israel and the arrests of fellow believers. Al-Islambuli was sentenced to death; he was only 24 years old.[43]

After the tragic murder, Sadat's vice-president, Lieutenant General Husni Mubarak, took the throne. He released the secular thinkers whom Sadat had put behind bars, and imprisoned Islamists in their place. Mubarak's attitude towards Islamists has been a mixture of reconciliation and repression – although as the 1990s drew on, repression played an increasing role. The Emergency Law, invoked after Sadat's assassination, has given Mubarak great leeway in suppressing the Islamists. The law is still in force, the argument being that it is needed to ensure national security. Currently there is a proposal to replace the Emergency Law with a Counter-terrorism Law. This would give the authorities even more extra-legal powers to silence the opposition (see Chapter 6).

Like Sadat, Mubarak started to use al-Azhar scholars as his mouthpiece. A government body, al-Azhar sung the praises of the Mubarak regime's Islamic credentials. Al-Azhar sheikhs conducted 'conversion tours' in prisons, during which they tried to convince the Islamists that their interpretation of Islam was wrong. Mubarak allowed the secular opposition to function more freely, and made only slight amendments to Sadat's Open Door economic policy, to relations with the West, and to the peace process with Israel.

The gap between the Brotherhood and other Islamists widened after Sadat's murder. The Muslim Brotherhood made a clear separation from the radical movements, and started to infiltrate student organizations and professional syndicates – therefore using legal means to co-opt the state.

In prison, the armed Islamist groups grew ever more radical, although their means differed. *Al-Gama'a al-Islamiyya* intended to continue their activities in their own mosques and on university campuses in order to recruit more supporters. *Al-Jihad* on the other hand thought it best to continue the armed struggle – its activities shifted almost entirely underground.

One of the detainees arrested over Sadat's assassination was Ayman al-Zawahiri, nowadays better known as Osama Bin Laden's right-hand man. Al-Zawahiri was a surgeon from a prominent, religiously observant medical family. As a young man, he had already participated in revolutionary activities as a member of a small group, and he believed in Qutb's interpretation of *jihad* as fighting against an un-Islamic regime. He had also spent some time in Afghanistan, as a medical doctor with the Red Crescent (the Islamic equivalent of the Red Cross).

Fuad Allam met al-Zawahiri during the post-assassination arrests.

Ayman al-Zawahiri was very well-mannered, very polite, very calm, very modest and very shy. He spoke only a little – to the extent that when, several years after, I saw him on a tape from Afghanistan, I thought it cannot be true – he spoke so fiercely and aggressively…When he was in Egypt he was a decent person with high morals. You were compelled to feel sympathy towards him.

Like his idol Sayyid Qutb, al-Zawahiri also claimed to have been exposed to severe torture in prison. Allam denies that torture was exercised in interrogations, or in prisons.

All the accused in the world will claim to you that they have been tortured. But there should be a distinction between various things. In earlier times, in Egyptian prisons it was permissible to punish an inmate who committed a crime within the prison by whipping. The prison director had the power to order 30 or 50 lashes.

Inmates don't want to obey prison rules, or allow investigation by the prison authorities but rather wanted to bring all kinds of forbidden objects inside prison. As you know, no sharp tools, knives, penknives or cooking utensils are allowed. Those who commit these acts inside prison answer to the lash. They try to paint this as torture.

But I cannot say that torture never occurs (here he raised his voice); everywhere in the world there are exceptions [those who don't obey]. It could be that there are police officers who torture, but this is neither common nor sanctioned. There are police officers who make mistakes, and we take them to court. The state does not condone torture.

Torture or not, something did happen to al-Zawahiri. People who knew him have said that by the time of his release from prison in 1984, he had turned into a vengeful radical, who climbed all the way up to the executive board of *al-Jihad*. The organization didn't approve of *al-Gama'a* spiritual leader, 'Umar 'Abd al-Rahman (who had issued the lethal *fatwa*

HOLD ON TO YOUR VEIL, FATIMA!

against Sadat). *Al-Jihad* continued its penetration of the army and police. Like a*l-Jihad*, *al-Gama'a* considered the Muslim Brotherhood (which had participated in the 1984 parliamentary elections) to be, at heart, merely a club of conservatives.[44]

Although Sadat had equated the Brotherhood with radical groups, a visible change could be detected in the Brotherhood's thinking after senior members had served time in prison beside other members of the rest of the opposition. The Brotherhood started to approach the Left more vigorously, and decided to use parliamentary means to reach its goal.

In the elections of 1987 the Brotherhood allied with the Liberal and Labour Parties under the slogan 'Islam is the solution'. The Labour Party's mouthpiece *al-Sha'ab* was edited by Adil Husayn, a former Marxist who had later found Islam. Under his guidance, the Labour Party sailed further from socialist principles, towards the Islamists. Although electoral fraud was apparent – indeed Islamists had been arrested before the elections – the Islamic alliance gained 60 seats, a whopping 36 going to the Brotherhood.

Now that it had the largest single bloc in parliament, and two newspapers – *al-Sha'ab* and *al-Ahrar* – were promulgating its ideology, the Brotherhood felt stronger. It seized anew upon its main policy: the immediate implementation of *shari'a*. Other policies included promoting Islamic banks (which don't charge interest) and cutting off diplomatic ties with the United States and Israel. The Brotherhood was so drunk with power that some of their MPs even suggested suspending parliamentary session during prayer times, and establishing an Islamic Caliphate. However, the Supreme Guide argued that *shari'a* should be implemented gradually.[45]

The young former Brother explained how the imposition of 'superior' morality was the norm within the organization:

36

My family was always religious, they became more so when my brother and I became more pious. They were excited at first, but then they started getting worried when we taped over all our music and replaced it with Qur'an recitation instead; when we started to give our mother instructions to dress more modestly, even though my mother has been wearing the veil since the 70s, but we still didn't think it was long enough, we thought she should wear the khimar [waist-long scarf], like the rest of the Sisters, and that she should not wear medium high heels, nor perfume...

And then we stopped watching TV. This was a big thing in our family of course, because like in any Egyptian family, it's on all the time – we would just walk out the room. So it really divided our house. And made them feel guilty, that they were not good enough for us. Then they started to get worried about our safety and our freedom, and started to talk us out of it – which of course made us even more stubborn.

Because the Brothers also feed you with these stories about the younger followers of the Prophet, how they completely severed their ties with their infidel families when their families refused to join the new religion with them. So you relive all these experiences with the Brothers – the entire experience of a young Brother is reliving the early days of Islam entirely. From waking up in the morning, to going to school, to organizing elections ... the example of the Prophet is not in the background of your activities, it's in the foreground. You are reminded of these stories constantly.

As for the radicals, they wanted *shari'a* here and now. Although the leadership of the radical groups was imprisoned, it didn't disable the scattered 'clusters'. Mubarak and al-Azhar's sheikhs failed to convince the Egyptian public of its Islamic credentials, and different groups – including the political opposition – started to demand the imposition of Islamic law. The secret police did not succeed in infiltrating all the campuses, where the Islamists still reigned supreme in the main student bodies. Through them, the Islamists pushed for the Islamization of tuition, for example, demanding gender segregation in tuition and public transportation.[46]

At the same time hundreds, if not thousands, of *al-Jihad* and *al-Gama'a* fighters, *mujahidun*, travelled to Afghanistan to fight with fellow believers against Soviet forces. Sadat had already endorsed this program – the United States was then Sadat's new friend to whom he listened over foreign policy manoeuvres. Perhaps the Egyptian leadership thought that this would be a convenient means of getting rid of various Islamists from the domestic scene. But some of the fighters returned, to strike against the Egyptian regime.

In Egypt, *al-Gama'a* re-surfaced, implementing 'forbidding of evil and commanding the good' by such means as trying to stop musical performances and plays. However, it was at the beginning of 1986 (a year of recession) that *al-Gama'a* really made itself noticed through its attacks on alcohol sellers, singers, and video rental shops. That autumn, it ambushed a beer delivery lorry from a government brewery on the open road, and threw the merchandise along the road and into the Nile. The security forces intervened, which lead to a bloody confrontation in a mosque in Asyut.[47]

According to Tal'at Fu'ad Qasim, then a member of *al-Gama'a's* governing council, the group established an armed wing in 1987 as a reaction to the use of force by the government. In the following year, they got hold of some ammunition, which they intended to use against tourist targets. However, the security forces got an inkling of the plan before they could carry it out. *Al-Gama'a* held tourism as the instigator of corruption and immodesty; claiming that scantily clothed female tourists corrupted the minds of Muslim youths. But by attacking tourism, they could indirectly attack the government, which was heavily dependent on tourism revenues. Qasim himself put it this way:

First, many tourist activities are forbidden, so this source of income for the state is forbidden [...] Second, tourism in its present form is an abomination: it is a means by which prostitution and AIDS are spread by Jewish women tourists, and it is a source of all manner of depravities, not to mention being a means of collecting information on the Islamic movement. For these reasons we believe tourism is an abomination that must be destroyed. And it is one of the strategies for destroying the government.[48]

Armed attacks increased steadily. In 1990 *al-Gama'a* shot Rifa'at al-Mahgub, Speaker of the Parliament. Tourists, ministers, police and security forces, and in the south the Copts (although *al-Jihad* left them alone) were targeted. The skirmishes with the Copts were a part of *al-Gama'a's* anti-government campaign, but it was also related to inter-clan vendettas, common in the south. This gave the government a good reason to warn the populace of the dangers of the Islamists: supporting them would lead to sectarian strife.[49]

Hisham Kassem, the then chairman of the Egyptian Organization for Human Rights (EOHR) and publisher of the now defunct independent magazine *The Cairo Times*, followed the fighting between the Islamists and the government from these two standpoints. His hair and moustache greying, forty-something Kassem is a sharp observer, who gestures eloquently with his hands, as if to make sure the listener gets his point. He described the tactics of the groups like this:

Jihad was more underground, it never bothered to attack small targets, and it didn't believe in proselytizing. The difference between al-Jihad and al-Gama'a is the 'explanation of ignorance' clause: al-Gama'a believed that people had time to change their perception, once they heard about Islam.

But al-Jihad argued that people had 1400 years to learn about the Qur'an, and if they didn't embrace it — it was their

fault. They can be killed. Al-Jihad mainly used bombs, and
although some Muslims died in the attacks, it wasn't a problem
because they would go to Paradise [according to al-Jihad].
Almost all the attacks which involved firearms were conducted by
al-Gama'a – they had specific targets.

1992 was a particularly grim year; in many ways it was a
watershed because fighting between the government and the
Islamists escalated. For *al-Gama'a* the trigger for intensification
of violence was an assassination of one of its leaders. The
Algerian civil war had begun, so an atmosphere of violence
was very much present. The attacks even targeted individuals:
a member of *al-Gama'a* killed a secular thinker Farag Fuda
(see Chapter 7).

The following year, a bomb exploded in a coffee shop
in central Cairo's Tahrir Square. Three people were killed
and eighteen injured. The same day, on the other side of
the Atlantic, in the underground car park of New York's
World Trade Center a car bomb went off. Six people died and
about a thousand were injured. The US investigations led
to the arrests of, among others, *al-Gama'a*'s spiritual leader,
Sheikh 'Umar 'Abd al-Rahman. Currently, he is serving a
life-sentence in the United States.

Both *al-Jihad* and *al-Gama'a* tried to murder selected
ministers. In 1993, the Minister of Information Safwat
al-Sharif was wounded by a sniper's bullets; later the
Minister of Interior Hasan al-Alfi was lightly wounded in
a similar attack, but the Prime Minister 'Atif Sidqi avoided
altogether a car bomb with his name on it. Even President
Mubarak became a target of *al-Jihad*. In 1995, it tried to
repeat history when Mubarak attended an OAU (the former
Organisation of African Unity) summit in Addis Ababa.
Mubarak's car was shot at, but the President escaped with
only a fright.[50]

Clashes between militant Islamists and the security forces had become daily fodder for the newspapers. Pictures of military trials showed bearded men with the fiery eyes of a sect member waving Qur'ans. Looking at these pictures and videos brought to mind the word 'brainwash'. Their prison conditions were often gruesome, as Hisham Kassem explained:

> Five prisons were built for the Islamists, which were designed in a way that they practically crushed the inmates. For example diseases like scabies and tuberculosis spread freely, and they didn't even try to prevent them.[51]

In the militants' southern eyries – Asyut, Minya, Suhag – the fighters hid in sugarcane fields, and periodically shot up passing trains or Nile cruise boats. In the early spring of 1996, I was travelling by train, admittedly nervously, to Luxor. Rumour had it that the Islamists were only targeting the first-class wagons, where most of the foreigners would be travelling. On either side of the railway tracks, the sugarcane had been cleared, so that the militants couldn't hide in it.

Despite these measures, some tourists did, however, die in these attacks; tourism, a vital source of revenue for Egypt, suffered as a consequence. The first major incident occurred in spring 1996 when a bus parked in front of the Europa Hotel, near the pyramids, was fired upon: *al-Gama'a* militants killed 18 Greek tourists. Subsequently, the group expressed its regret for the incident, claiming to have mistaken the Greeks for Israelis.

The following year was even worse. In September, a former night-club singer escaped from a mental asylum and opened fire on a German tourist bus in Tahrir Square, right in front of the Egyptian Museum. The bus driver and nine others were killed. In 1993, the same perpetrator had killed four foreigners in a coffee shop in the Semiramis Hotel. This incident demonstrated that not all the bloodshed was committed by organized Islamist groups; random individuals were involved too.

Only a month after the Tahrir Square incident, a shocking event took place in Luxor. At the temple of the ancient ruler, Queen Hatshepsut, six armed *al-Gama'a* members started to shoot into the temple courtyard. The policemen guarding the site were killed first, then 58 tourists. The bloodbath shocked all of Egypt, even the Islamists, such that *al-Gama'a* even issued a statement claiming that the attackers had acted without *al-Gama'a* leadership authorization. The Luxor massacre was the last link in the five-year chain of attacks in the 1990s – which claimed over 1200 lives – between the government and the Islamists.[52]

Both *al-Jihad* and *al-Gama'a* have subsequently declared a truce in Egypt. *Al-Jihad* has split both geographically and into smaller groups. It is no longer believed to be a major force in Egypt. However, *al-Jihad*'s military leader (and Osama Bin Laden's second in command) Ayman al-Zawahiri has gained a somewhat dubious reputation abroad. The CIA believes that al-Zawahiri and Bin Laden were responsible for the killing of American soldiers in Somalia in 1993; the bomb attacks on US embassies in Kenya and Tanzania in 1998; attacking the USS *Cole* missile destroyer in Aden, Yemen, in 2000; and the 9/11 attacks in New York and Washington, DC.

Bin Laden and al-Zawahiri had met during the Afghanistan campaign, and spent time together in Sudan until Bin Laden was expelled in 1996. Al-Zawahiri signed a co-operation agreement with al-Qa'ida (Bin Laden's group) in 1998, when they established the 'International Islamic Front for Jihad on Jews and Crusaders'.[53] According to their manifesto, killing American soldiers and civilians was a Muslim's duty – thus they expanded the Qutbian vision of justified fighting against un-Islamic rule: foreign countries and civilians were now legitimate targets. In 1997, *al-Gama'a* issued a statement in which it declared that it had abandoned violence. But it wasn't until 2003 (when Makram Muhammad Ahmad, the editor of *al-Musawwar* magazine, was allowed to interview Islamist inmates in Tora Scorpion prison) that the initiative re-appeared in the public eye. Some of them are 'waiting for the rope' – as they put it themselves, and the majority of them have been imprisoned for more than 20 years. Among the interviewees was *al-Gama'a* leader Karam Zuhdi, serving a life-sentence.[54]

The interviews were published in a book titled *Conspiracy or Repentance*, which refers to the author's presumption that the initiative is just a strategic move by the Islamists. In the book, the Islamists claim that they came to the conclusion that attacking the state, Christians and tourists was wrong. They also say that killing Sadat was wrong, because he was a legitimate ruler. They admitted having misinterpreted the Qur'an and other texts, and to having taken things out of context. Their interpretation of *jihad* has also been revised – according to their new belief, *jihad* is only a means, not the aim. "Now the aim is to guide the Lord's creatures, and call them to God... *Jihad* is just a means to guide mankind; killing is not an end in itself, but rather a horrific deed..."[55]

The convicts claimed that the military wing of *al-Gama'a* has been disbanded, and that the leadership became unanimously convinced of the need for a peace initiative by 1999 – only the so-called 'leadership abroad' was an exception, they said. The imprisoned *al-Gama'a* members also condemned the 9/11 attacks, and reminded the interviewer that Muslims were among the dead as well. The interviewees had committed many serious crimes – killing Copts, robberies, murders of politicians and tourists – but they still didn't admit that they themselves were guilty. They repeatedly referred to 'youngsters' who didn't understand, although they themselves were those very youngsters.[56]

Nonetheless, the government rewarded them by releasing more than 900 members of the *Gama'a*. Yet it is difficult to judge how genuine the peace initiative was: according to many observers, these groups had no other choice but to put their weapons down, because they had been genuinely crushed. Hisham Kassem doesn't think it is credible.

> The initiative came from someone who was already lying on its back. When you have already been defeated, you cannot make initiatives anymore. That's why no one took it seriously. And why should they? Their history and culture is scary – that it is ok to lie, and deny other peoples' values. The initiative was just good press material.
>
> The question is not whether they should be trusted or not – that answer is an emphatic 'no'. The question is rather could those incredible circumstances [Sadat supporting Islamism, Afghanistan] which led to the ascendancy of Islamism occur again? The answer is no. Police cruelty and collective punishment has scared people in the south. But the poor south is still there.

And poor Sinai. The peninsula on the Red Sea, a major tourism region, has become the latest venue for terrorist attacks – after seven years of calm. Its native population, the Bedouins, were usually ignored – if not actively discriminated against – in the development of tourism projects. Traditional Bedouin lands, not always officially registered, were confiscated for tourism development, which mostly benefited people from the mainland. Neglected in national development plans, outside the Red Sea Riviera, the Sinai was (and remains) one of the most impoverished areas in Egypt after Upper Egypt.

44

In October 2004, a truck bomb at the Taba Hilton Hotel (right on the Egyptian–Israeli border) killed 34 tourists and Egyptians. Simultaneously, a smaller car bomb killed three Israelis and a local Bedouin on a near-by beach. A shock-wave washed through Egypt, because people had thought that the cycle of violence was over. Initially al-Qa'ida and Palestinians were blamed for the attack: thousands of mainly northern Sinai residents were arrested, and – according to human rights organizations – tortured.[57] The Egyptian authorities declared that a new group called *Tawhid wa Jihad* (Oneness of God and Struggle) – consisting of Bedouins and northern Sinai Egyptians of Palestinian origin – was responsible.[58]

In the end, 15 people were brought to trial in February 2006. But before the verdict was handed down, an even more devastating attack took place in Sharm el-Sheikh, the Sinai's largest holiday resort – and the President's choice for his vacation residence and conference venue.

23rd July is the commemoration of the Free Officers' 1952 Revolution. In 2006, the celebration turned to tragedy in a deadly attack. Three bombs went off: one in the centre of Sharm el-Sheikh's old market; another near a taxi stand in Na'ama Bay, and the most deadly blast at the Ghazalah Hotel. Over 70 holidaymakers were killed, the majority of them Egyptians. The most recent terror attack in Egypt took place in Dahab, a smaller holiday resort on the Red Sea. On 24th April 2006 – Sinai Liberation Day – three bombs went off almost simultaneously, killing 23 people.

What unites the latter two attacks is the fact that they took place on Egyptian national holidays, and so most casualties were Egyptian holidaymakers. Many Egyptian commentators believed either that these attacks were in revenge for the arrests and mistreatment that followed the Taba bombing – or a blood-soaked message to Mubarak.[59]

However, many details of the perpetrators, their motives and modus operandi remain murky.

Ahmed Sayf al-Islam – a veteran human rights lawyer and activist – was defence lawyer for the alleged *Tawhid wa Jihad* members charged with the Taba bombing. Shaggy-haired, Cleopatra-smoking Sayf al-Islam told me in November 2007 that he is still puzzled by the whole affair:

> It is difficult to determine whether the government was behind it, or whether there really was a group by this name. First, all the confessions were made under torture. Secondly, this group didn't have a single [unified] ideology. Some of them said – even in their confessions – that they wanted to train anyone who wanted to know how to use weapons, regardless of their different ideology. Others talked about the importance of imposing a unified Islamic vision. But they didn't have a common Islamic vision, but rather were unified by a common goal. This has been the change within the Islamic organizations.
>
> (But) all the command elements in the organization were killed, and there is nothing written, or at least the police didn't present anything written about their politics, world view or their religious vision – it's all hearsay. The only thing they (police) said about their ideology was that they considered the government *kafir* [infidel] and that they wanted to help the Palestinians in their struggle against Israelis or Jews – their answers varied. But there is nothing about domestic politics.

What seems to emerge from this picture is that the extraordinary sons of ordinary families (like Atta) are still drawn to extremism, no matter how much the government is trying to put a lid on it. The reasons for their grievances are still there: poverty, injustice, a dictatorial political system which to them is not Islamic enough. Although the backbone of the Islamist organizational infrastructure in Egypt has been crushed, there is simply no way of knowing whether single attacks – inspired by the global al-Qa'ida 'brand' for example – will take place. Hisham Kassem pondered:

> Any organization needs logistic support to come from abroad. And the operations that took place here in Cairo were nail bombs: something for which you and I can just go and buy the ingredients from a shop, and put them together. We know that the economy has deteriorated further and there is more desperation – which was the original reason (for attacks). But it's difficult to outline how things could evolve.

It is also too early to predict what impact the latest reconciliation move will have on global *jihadis*. Sayyid Imam (aka Dr Fadl), a mentor of Ayman al-Zawahiri and an important *al-Jihad* ideologue is the latest figure to renounce his militant ideology. Dr Fadl was extradited from Yemen to Egypt in 2004 and is being held in Tora prison where he wrote his revisions which he publicized in November 2007. The essence of his recantation was that 'clashes' in different countries, where people were killed for their nationality, colour of their skin or their ideology, were a violation of Islamic law. While he remains ideologically committed to the application of *shari'a,* he rejects violence in bringing it about. He later went on to criticize Bin Laden and al-Zawahiri, calling the 9/11 attacks immoral.[60]

Still, no matter how many dramatic headlines these attacks or ideological revisions have gained over last three decades, it is a conflict that is not ripping Egyptian society apart. Most Egyptians are quietly religious, but they don't share the agenda or means of the radical movements. Most can look at religion with some distance and a sense of humour.

One evening in the salon of the late Nobel Laureate Naguib Mahfouz, playwright Ali Salem told this decades-old joke to his amused host:

Two women – a priest's wife and a sheikh's wife – lived as neighbours in a small village, in impoverished southern Egypt, sharing a modest roof top. Every morning the sheikh's wife woke up, humming away happily, hanging her underwear to dry, and combing her hair.

One morning the priest's wife asked her Muslim neighbour about the secret of her never failing good mood.

"Well, in the evening I cook chicken with broth for my husband, and sometimes – for the sake of change – I offer him fish or duck, so that he doesn't get bored with the same food. After the meal I give him a massage and he, in his turn, gives me fantastic sex."

The next day, when the priest came home after work, he couldn't find his wife anywhere. All that was left of her was a note on the bed, which read: "Islam is the solution."

Notes

--

1 See e.g. Wright, 2006:304–310, 366.
2 Al-Sayyid Marsot, 1985:73–90.
3 Al-Banna didn't know any foreign languages, but he was an avid reader of translated literature, especially European history.
4 Mitchell, 1969:1–11; Commins, 1994.
5 Ayubi, 1991:132.
6 Mitchell, 1969:246–249; Commins, 1994:135–137.
7 Wafaa's son is Switzerland-based moderate Islamist Tariq Ramadan.
8 Badran, 1996:182–183.
9 I have used Marmaduke Pickthal's Qur'an translation, available online at: http://www.usc.edu/schools/college/crcc/engagement/resources/texts/muslim/quran/.
10 Wendell, 1978:155; Abed-Kotob, 1995:332.
11 Carré, 1983:28; Mitchell, 1969:30.
12 Hasan al-Banna's brother Gamal al-Banna thought that his big brother's good physique was a result of his mother breastfeeding him until the age of two. For more on the scouts, see Commins, 1994:146.
13 Ayubi, 1991:133–134; Mitchell, 1969:31–33.
14 Mitchell, 1969:58–71.
15 Kepel, 1993:38–41; Wright, 2006:10–24.
16 Tripp, 1994:154–157.
17 Hiro, 1989:66; Mitchell, 1969:88–104.
18 Mitchell, 1969:133–162; Tripp, 1994:160.
19 Qutb, 1993:9–21, 44, 98–104; Qutb, 1995:198–199.
20 Qutb, 1993:62–78, 81–85.
21 Tripp, 1994:164–165; Kepel, 1993:30–35.
22 Al-Sayyid Marsot, 1985:123–127; Laqueur & Rubin, 2001:99 (Nasser's speech); Shlaim, 2000:236–250.
23 Wickham, 2002:98.
24 Ibid.:37–41.
25 Rodenbeck, 1998:318.
26 Gamal al-Banna's office still has the table over which this oath took place.
27 Ayubi, 1991:141–143; Ramadan, 1993:164–166.
28 Esposito, 1994:160–161; Al-Sayyid Marsot, 1985:132–135; Shlaim, 2000:318–322.
29 Heikal, 1983:252–253.
30 Ibrahim, 1980:437–440, 446–449.

31 Ayubi, 1991:177.
32 Ramadan, 1993:157; Hiro, 1989:70 71.
33 Sayyid Ahmed, 1991:72, 85, 140.
34 Kepel, 1993:73–81; Ibrahim, 1980:425, 436–443.
35 Wickham, 2002:117.
36 Faraj, 1991:137.
37 Ibid., 1991:127–133, 136–139.
38 Wickham, 2002:96–97; Heikal, 1996:245.
39 Egypt and Iran do not have diplomatic ties to this day, although lately their relationship has warmed up slightly. On the Mecca attack, see Trofimov, 2007.
40 Wickham, 2002:117–118.
41 Kepel, 1993:205.
42 Ibid.:192.
43 For a detailed description of the events, see Heikal, 1983:252–265, 268; Dekmejian, 1985:87–89, 97–99; Kepel, 1993:205, 210–214.
44 Wright, 2002; Azzam, 1996:121 (footnote 1).
45 Ramadan, 1993:173–177.
46 Hiro, 1989:83–86.
47 Ramadan, 1993:162–163.
48 Mubarak, 1997:321.
49 Azzam, 1996:113–114.
50 Weaver, 2000:174–177. Relations between Egypt and Sudan have been troubled for a long time because Egypt accused Sudan of the assassination attempt.
51 See also HRW, 1995.
52 See Weaver, 2000:257–259; Mubarak, 1997.
53 Wright, 2002.
54 Zuhdi was released in September 2003. He has not given any interviews, and has returned to his hometown Minya.
55 Muhammad Ahmad, 2003:33–36 (quote page 35), 108, 121–122.
56 Muhammad Ahmad, 2003:44–46, 50, 88–89.
57 See HRW, 2005/2.
58 Back in Cairo, six months later, a strange, violent sequence took place. A man threw himself from a central Cairo flyover, next to the Egyptian Museum, as police were chasing him. He was carrying a bomb, which exploded as he hit the ground, injuring eight people, among them tourists. He was allegedly wanted in connection with a deadly nail-bomb attack in the Khan el-Khalili bazaar earlier in the month. A little later, the attacker's sister and wife shot at a tourist bus near the Citadel. They then turned the guns on themselves. Over 200 people were arrested in the aftermath in the poor neighbourhood of Shubra el-Kheima. In August 2007 four people were sentenced to life imprisonment, four

receiving shorter sentences. See 'Harsh aftermath', *al-Ahram Weekly*, issue no. 859, 23–29/8/2007.
59 See ICG, 2007. Gazan involvement has also been suggested, in the so-called Dahlan files that were discovered after the Hamas take-over, see http://arablinks.blogspot.com/2007/06/egyptian-paper-documents-show-dahlan.html.
60 See HRW, 2005/5. *Al-Masry al-Youm* started to publish excerpts from *Tarshid al-Jihad if Masr wa a-'alam* from 18/11/2007, issue no. 1253 onwards. See also Jarret Brachman, 'Leading Egyptian Jihadist Sayyid Imam Renounces Violence' in *CTC Sentinel*, December 2007, Vol. 1, issue 1.

2

Only as a mother is she a real woman

— ‑

"Where are you from?" the taxi driver inquired and leered through the rear-view mirror. Beige fake-fur carpet decorated the dashboard; resting on it were a Qur'an and a plastic dog with a mobile head, which swung as the car went round corners. A used CD hung from the rear-view mirror, reflecting the sun in sharp rays, but the driver didn't seem distracted by it.

"From Finland," I replied, looking out of the window, stuck in a midday traffic jam.

The driver digested the noun, but clearly his brain didn't register a country by that name. He gave me suspicious glances via the mirror, as if I had made up this country called *Finlanda*.

"What are you doing here?" was the next question. "Studying?"

How nice that someone would take me, in my thirties, for a student still! I told him that I was a journalist.

"Are you married?" he asked, going straight to the point. Egyptians don't consider inquiries about one's civil status to be private matters, at all.

"You have to take an Egyptian husband, you will start a home, have children and stay here!" he suggested, winking his eye and giving me the kind of look that suggested he wouldn't mind volunteering.

These conversations are pretty harmless, but they reveal something about the way in which Egyptian men perceive foreign women. If you're not married, it means that you are looking for a husband, and anyone can volunteer as a candidate. If you are married to a foreigner, it's only half ideal, because Western men are thought to be a bit sissy. Only Egyptian men are *real* men, many locals believe. Perhaps that's why they think that men of every age, appearance or social class have a right, if not a duty, to call out to women, which are meant as compliments:

Hilwa...Sweet...
Eh il-halawwa di? – What's this sweet thing?
Eshta – Cream
Asal – Honey
Mozza – Babe (and an old word for a prostitute)
Ah, lahma abyad! – Ah, white meat!
Ya Allah! – Oh my God!

These sugary utterances are often accompanied by a smacking of the lips and a daring look – and this treatment is given as generously to local women. And sometimes it's more than words; sometimes young men purposely pass you in the street so close that shoulders touch, unless you have time to dodge it.

Leering is another daily nuisance. The most dedicated ones will follow you block after block and whisper obscenities in Arabic. Then they wait for the moment when they reach you, and utter probably the only English words they know: *I want to fuck you.* This is when a handbag often transforms itself into a mace, and shouting draws negative attention to the sleaze-ball – all in the hope that public embarrassment will teach him a lesson.

Crowds are a haven for whisperers and squeezers of women's behinds. In the Middle East, I've never been groped as much as in Egypt: in a bus, bazaar, street, at *mulid* popular feasts, at a techno rave… Punishing the perpetrator is very difficult in these circumstances, because you simply don't know who did it. Voicing loud protests will usually attract the attention and protection of older gentlemen, who offer to keep restless fingers at bay, and steer the embarrassed victim away from the badly behaving crowd.

It is no exaggeration to say that most Egyptian and foreign women have had similar experiences. In July 2008 the Egyptian Centre for Women's Rights (ECWR) published a first-of-its-kind study on sexual harassment. The results supported women's real life experiences: 83% of Egyptian women and 98% of foreign women reported exposure to sexual harassment, roughly half of them on a daily basis.

The most shocking part of the survey was that 63% of the men surveyed readily admitted to harassing women. The men also claimed that women wearing revealing clothes are more likely to get harassed, although the study found that modest clothing was not an effective repellent for harassment. While men of all ages engage in this activity, the average profile of a harasser is a 19- to 24-year old microbus or taxi driver – or with foreigners, usually a police officer or security personnel.[1]

Yet most Egyptian women don't answer back to gropers, because they fear that scolding might be interpreted as making a move, or as a sign of interest. Staring back is not an option either, because it would immediately be taken as encouragement. Moreover, women rarely report sexual harassment to the police – only 2.4% of the women in the ECWR survey filed reports.

Soon after the survey had sparked a debate in the Egyptian media, a brave woman called Nuha Rushdi made the headlines. In broad daylight, she had been groped repeatedly by a man driving beside her, while she was walking on the curb. Rushdi took him to the police station, filed charges, and the man, Shirif Gum'a, was sentenced to three years imprisonment and a LE5001 fine.

What seems to be a new phenomenon is group harassment on religious holidays. During Eid al-Adha in 2006, several women were harassed in downtown Cairo. Some of them were chased by packs of men, while others had to take refuge in shops. Bloggers, such as 'Wounded Female from Cairo', brought these ugly events into public consciousness:

> We felt like we were in a war – I had my self defense spray (*sic*) was emptied on the endless number of guys who surrounded us and yet still wasn't enough.
> We, girls, had our butts, breasts, and every inch of our bodies grabbed. I end up slipping into a car that was parking on the road side when I tried to catch one of the mother fuckers who insisted and never gave up on grabbing my butt. So, I end up with a deep cut in my right hand palm and another one on my thumb of the same hand as I slipped into the car's headlight that broke and cut my hand. 6 stitches on my hand palm cut and 3 on my thumb – still my anger is pretty fresh in the deep inside of me that makes want me to put all Egyptian men on fire right now for what they have caused.[2]

As usual, the government tried at first to deny that these events took place. Yet videos posted on YouTube prompted a Dream TV talk-show to tackle the issue, bringing the topic into Egyptian living-rooms, and some independent newspapers covered the issue as well. Most Egyptians were shocked by the news, yet the same thing happened in 2008, this time in Muhandiseen, during Eid al-Fitr when a group of women were harassed by a mob of young men.

As a response, in their usual way, the Egyptian police rounded up about 400 boys between the ages of 15 and 17 in November. While the police were wondering what to do with them, the First Lady decided to give her assessment on the situation. In her opinion, Egyptian men always respect Egyptian women and, contrary to the media's exaggeration, Egypt's streets are safe. "Maybe one, two or even 10 incidents occurred. Egypt is home to 80 million people. We can't talk of a phenomenon. Maybe a few scatterbrained youths are behind this crime. And maybe some people wanted to make it seem as though the streets of Egypt are not safe so girls and women stay at home. This could be their agenda," she said.[3] I wonder, when was the last time Ms Mubarak walked in the street all by herself?

In time, one gets used – or numb – to the whistles and whispers, and shuts one's ears. Another way to solve the problem is to wear sunglasses (they can't see what you're looking at) and an MP3 player (you can't hear what they are saying). An assertive pace and a determined face may deter the worst cases from approaching. But the only way to completely avoid harassment is to walk with an Egyptian man. The disregard for foreign men is so deep that I got calls even when I walked with my father. Or perhaps they don't expect to be understood, they just want to say that *hilwa* anyway, as if it was hard to kick the habit.

People often ask me what it is like to live in Egypt as a foreign woman. Apart from the harassment, I don't think living in Egypt as a woman is any harder than in any other developing country. The principle of 'when in Cairo, do as the Cairenes do' applies, and one has to take into consideration the different cultural values. For example, a woman has to think hard about what to wear (i.e. how much do you need to cover up), which route and which form of transportation she is going to use.

At first I covered myself in long skirts and loose t-shirts; but I didn't notice a significant difference on the harassment level if I wore jeans or a tighter top. In parallel, and despite the simultaneous trend toward veiling, many Egyptian women have liberalized their dress style to more tightly fitting garments – but still cover up arms and legs. Still, if you choose to wear spaghetti strap tops and a miniskirt in central Cairo, then you're really asking for trouble.

On the other hand, in one-to-one dealings Egyptian men (apart from taxi drivers) are usually businesslike and straightforward. I can't recall a single situation where, for example, an interviewee ever condescended to me (except on occasion with the Muslim Brothers) or questioned my professionalism because I'm a woman. On the contrary, being a woman is often a plus.

Once I was doing a TV interview with a spokesman of the *al-Gama'a al-Islamiyya*. My male colleagues had warned me that he is presumptuous towards foreigners who don't speak Arabic up to his standards. With this advice in mind, I wrote down the questions carefully in formal Arabic and dressed conservatively. Before we started filming, this heavy-set man in a pin-stripe suit turned my business card between his fingers and said: "Haven't we met somewhere before? I would remember an attractive woman like you." That moment I knew that I didn't have to get my head around Arabic grammar.

At the same time, as a foreigner, an outsider, I'm freer than Egyptian women. I can live alone without too much hassle, although I remember once I had to explain to laundrette workers that in my country young people do live alone, and that most of them actually wait eagerly to leave home. They couldn't comprehend at all why someone would want to live alone; surely you need to have your family around you. And there was no one to protect me if I lived alone!

My Egyptian female friends who live alone (such as when their father has passed away, or in rare cases, when they have their father's consent, hence the liberty) have to choose the area they live in very carefully, and they make sure that the *bawwab* (the porter) knows that he is there to guard only her door, not her morals, and does not keep count of the men who visit the woman's flat.

In addition, I do not have to follow the same moral codes that restrict the lives of Egyptian women. Concepts that might today sound alien to a Western woman – such as honour, chastity, virtuousness and virginity – are essential concepts for most Egyptian women. Women's position is prescribed by Islamic family law, traditions and patriarchal values, but more and more by the challenge of balancing these with modern day demands and the imposition of Western culture.

But the picture is multifaceted: for some people, life is one great suffering, whereas others have found happiness and balance – just like anywhere else in the world. Yet particularly the poor, uneducated – the majority of – women probably don't even question their position, or see it as particularly bad.

The debate over women's position in an Islamic-Arabic society, which started over 100 years ago, is still heated. Although the emphasis now is different, the fundamental questions have remained remarkably similar. What should we think about women's work? What does Islam say about

women's position in the society – is a woman's primary role
to be a wife and mother? How should women move about
and behave outside their home? Do women have the right to
take control of their bodies?

The Egyptian women's movement has managed to change
a variety of perceptions. Few now would publicly question
the right of women to study, or to vote. However, the exercise
of these theoretical rights is an altogether different matter,
particularly in rural areas.

Modern Egyptian women are visible in all public arenas:
they participate in social debate and economic activities, they
practise medicine and law, and work as diplomats and pilots.
The Western stereotype of a Muslim woman hidden beneath
a tent, 'between a fist and the stove', and living a life of
submission is as far from reality as claiming that all Finnish
women are always and everywhere equal with Finnish men.

Although the picture is getting brighter, it is still not
rosy. Working women have to manage two jobs, because
most Egyptian men still don't help or share domestic chores.
Few women question this situation and ask their husbands
to help, because this is not generally the Egyptian custom.

In fact, many Egyptian women would rather stay at
home than seek external employment: women make up
only 20% of the formal Egyptian workforce. When you meet
Egyptian women, they don't ask first what you do for living,
but rather want to know if you're married and if you have
children. Or sometimes when I ask women what *they* do for
a living, they give a nonchalant answer: "I'm just at home, I
have two kids – and it's so much work!"

Yet you don't see many high-ranking women: women
hold only 1.98% of parliamentary seats (2005 parliament[4])
and a tenth of all top management positions. Women's overall
literacy is much lower than men's, only 57.3% of women can

read,[5] although this varies by social class. Girls are more likely to drop out of school, and most of them still have to endure painful female genital mutilation (FGM), particularly in the south. Domestic violence is rampant, and the laws governing the role of women put them in an unequal, weaker position to men.

For a woman was not created in order to remain within the household sphere, never to emerge. Woman was not created to become involved in work outside the home only when it is directly necessary for household management, childrearing, cooking, kneading bread, and other occupations of the same sort [...] No, upon my life![6]

These are the words of Zaynab Fawwaz in 1891, printed in the Cairene *al-Nil* newspaper. Born in Lebanon and buried in Egypt, Fawwaz was one of the pioneers of the Egyptian women's movement, women who wanted to shake up the patriarchal society.

The dawn of the Egyptian women's movement coincided with the time when Egyptians were reflecting on their identity vis-à-vis the West – like today. Egypt had been under British control since 1882, which gave rise to nationalistic aspirations, but also to admiration for European civilization. In the 1890s women began to become active in the literary discourse: newspapers published writings by women (special women's magazines also existed), which contemplated women's position. Writing was considered to be 'appropriate' because women didn't necessarily have to leave the house.

Modernists, who in the mid-19th century had argued for new Qur'anic interpretations, and independent reasoning (*ijtihad*) instead of following traditional texts, were the first ones to make demands for women's education. The most renowned of the Modernists was a judge called Qasim Amin, who in 1899 published his manifesto, *Woman's Liberation* (*Tahrir al-Mar'a*). Qasim and other Modernists called for a woman's right to education and to work, because it would benefit the whole nation. A lack of education was seen as the main reason for women's backwardness.

In 1832, the first educational avenue for Egyptian girls had opened: the School for Hakimahs, or medical aides. But it took a further 40 years before the first state school for girls was established, which was mainly for upper-class girls, and had only a few pupils. Yet little by little, more girls' schools were built, although well-off families still preferred their daughters to study at home with a tutor. Higher education for women was even longer in coming – women were only allowed to enrol at the Fu'ad University (now the Cairo University) for the first time in 1929, with four eager students. In 1941 a woman called Suhayr Qalamawi made Egyptian history by becoming the first female holder of a doctorate.[7]

Nevertheless women had very little room to manoeuvre, especially in the upper classes. Huda Sha'arawi[8] – a pioneer of the feminist movement in Egypt and the wider Middle East – represented the last generation to live in a harem. In Egypt, the harem was a part of a household reserved for women only, separated from the men's quarters. Only the most affluent could afford this arrangement. Outside the household, segregation between sexes was effected by veiling, which covered the hair and most of the face. This practice not only separated upper-class women from all men, but also from women of other social classes.

Egyptian feminism[9] was connected to the modernization debate, the national awakening and anti-imperialist struggle.

Organized feminism of the 1920s quickly branched out in two different strands. Huda Sha'arawi's feminism was characteristically pro-Western – appealing to upper- and middle-class women – and had a secularist touch. Alongside Sha'arawi's trend functioned a more marginal Arab feminism, drawing from Islamic culture, with a critical view of the West.

Both of these strands (and Arab feminism in general) differ from Western feminisms in that they haven't called for women's liberation as individuals, or women's sexual liberation (Nawal el-Saadawi is an exception). Family and marriage have remained as the central focus of women's lives, and almost an unquestionable concept is the role of woman as a wife and mother, not as an independent (of a man) or unmarried individual. Nevertheless, Arab feminism argues that a woman has a right to self-development.

Huda Sha'arawi was born into an aristocratic family: her father Sultan Pasha was a wealthy land-owner and a member of the Egyptian Chamber of Deputies. Her mother, a concubine, was of Circassian origin and much younger than her father. (Up until the early 1900s it was common to give girls from the Caucasus as wives or concubines to elite families: they had instrumental, status value.) Huda's father died when she was 5 years old. Because the household didn't have another adult male, Huda's cousin 'Ali was ordered to be their legal guardian. He was later to become Huda's husband.

At a tender age, Huda learned that her brothers had more privileges than her. Huda wanted to learn Arabic grammar, in order to do better in her Qur'an studies, but this was forbidden because of her gender. This restriction didn't stop her from memorizing the entire Qur'an by the age of nine very rare for a girl. She also studied subjects which were deemed 'appropriate' for girls, such as Turkish, calligraphy, French, and the piano. Around this time her household was visited by a female poet, Sayyida Khadija al-Maghribiyya, who planted in her mind the idea that women can be equal to men through education.

Her childhood came to a symbolic end when she donned the veil at the age of 11. This meant that her movements were restricted to the women's side of the house, while outside the home she had to wear the veil. When she was 13, she was married off to her guardian-cousin 'Ali who was 40 years old at the time. Previously, Huda had thought of him as her father or older brother, and tells in her memoirs that she both feared and respected him.

'Ali already had a concubine and children by her who were older than Huda. Huda's mother tried to get the marriage-contract[10] to free 'Ali's concubine, who was a 'former' slave.[11] This would have made Huda's marriage monogamous, but 'Ali refused to sign the contract. He continued with his concubine and she became pregnant again. Huda used this as an excuse to move back in with her mother – for seven years. This was a very unusual arrangement, but crucial for Huda's inner growth.

That seven year period changed Huda's life: as a married woman she had more liberties. This was a time of education and socializing – she had several foreign friends who pursued these kinds of activities. The most important of her friends was Eugenie Le Brun, a.k.a. Madame Rushdie, a Frenchwoman who had converted to Islam before marrying an upper-class Egyptian man.

Huda was the youngest member of Madame Rushdie's Saturday salons, a venue for elite women to share ideas on women's issues. Because most of the salon participants were foreigners, a woman's position was observed from an outsider's perspective. Egypt was seen as backward, and the veil as a hindrance to women's development. Madame Rushdie was of the opinion that foreigners got the wrong idea of the veil, that it was used as a mask for immorality. However, she argued that women's backwardness didn't derive from Islam, but from die-hard habits of the patriarchy. Similarly, she held that the veil was an invention of the patriarchy, not of Islam.

Eventually, a reluctant Huda returned to her husband. Soon she gave birth to a daughter, and then a son. She even breastfed them herself, although within the Egyptian elite it was customary to hire a wet nurse. Yet, she wasn't going to give up the women's discussion club. Indeed, she became even more independent-minded after the death of Madame Rushdie.

Huda organized speeches and lectures for women, and helped to establish a charity organisation, Mubarrat Muhammad Ali, which provided free medicine and health consultations for poor families. In Egypt, both Muslims and Christians share a tradition for charity; this served as a meeting point for women: here, harem women's space expanded to the realm of public life. Elite ladies on their part thought that lower-class women would be liberated by the knowledge the centre provided.

The years 1919–1922 have been called the era of public feminism. It was also the beginning of national awakening and abandoning of the harem system – men and women from all walks of life, in cities and the countryside joined the fight for independence. Except in traditional religious circles, feminist women's activities were looked upon with approval, because women were fighting for the common good, against colonialism.

The major event that started the national movement was the demand of the Egyptian delegation – the *Wafd* – for independence from Britain. Huda's husband 'Ali was the treasurer of *Wafd*, so through him Huda was able to follow current political affairs as they happened. The delegation's demands weren't met, so Cairenes rioted, and went on strike. Huda was busy organizing demonstrations against the British and supported the strikers. She wrote in her memoirs that she had never been so close to her husband as in this time of national awakening.

The *Wafd* transformed itself into a political party, and Huda was elected as the chairwoman of the women's division. But before long there was friction between the men's and women's committees; women felt sidelined when it came to political decision-making. Yet women also played an important role as messengers via domestic social networks. It has been argued that the women's role was also important in keeping up morale – as often is the case with independence struggles.

Britain gave Egypt its independence in 1922. In the same year, Huda's husband 'Ali passed away. A year after independence, the first People's Assembly was formed, but not a single woman was given a seat, even though they had been struggling for independence side-by-side with men. Women had fully taken their place in the public sphere, but now the message seemed to be: go home, and don't worry about politics.

Feminist scholars of Egypt refer to 1923 as a watershed: women's activity became visible, public. Although the majority of upper- and middle-class women still wore the face-veil, with the societal upheaval, their milieu expanded from their homes to the streets. The feminist awakening culminated in establishing the Egyptian Feminist Union (*Al-Ittihad al-Nisa'i al-Misri*), or EFU. Huda Sha'arawi was elected as its president with little dispute. And she was about to perform a dramatic act of defiance.

In that year, three founder-members of the EFU took part in a conference of the International Alliance of Women in Rome. On their return, they did something unprecedented: at the Cairo railway station, they discarded their face-veils.

As scholar Margot Badran points out, this wasn't just a symbolic gesture, but a powerful political statement. It meant leaving behind women's invisibility and the demure life of the harem. (One has to bear in mind that Huda could afford such a gesture – she was an independently wealthy widow – the other 'drama queens' were unmarried.) However, most women couldn't just take off the veil (Huda continued to keep her hair covered) without familial support.[12] Forsaking the veil was never a part of the EFU manifesto, but a voluntary, individual choice.[13]

The new People's Assembly issued a constitution, a year in the drafting, which proclaimed that all citizens regardless of their race, religion or mother tongue were equal before the law. A citizen's gender wasn't mentioned, and women were left without suffrage – the issue closest to Huda's heart. She recounts in her memoirs how disappointed she was with men, and with the new watered-down constitution:

> Exceptional women appear at certain moments in history and are moved by special forces. Men view these women as supernatural beings and their deeds as miracles.[...] In moments of danger, when women emerge by their side, men utter no protest. Yet women's great acts and endless sacrifices do not change men's views of women. Through their arrogance, men refuse to see the capabilities of women.[14]

The EFU manifesto is usually described as liberal feminist, because they called for women's political rights, provision of basic education to girls, professional equality with men and enhancing women's working conditions. The EFU was heavily involved in charity, ran a clinic for women, published two papers, organized workshops for poor girls, and offered child-care for working mothers. One of the main activities were literacy campaigns, because most Egyptian women were illiterate. In addition, the EFU campaigned against prostitution, sustained and regulated by the former British administration.[15]

The Feminist Union was personified by Huda Sha'arawi, who dedicated her life to the organization, right up until her death in 1947. Indeed, thanks mainly to her monetary contributions, the EFU was financially independent. From the onset, the EFU's target group were the upper- and middle-class women of Egypt's major cities, who were seen as the key actors realizing the feminist ideology. It wasn't until the 1940s that the EFU reached rural areas and working-class women.

There is no denying that Huda Sha'arawi admired European individualism. Badran suggests that Huda supported a secularist approach, although she often referred to Islam in her arguments. Particularly during the early stages of the EFU, women drew on Islamic role models for women's political participation: women who had been active in the formative years of Islam, such as the Prophet Muhammad's wives Khadija (an independent, wealthy entrepreneur) and 'Aisha (the transmitter of traditions, *hadith*, who also participated in armed struggle and politics).

In addition to setting forth the feminist agenda, the list of EFU accomplishments included a new law on minimum age for marriage, which was set at 16 for girls (it hadn't been defined before, girls were married off at puberty) and 18 for boys. Even then feminists argued that women should first educate themselves and only then marry. Hard as they tried, these early feminists weren't able to restrict men's easy recourse to divorce and polygamy. But Sha'arawi's work was eventually acknowledged by the state – before she died she received Egypt's highest decoration, in recognition of her struggle for women's rights.[16]

Alongside these developments, other women's movements sprung up, criticizing EFU for its elitism. The EFU was accused of being under foreign influence, a mouth-peace of imperialists. Critics have often used this argument against feminist movements in Egypt and in other Arab countries – even today.

The guiding light of Egypt's Islamist women's movement was Zaynab al-Ghazali. For about a year she was a member of the EFU, but left the group in order to set up her own organization, the Muslim Women's Association (MWA) in 1936, which was at first affiliated with the Muslim Brotherhood. She was only 18 at the time. This is how she explained her decision to scholar Valerie Hoffman in an interview in 1981:

> I was working with Mrs. Huda al-Sha'arawi in the women's movement, which calls for the liberation of women. But I, with my Islamic upbringing, found that this was not the right way for Muslim women. Women had to be called to Islam, so I founded the Muslim Women's Association after I resigned from the Feminist Union.
> ...Islam has provided everything for both men and women. It gave women everything – freedom, economic rights, political rights, social rights, public and private rights. Islam gave women rights in the family granted by no other society. Women may talk of liberation in Christian society, Jewish society, or pagan society, but in Islamic society it is a grave error to speak of the liberation of women. The Muslim woman must study Islam so she will know that it is Islam that has given her all her rights.[17]

Nevertheless, the activities of the MWA were quite similar to its secular counterpart. It organized lectures for women, ran an orphanage and provided stipends and family counselling for less well-to-do families. The MWA also integrated unemployed women and men into its activities by assigning them religious activity tasks. Al-Ghazali held that the MWA had an agenda (aligned with the Muslim Brotherhood's) that Egypt should be governed by *shari'a* – Islamic law – not by secular legislation. She was therefore in favour of establishing an Islamic state.

Hasan al-Banna, the leader of the Muslim Brotherhood envisioned the MWA as part of his organization, but al-Ghazali insisted on her independence. They had a friendly relationship, which goes to show that al-Ghazali was an unconventional woman for her time. But although she argued that woman's primary role was to be a mother and a wife, and bring up an Islamic society, she chose a completely different path in her personal life.

She married twice – the first marriage foundered because her spouse didn't approve of all her time being devoted to Islamic affairs. As part of her second marriage contract, she stipulated that her husband should support her work. According to her, their union was based on companionship and love. This is the ideal in many Islamist writings.

Al-Ghazali was imprisoned in the mass arrests of the Muslim Brotherhood in 1965, which signalled the end of her association. She claims to have been tortured repeatedly – by flogging, making her stand in a cell full of water, and by using dogs: "Within seconds the snarling dogs were all over me, and I could feel their teeth tearing into every part of my body. [...] I expected that my clothes would be thoroughly stained with blood, for I was sure the dogs had bitten every part of my body. But, incredulously, there was not a single blood-stain in my clothes, as if the dogs had been my imagination only. May God be exalted!" she wrote of her experience.[18]

She was sentenced to 25 years of hard labour, but was released after six years. After her release, she wrote extensively in *al-Da'wa* (the Muslim Brotherhood's mouthpiece), and established herself as a lecturer and preacher of Islam.[19] She died at home in August 2005, after a long illness.

Another colourful character in Egypt's early feminist movement was poet and activist Doria Shafik, a protégée of Huda Sha'arawi. She followed the secularist path paved by her idol, trying to popularize it. The 'Perfumed Leader' as she came to be known,[20] Shafik finished her doctoral thesis at the Sorbonne and returned to Cairo in 1945, ready for action.

Initially she tried her wings with the EFU, but disagreements led to her setting up her own organization, Daughter of the Nile Union (*Ittihad Bint al-Nil*), publishing a magazine by the same name three years later. She demanded full political rights for women, and Bint al-Nil even had its own small militia, a sign of the times. Shafik organized demonstrations, and marched into the parliament, interrupting a session. Bint al-Nil participated in the political upheaval prior to the Free Officer's coup in 1952 – all Cairo was in flames in January, anti-governmental activity at its peak.

Drama queen as she was, she knew how to stage a scene. When the People's Assembly convened to draft a new constitution, Shafik objected to the fact that not a single woman sat on the Drafting Committee. She informed the media that she and her fellow sisters were going on hunger strike 'until death', for comprehensive rights for women. The governor of Cairo came to see the 14 protestors, and gave his word that women's demands would be met. That was the end of the strike.

The constitution of 1956 granted women's suffrage, but women had to apply to vote – the same condition didn't apply to men. Shafik protested again, and the next year did something which shows that she miscalculated the political atmosphere. She announced, to President Nasser and to the domestic and international media, that she would go on another hunger strike 'until death', because her human rights had been violated in two areas: Israel was still occupying Egypt (withdrawal from the Sinai was slow after the Suez crisis), and Egypt's dictatorship was leading the country into bankruptcy and chaos.

Shafik marched to the Indian embassy (she had been to India and met Nehru), and started her hunger strike until death, this time for real. This deed was too much for everyone else – the Egyptian government couldn't arrest her at the Indian embassy, and the two countries were having delicate consultations at the time.

Even her own Bint al-Nil organization abandoned her, and forced her to resign. Other women's organizations declared that she was a traitor. Nasser eventually put her under house arrest and shut down *Bint al-Nil* magazine. Shafik had clearly misread her own popularity as against Nasser's. Nasser was at the peak of his popularity, and Shafik's dramatic action was seen as being directed abroad. She continued writing from her domestic 'prison', but went through several nervous breakdowns before finally committing suicide by jumping off her balcony in 1976.[21]

Although women won suffrage in 1956, the price they paid was that all women's rights organizations were either banned or integrated into the state machinery. The Egyptian Feminist Union became the Huda Sha'arawi Association and was re-focused solely on charity. On Nasser's watch, Huda Sha'arawi's beautiful house off Tahrir Square was demolished, and it is now a drab parking lot.

A couple of years ago, I went to see Sha'arawi's niece Muna at her home in Garden City, in a high-ceilinged villa which has seen better days. Shaggy-haired and bespectacled, Muna was wearing a worn-out, whitish t-shirt – she didn't exactly resemble what I imagined the scion of an aristocratic family would look like. Maybe the 1952 Revolution and nationalization of assets had something to do with her laid-back looks. Yet on closer inspection, she bore her grandmother's round features and wide, serious eyes.

She remembered her grandmother well. "She was always friendly to children, despite being busy with the Feminist Union." Although her grandmother established several health clinics, she had one undoubtedly unhealthy habit. "She was a chain-smoker: her room was always full of tobacco fumes," Muna recalled.

Muna Sha'arawi and her sister often used to attend meetings of the association named for their grandmother, but lately less and less so. This is hardly surprising, as it has experienced a serious curtailment, and now functions under the Ministry of Interior – a far cry from its glory days. The Association still follows much the same line of activity: it runs three day-care centres for pre-school age children (I was shown a pleasant yellow room with plenty of toys), an orphanage, a family planning clinic and a dormitory for female university students. The students have an impressive library at their disposal – although it hasn't been updated since Sha'arawi's days. Even so, one can appreciate Huda's fingerprint here: the association still supports women's work, studying and healthcare.

During Nasser's time the women's movement fragmented because of the government's tighter control over it. Nawal el-Saadawi (born in 1931) represents the appearance of sexual feminism in the 1970s. She was the first Egyptian to tackle publicly issues which had previously been taboos: female genital mutilation (FGM), motives for veiling, and sexual abuse of women. A widely translated author, el-Saadawi's main theme is the fight against the patriarchal-capitalistic system, although she also unveils the double standards in Egyptian society. She, too, has a taste for headlines – in 2005 she ran for president in Egypt's first multiparty elections.

I met her for the first time in summer 1999 just after the first part of her autobiography had been published in English.[22] I had been taking turns to read it with a German colleague, Hannah, getting ready to meet the country's most vocal feminist. While el-Saadawi has been praised in the West as a defender of women's rights, and for having inspired many secular Arab feminists, in her own country she excites controversy, even hatred, possibly deliberately in part. No one, however, can accuse her of resting on her laurels, even in her 70s: at the time of the interview she was busy setting up a new umbrella organization for different women's rights groups.

She received us in her home, in a high-rise apartment building in the suburb of Shubra. Her home was a tastefully decorated intellectuals' abode, with the Oriental *mashrabiyya*, carved wooden furniture, and overflowing bookshelves. And if there ever was need for an extra inspiration, she could see the Nile from her balcony.

El-Saadawi is a physician by training and she used to work for the Ministry of Health – until she was fired for her writings. The reason was her first non-fiction book, which was provocatively titled *Women and Sex*. It was banned shortly after its 1970 publication.[23] The book had such a lasting impact that her critics still see her as 'the sex author'.

The organization she founded, the Arab Women's Solidarity Association (AWSA), is no longer allowed to function in Egypt, and only its international branch remains active. It was banned in 1991 – el-Saadawi thinks it was due to AWSA's stance against the Gulf War. The new NGO law of 1999 gave the Government a stronger hand to interfere in the governance and funding of NGOs. The motive for this stricter control was probably the government's fear of foreign funding for political organizations, which might 'harm Egypt's national interests' as the standard government line stated.

Talking to us in her living-room, el-Saadawi said that the invitation to join the new union was open to all women's organizations, including Islamist women. "The idea of the union is not to erase differences, but to work on the common ground," she emphasized. The relationship between secularists and Islamist women hadn't exactly been warm, and el-Saadawi was well-known for her critique of Islamists. It was therefore a bit surprising to hear her acknowledge that even Islamists had some enlightened and progressive thinkers.

In 1981 el-Saadawi was imprisoned for a few months, along with the rest of the opposition, but was released by Husni Mubarak after Sadat's assassination. In the 1990s el-Saadawi received death threats from the Islamists, so the government ordered 24/7 security and a personal bodyguard; el-Saadawi opted for voluntary exile in the United States.

Since her return to Cairo in 1996, she has concentrated on literary pursuits. Her fictional writing is characterized by certain pessimism: women seem to be victims of their circumstances, incapable of making choices. "People have called Woman at Point Zero pessimistic, but I think the protagonist's death symbolizes resistance, and it's fighters that I want to write about," she explained and emphasized her training as a doctor. "I want to portray fleshy people, suffering, the physical and psychological agony of women, but also of men."

She sees class and patriarchy as inseparable. "I don't make a distinction between politics and women's issues either. I believe that I serve Egypt best by criticizing it because it's supposed to improve the society," she argued. Yet she finished the interview with a pessimistic note: even in the West women shouldn't delude themselves that they have attained equality. "Women's position is bad everywhere. We are all in the same boat."

El-Saadawi's Women's Union never materialized. In August 1999, Egypt's leading newspapers carried an official notice from the Ministry of Interior, stating that el-Saadawi was trying to set up an illegal organization. The new NGO law hadn't come into effect by then, and the press accused her of taking advantage of the transitional stage. In a statement, Mirvat Tillawi the Egyptian Minister of Social Affairs said that she wouldn't allow the new law to be abused in this manner.

Under the previous law, NGOs had to register at the Ministry, but according to the new law this was supposed to happen automatically; el-Saadawi had even followed the old law's stricter regulations. The whole affair was rather strange, because the government had previously objected to the Union for altogether different reasons. After having initially cooperated with her, the Ministry all of a sudden announced that it didn't recognize 'women' as a category for an NGO.

A further twist to her bureaucratic struggle occurred just before el-Saadawi's press conference in August 1999. She received a letter from the Ministry stating that they had already received an application from 200 organizations wishing to unite under one union. The letter stated that two unions in the same field simply cannot exist. The law itself doesn't actually state that, so it was almost certainly plain politics: el-Saadawi had long been a thorn in the government's side, and having her leading a women's union would certainly have meant more criticism.

But a new union was definitely in the making, and it saw daylight in 2000. It was called the National Council for Women (NCW). Minster of Social Affairs Tillawi was chosen as the Secretary General and the Chairwoman was none other than the First Lady, Suzanne Mubarak. In theory it was an independent organization, but in practice it was far from autonomous. Its headquarters were in the same building as the ruling National Party of Democracy. The NCW has more or less nationalized the Egyptian women's movement – which was probably the intention.

The secular feminism represented by el-Saadawi has always been, and remains, marginal in Egypt. Today, although the NCW has tried to bring it under one roof, the women's movement is still fragmented: there are up to 16,000 NGOs active in enhancing women's position in various fields.[24]

With the rise in religiosity, female Islamist voices have also become louder. Islamist women's organizations and networks have spread through their grassroots work. These groups often function as charitable organizations in the vicinity of mosques, giving them direct access to their beneficiaries.

Sherine Hafez, who studied Islamist activists (female preachers, charity workers), claims that no subject has motivated Egyptian women with such vigour as Islamist activism since the struggle for independence. It is open for all women, regardless of their social class, and it combines academic and social activities. "Many of their goals may appear modernist and even secular feminist, yet the aspect of authenticity remains central as a guiding framework. They insist on political participation for women as a legislated right by Islam."[25]

By "authenticity" she means Islam, but often these women are also nationalistic and anti-Western. Female Islamists consider Islam as a force to liberate them from Western oppression and from Western gender roles, rather than liberation from the rule of men. Islamists see gender roles as mutually supportive, and they therefore don't call for equality between sexes. Due to their anti-Western stance, they usually dislike the term Islamist-feminist.

Islamist women employ religious zeal, virtuosity and high morals for personal enhancement. Hafez argues convincingly that Islamist women don't fit the Western concept of women's empowerment because "...while they submit themselves to structures of authority that privilege men, they paradoxically empower themselves in dealing with men by acting in accordance with prevalent norms of ideal female behaviour."[26]

These women therefore believe themselves to be good Muslims, even 'higher' than men when it comes to their faith. These women are trying to achieve the ideal attributes of Islamist women, such as faith, virtue, morality, modesty and closeness to God. In other words, if a woman is a good Muslim, she can make society better. Yet Islamist women have been criticized for supporting and strengthening – maybe unwittingly – Islamist political forces which would, once they gained power, establish authoritarian theocracies in which women's position would undoubtedly be worse.[27]

This aspect came to my mind when I was following the Muslim Brotherhood electoral campaign in 2000. Quite a few of the wives, sisters and daughters of Brotherhood activists wore the *niqab* face-veil, in which only the eyes – if that much – are visible. Wearing the *niqab* usually signifies a more rigid interpretation of Islam, and at that time *niqab*s were even more rare than today. I couldn't help wondering if the *niqab* was the Muslim Brotherhood's ideal uniform for all women.

One of the most distinguished female Islamist theorists is Hiba Ra'uf, Assistant Professor of Political Science at Cairo University, and a regular contributor to the islamonline.net website. We first met when I was doing research for my MA thesis, and I wanted to know more about her ideas on the role of women in (theoretical) Islamist society.

She had suggested meeting at a coffee shop near the US and British embassies in Garden City, and she arrived arm in arm with her husband Ahmad Abdallah. She was wearing a long, cream-coloured *khimar* veil – a more conservative form of veiling than the one she first wore at the age of 13. In those days, the veil was more than a sign of religiosity – it was a show of rebellion, particularly in the German school run by Catholic nuns that she attended. "The message was always that the West is better. When I took the veil, the headmistress said with contempt that I might as well go to study at al-Azhar, as if that was something inferior," she told me.

Ra'uf's family was somewhat religious, but her real 'awakening' came after neighbours and friends introduced her to Qur'anic study circles. She also became acquainted with the Muslim Brotherhood, although she never formally became a member, and with the Deobandi group *Tablighi Jama'at* – a missionary group of Indian origin.

At university she was active in Islamist circles, but her MA dissertation topic differed from the traditional thinking of Islamist gender roles. While Islamists emphasize biological differences between men and women, Ra'uf claimed, basing her arguments on Islamic jurisprudence (*fiqh*), that there is nothing to stop women from pursuing even the highest official positions in a society. Like many Islamists in general and Muslim feminists, she has called for more independent reasoning, *ijtihad*.

Ra'uf urges a stronger role for women in the society – a woman can be a judge or a president (although she does not regard the role of the latter as central to an Islamic society.) Hiring and political appointments should be based on qualifications, and that's why she doesn't support gender quotas for low ranking jobs.

She argues that military service should be obligatory for women as well, because women should be more active not only in the governance of an Islamic society, but also in its defence. "As women, we have been used in many cases as tools for revenge – for example the mass rape of women in Bosnia. Women should learn how to protect themselves as well as their country. The idea is that women should have obligatory training for defence and first aid and related topics, and be ready to defend the country when needed," she listed. Here her view doesn't differ much from Western feminists – feminist associations often advertise self-defence classes.

For Ra'uf, what is missing from feminist discourse is an appreciation of motherhood and family values. She promotes the concept of the 'political mother' as a tool to empower women in their domestic role as educators and transmitters of culture and values. For this mother of three, the family is a microcosm of society: just values of a family can also be the basis of the whole society.

"I'm against representative democracy. I am supportive of direct democracy, in a system where the state is marginal and civil society strong," she argues. This model is the Islamist ideal, present in the theories of al-Banna and Qutb. Similarly, the Islamic council, the *shura*, can function as the basic component of a democratic family. If a member doesn't abide by the rules, she or he can be expelled (but to where?). Ra'uf is keen to emphasize that the model is an ideal, and that the only recipe she has for its realization is education.

A common theme in both the Islamist and secular movements is the perception that patriarchy, not Islam, is to blame for women's inequality. The so-called classical patriarchal belt extends from North Africa to the Islamic Middle East (including Turkey), and South and East Asia (Pakistan, Afghanistan, North-India and rural China). Characteristic of this area are extremely restrictive moral codes for women, rigid gender segregation, and an ideology which links family honour to female virtue.[28]

Muslims are quick to point out that Islam gave women rights which didn't exist in Judaism or Christianity or in pre-Islamic societies. Islam gave each woman the right to contract her marriage, receive dowry, retain control of property and receive inheritance.[29] The then common practice of burying female babies alive ended with the onset of Islam.

Overall, women's freedom of choice has been very limited within the patriarchal belt. Women generally constitute a less important part of the population, women's literacy is lower than men's, women's school attendance is lower, the fertility rate is high as is death in childbirth, nor do women participate in the formal workforce in large numbers. In general, the hold of patriarchy is stronger in the countryside than in cities.[30]

Nowadays the hold of patriarchy is diminishing due to a combination of financial factors – men cannot afford to support women as they used to, while modern women are more mobile and work. Yet women's work is still a topic of hot debate in these societies. Although in Egypt women have worked outside of the home since the days of Muhammad 'Ali (1805–48), every now and then conservatives point out that women's primary role is at home, as a mother and wife.

Islamists in particular believe that men and women have different roles. They fear that if women go to work, they might lose their feminine attributes. Scholar Valerie Hoffman-Ladd has listed the common fears of Islamists (and other traditionalists) stemming from women working outside their homes: "They will abandon their natural role of motherhood, which is their social and religious duty, they will lose their femininity, and they will be unable to provide the right kind of comfort to their husbands."[31]

Women are often considered to be men's servants, who have to please their husbands after a long day of work. Muslims who argue this refer to the Qur'an, which states that men are guardians for women:

> Men are in charge of women, because Allah hath made the one of them to excel the other, and because they spend of their property (for the support of women). So good women are the obedient, guarding in secret that which Allah hath guarded. As for those from whom ye fear rebellion, admonish them and banish them to beds apart, and scourge them. Then if they obey you, seek not a way against them. Lo! Allah is ever High, Exalted, Great. (4:34)

This has certainly been problematic for feminists, because it puts men and women in unequal positions, and even allows physical punishment of a wife's disobedience. Whether men take this licence literally or not, in Egypt, domestic violence is rampant. But as often is the case for statistics in Egypt, it's impossible to get any reliable figures.

In 2003, Iman Bibars, head of the Association for the Development of Egyptian Women (ADEW) established a shelter for women, which became known as *Bet Hawa*.[32] Always well-groomed, Bibars is a rare case of someone who will openly declare that she is a feminist. She received her 'calling' after reading Nawal el-Saadawi's work. Today, Bibars is among the most influential secular feminists in Egypt: she even brought Eve Ensler to perform her *Vagina Monologues* in Cairo – by invitation only – but it was still a shocker for many of the audience.

Her interest in female domestic violence stems from research for her doctoral thesis. She interviewed 444 women in Manshiet Nasr, a low-income Cairo neighbourhood, and found the result shocking. "96% of the interviewees had been beaten or severely abused," Bibars told me. The Nadim Center, which supports victims of torture, had produced similar results: almost half of Egyptian women become victims of violence in some stages of their lives. It is mainly domestic violence and beating, which occurs in all social classes, and within both Muslim and Christian Egyptian communities.

According to Bibars, women become accustomed to physical and psychological violence first through their father, then their husbands. "Women grow up hating beatings, hating themselves and they can't see a way out. Myths about women liking beatings, or having deserved it, are women's own protection mechanism. This way they can retain their dignity," Bibars believes.

Women often believe that a man has the right to punish his wife – particularly if the woman doesn't want to have sex. Bibars argues that Egypt is engulfed in a culture of violence: violence is an acceptable part of children's upbringing. The entertainment industry is also full of violence: in Cairo, parents take even small babies to watch action movies. Sex is censured, violence is not.

Yet according to the modern interpretation of the Qur'an, beating is only the last resort to discipline a wife. But the sura still maintains that a man is the head of household who provides for his wife, and makes the most important decisions in the family. Islamists are afraid that if women try to alter this balance and abandon their traditional roles as mothers, then society will slip into chaos. Like conservatives around the world, Islamists perceive everything through the lens of religion, and regard family as the core of society. They accuse feminists of lacking morals and devaluing domestic work. Blurring of gender roles scares them.

Islamist theoretician Muhammad al-Bahi has argued that if men are not in charge of women, women will lose all their human values, leading to the disintegration of family. She will lose her femininity, ability to participate in marital life and taking care of children. He also warns about the perils of women's financial independence: it will lead to women choosing for themselves whom they will marry, where they will live and whether they will have children.[33] What a scary scenario! In other words, Islamists look on women as children, devoid of understanding and discretion.

Girls' schooling is therefore not a high priority in many families. Girls' school attendance (90%) is slightly lower than boys (92%), but there are huge internal differences. While in Cairo and Alexandria 100% of girls attend school, in the rural southern town of Suhag only 75% of girls went to school (in the south also boys performance was weaker).[34] In Upper Egypt particularly, girls drop out of school more often than boys, because the girls are needed in agricultural work. Parents don't believe in girls' schooling – it is more important to get them married.

Public spending on education is on the decline: in 1990/1991 the state spent 5% of GDP on elementary and secondary education, but by 2008 it was only 3.25%. A large proportion of these funds are earmarked for higher education and administrative personnel's salaries. That is why the level of primary education in Egypt is worse than in many other developing countries.[35]

The miserably poor state of education is often the reason for dropping out. Classes are overcrowded, tuition is based on rote learning and school buildings are often in poor repair. According to an unpublished study completed in 1996, 77% of elementary schools had to arrange tuition in two shifts because they simply had too many students.

Furthermore, of the schools sampled, 80% didn't have adequate libraries and 10% of the school buildings were in such a bad shape that they had been declared dangerous. A typical classroom had a cracked chalk board, broken windows and not enough seats or desks for everyone. Hygiene also left a lot to be desired – 70% of the toilets were in such a bad condition that they were a source of 'pollution and disease'.[36]

Although education is in theory free, a big chunk of the family budget is nonetheless spent on it. In parallel with public education runs a system of private tuition: in practice the whole school system has been privatized. The reason for this strange arrangement is teachers' low salaries (less than €100 per month) and their consequent lack of motivation.

In principle, giving private lessons is forbidden, yet some estimates claim that up to 70% of pupils and students resort to private lessons. Sometimes, teachers simply don't show up for classes, and students are forced to pay separately for education, even in governmental schools. According to statistics, Egyptians spend up to LE13 billion per year on private tuition fees.[37]

The poorest cannot afford this system and take children out of school earlier – poverty is indeed one of the main reasons for dropping out of school. In the countryside, parents' attitude is crucial for girls' education. A population and health study in 2000 asked mothers of 6- to 15-year-old children if they would rather send a daughter or son to university. 53% of the respondents said it would depend on the child's skills, 39% would send a boy and only 8% would give a girl the opportunity to pursue higher education.[38]

Currently less than a fifth of women have joined the formal work force. Yet not only Islamists and traditionalists but also ordinary women argue that not all work is appropriate for women. For example, the Muslim Brotherhood's first female candidate for the 2000 parliamentary elections, the *khimar*-wearing former bank employee Jihan al-Halafawi thinks that women can follow her example, but within the limits of decency. "For example the work in TV or cinema, where women are not properly dressed [unveiled] is not appropriate," she told me during her campaign. (See Chapter 8 for more on Jihan al-Halafawi).

Legislation also places some limitations on women's work. Egypt's labour law lists some 30 jobs which are forbidden to women. The first category consists of morally dubious work: women are not allowed to work in bars or casinos, except in those approved by the Ministry of Tourism, or unless they happen to be oriental dancers above a certain age. Women are also not allowed to participate in the production of alcohol.

Other jobs off-limits to women are due to their dangerous or physically demanding nature: women are not allowed to work in mines (who would want to?), manufacturing explosives, pesticides or cement; expose themselves to radioactivity or handle lead or mercury (how many men would want to handle them either?) or work as porters in harbours or warehouses. Pregnant and breast-feeding women get a special mention: they are not allowed to deal with substances containing petrol.[39]

Most working Egyptian women are teachers or in healthcare. Since the 1960s, women's presence in the work force has increased by 50%, but it is still one of the lowest in the MENA region. According to a study by Cairo University, only 18% of women work outside the home. Women also leave the work force early – most working women are 20 to 24 years old (for men the age is 25 to 39). One fifth of working women don't get paid (particularly for agricultural work), while only 8% of men work for free. Most women work in the public sector (41%), while a significant number try to make a living in the informal sector (35%), for example as street peddlers or as seamstresses.[40]

A good example of grey area work is the thousands of women who work as maids or cleaning ladies. Middle- and upper-class Egyptian households, as well as foreigners, are pretty much obliged to employ a woman (or in rare cases a man) to wipe off the omnipresent Cairo dust. As a foreigner, Egyptians immediately see me as rich and privileged, therefore I would be considered stingy if I cleaned my flat, ironed my clothes or used public transportation. A foreigner cannot but support the micro economy.

Hala – my cleaning lady for many years – is a quiet, serious woman in her early 40s, who looks much older than that. She had the first of her three kids when she was only 18. That was the end of schooling for her, and she has now been cleaning flats for 16 years. Her husband works at a bakery, so the family is not the poorest of the poor because they both contribute to the family income.

Hala got into the household maintenance business because her mother is also a cleaning lady. It is a relatively good source of income, but I'm not sure what they think of their work. Some cleaners are ashamed of their work and conceal it from their neighbours. One thing is clear: she wants something better for her children.

Hala would like her children to study more, but her eldest son is mentally handicapped, while her teenage daughter just likes to sit at home and watch music videos. So Hala has pinned her hopes on the youngest one, a happy girl who likes computers and games. "I would like her to become a doctor, or a reporter like you," she told me when I visited their humble home. The youngest one attends a private school, which is several degrees better than the state schools. Hala has to balance between work and home, and she has planned her schedules in a way that she can pick up the youngest from school.

The prevalence of kindergartens has made it easier for women to take up work outside home. While before grandparents used to take care of children, now kindergartens and nurseries are taking over that role, at least for well-off families. Still, only wealthy families can afford private childcare, and state nurseries have long waiting lists.

Women who have managed to achieve the work–life balance have been able to manage successful careers in the male-dominated job market. A significant milestone for strengthening women's public role was reached in 2003 when the first female judge, Tahani al-Gibali, was nominated to Egypt's Constitutional Court. Al-Gibali, who is in her 50s, is a former board member of the lawyer's syndicate and a legal advisor for the United Nations.

The decision was praised, but to many it came embarrassingly late – particularly when in other Arab countries female judges aren't exactly a novelty. In Egypt women have been practising law since the 1930s, but they haven't been deemed qualified enough to act as judges – the first time a woman applied for a judge's position was in 1949. The Prime Minister at the time rejected Aisha Ratib's otherwise qualified application, referring to political reasons.[41]

Many people argue that the main hindrance for women's advancement in the field of law is the Supreme Judicial Council (SJC), which is in charge of nominations, approved by the President. Neither the Islamic law (*shari'a*) nor the civil code or the constitution forbids women from becoming a judge – men and women are equal before the law. Therefore, it is the regressive circles which insist that women's biology renders them unfit to work as judges. Previously the SJC has argued that women are not qualified, the job is too demanding and that it requires decision making and concentration. One judge explained his opposition to female judges this way:

> The nature of judicial work is very exhausting and requires that a judge not have his home in mind.... Judges are regularly transferred outside of Cairo... Will husbands allow their wives to live outside of the home? Will a family be able to bear it?[42]

Opponents have also used religious arguments; according to Islamic law, a female witness is only worth half of a male witness, so how could a woman be a judge? But lately, both the religious authority al-Azhar and the Muslim Brotherhood have come out in favour of nominating women to the bench.

Therefore it is attitudes, not legislation, that obstruct women from advancing to important positions. And although al-Azhar has supported nominating female judges, it has never accepted female board members of its influential Islamic research centre or Arabic language centre. Qualified women have applied in vain, because male boards have simply never voted for a female candidate.[43]

It is difficult to estimate how much, and what kind of impact presidential wives have played in the shaping of women's public roles. Gamal Abdel Nasser's wife Tahya stayed in the background, but Anwar Sadat's wife Jihan was, and remains, a controversial figure. At first she shied away from publicity, preferring the domestic sphere. But from the 1973 war onwards she took a more visible role. She studied, and later taught Arabic literature in Cairo University, did a lot of charitable work and participated in political debates – she even suggested female candidates for the ruling party's list. She also had a big impact on the family law (see below).

The current First Lady, Suzanne Mubarak, is the daughter of an Egyptian doctor and his English nurse wife. Like her predecessor, she first stayed at home, taking care of their two sons Alaa and Gamal. Once the younger son, Gamal, started school, Suzanne, like Jihan before her, decided to continue her studies. She studied political science part-time at the

American University in Cairo in 1972, under her maiden name Suzanne Sabet. (This was because by then her husband was becoming an important figure, named Vice-President in 1975.) She received her MA in sociology / anthropology, doing her thesis on a school project in a poor district of Bulaq, in which she also actively participated.[44]

When Husni Mubarak became the president in 1981, Suzanne first stayed behind the political scenes, although she did (and still does) a lot of charity work for children. But nowadays she is much more in the limelight and she has become, in a way, the leading figure of the women's movement, chairwoman of the National Council for Women (NCW).

Today, her face beams from the central Cairo billboards, advertising a literacy campaign. Her pictures decorate the state-owned newspapers' front pages, advocating women's and children's rights. For better or worse, the NCW has become the monopoly of the women's movement. Although female activists acknowledge her role, they argue that the NCW should not take part in the field projects, but act solely as the mediator between the NGOs and the government.

Although women have fought to get a foothold in business and the public space, probably the most obvious aspect limiting women's position is family law, which draws from Islamic *shari'a* law. For women's organizations, family law has been a difficult issue, because it favours men at the expense of women – in contravention of the constitution. Egyptian society may have changed, and with it gender roles, but men still cling to their power through family law, as if it was the patriarchy's last straw. It is family law which affects women's lives from cradle to the grave, because it includes rulings on marriage, child custody and inheritance.

In Egypt, family law is the only part of legislation which is based on *shari'a*. (The same applies to most other Middle

Eastern countries, except Tunisia and Turkey.) Other laws are adapted from Ottoman, French and British legislation.[45] *Shari'a* is not a solid, written law, but rather it is open for interpretations. The form and content of family law has always been a controversial issue – a battlefield for traditionalists and reformists.

The law is based on Islamic jurisprudence *fiqh*, which is derived from the Qur'an, Sunna, *hadith* literature, analogical reasoning (*qiyas*), and consensus of the community (*ijma'*). In addition, the four Sunni schools of law (*mathahib*) have their own interpretations of *shari'a* – Egypt follows the *Shafi'i* school.

Family laws were formulated with women's reproductive role in mind, and hence they made women dependent on their husbands or close relatives. For example, a woman's share of an inheritance is half of a man's, but in practice a woman's right to their half-share is not always respected – male relatives just take it for themselves. Also, a female witness is regarded as only half as good as a male – thus two female witnesses equal one male.

If a woman wants to get a divorce, the procedure is much more difficult than for a man. Custody is also problematic: by law, daughters stay with the mother until the age of nine, boys until seven, and then they return to their fathers. As strange as this may sound, this can be an enormous financial relief for women since it's very difficult to extract child maintenance from the fathers. Islamic scholars often point out that the economic constraints of the Arabian Peninsula in the early Islamic era affected the law: men supported women financially, and hence had bigger decision-making powers.

Sunni Islamic law was considered to be completed by the 10th Century AD, and for the next 900 years, in principle, it remained unchanged. The problem is that *ijtihad* (interpretation) is not applied to family law, unlike legislation dealing with other aspects of society. Indeed, new family legislation is often drafted with deliberately conservative overtones, so as to please the Islamists.[46]

In Egypt, family law was first formally codified in 1920, and modified in 1925 and 1929. The law remained unchanged until 1979 when the so-called Jihan Law (after President Sadat's wife) was enacted. The main innovation of this new law was to allow the wife, in case of divorce, to remain in the family abode. It also gave her the right to be notified if her husband was taking another wife, and the right to divorce if the husband was polygamous. But these equal measures were too much for the conservatives, who launched a fierce attack on this law, and it was repealed in 1985.

Women's organizations campaigned for new law, and it was finally enacted in 2000 after nine years of preparations – Islamists were blamed for the delay. One of the main innovations with the new law was to make women's access to divorce easier, the so-called *khula* process. This grants women an immediate divorce, if she gives up all financial claims, i.e. returns the dowry and other gifts from her husband.

However, in practice, women have to wait for months for *khula* because the family courts are chronically overstretched. Previously, women had to state a reason for divorce, such as a husband's neglect of the family, having a serious illness, or having just vanished. Impotence has also been upheld as a valid reason for divorce.

But if the wife wants to keep her dowry, the husband has to agree to the divorce. Often this doesn't happen, and the wife remains in an unhappy marriage. Getting a divorce is still much harder for a woman than if a man initiates it. To this day, a man can divorce his wife by uttering three times: "I divorce you" without having to resort to the courts

– registration suffices. This is in clear contradiction to the constitution, which states that women are equal before the law. In addition, husbands can still prevent their wives from obtaining a passport, or forbid them from travelling abroad.[47]

Another recent innovation was the establishment of family courts and a family fund, approved by the Egyptian Parliament in 2004. These courts specialize in handling cases concerning family law, and the hope is that they will ease and speed up the family dispute processes. Every court has three judges, a sociologist and a psychologist who act as arbiters. Women's organizations have called for designation of female judges to sit in these courts.

Supported by the Grand Sheikh and Mufti of al-Azhar, in 2007 the Supreme Judicial Council finally made a U-turn, and appointed 31 female judges. Most of them have been posted to preside over family courts, although not without protests from conservative male judges, who have claimed that their appointment contradicts *shari'a*.[48]

Another landmark was reached in March 2004, when mothers gained the right to pass their nationality on to their children. Previously an Egyptian woman married to a foreigner couldn't get Egyptian nationality for her child.[49] Prior to this new piece of legislation, children from these mixed marriages were denied free education or the right to work. Despite this recent change, children with foreign fathers are not allowed to join the Egyptian Army, or Police Force or apply for certain positions, 'for national security reasons'.[50]

Although the Qur'an sets men above women, elsewhere the holy book cherishes the importance of harmony and love between the spouses:

> And of His signs is this: He created for you helpmeets from
> yourselves that ye might find rest in them, and He ordained

between you love and mercy. Lo! herein indeed are portents for folk
who reflect. (30:21)

Islam actually has a positive attitude towards sexuality – as long
as it is within the confines of marriage. Marriage is therefore a
much bigger deal than in the West: it is the only approved
way to channel sexuality.

In the Middle East, lifestyles other than the heterosexual
family unit are looked down upon: living alone or leading a
happy single life is considered to be weird; unwed co-habiting
is rare. Getting married is the dream for many women, much
more so than having a successful career. The potential husband
has to be able to provide for the family, and many women
dream of quitting work after marriage.

Now more than before, young people are choosing
their spouses by themselves. At night, they gather on the
Nile Corniche in central Cairo, adolescent girls and boys in
their own groups, checking each other out. On the Nile-side
boulevard, couples sit on benches, planning their future,
holding hands shyly or walking arm in arm on the bridges
over the Nile. These courtship rituals retain an innocence which
has been lost in the West, perhaps due to the over-exposure
of sex.

But as in the West, finding a spouse via personal ads has
gained ground. In addition to traditional newspaper ads, one
can peruse potential spousal candidates on internet dating
sites – or more appropriately, marriage sites.

Despite these personal ads, getting married is still not
completely a deal between two people: according to tradition,
both families (and in particular the fiancée's brothers) participate
in the marriage negotiations. Families set the details and
the timeline for a marriage. The most important thing is that
the bridegroom commits to buying a home for the couple

– although renting a flat has become an acceptable alternative recently.

This requirement has become a huge headache, particularly for lower income couples, because salaries remain low, and saving up is almost impossible. Those with meagre means often build a flat adjacent (or above) their parents' house, but for those looking to maintain a middle-class lifestyle, it requires a more impressive household. Families also agree on the amount of the dowry (*mahr*). The bridal dowry is supposed to be earmarked for the furnishing of the marital abode.

It is possible to list conditions in the marriage contract, but women are often unaware of this option. For example, a woman can demand that her husband cannot take another wife. This is because, in Islam, men are allowed to take up to four wives.

> And if ye fear that ye will not deal fairly by the orphans, marry of the women, who seem good to you, two or three or four; and if ye fear that ye cannot do justice (to so many) then one (only) or (the captives) that your right hands possess. Thus it is more likely that ye will not do injustice. (4:3)

Some scholars have interpreted these verses as supporting monogamy, because treating wives equally is impossible in practice. Statistics support this view: polygamous marriages are not very common. According to 2004 statistics, out of a population of over 70 million (at the time), 3242 Egyptian men had four wives, 8350 were married with three wives and 151,920 had two wives.[51]

According to the 2000 *khula* law, husbands were obliged to inform their first wives of their intentions to take another wife. The law grants the first wife the right to divorce, if she so wishes, if her husband has polygamous intentions. But often men simply don't inform their first wives of 'additional family members', and pay bribes to the authorities to keep quiet.

The reasons behind taking a second wife are often socio-economic (to help out a widow or a divorcee, who are often looked upon as social outcasts), or sexual, particularly in cases where the first wife is not aware that her husband has another wife (effectively, he is maintaining a legal 'mistress'). This way the husband doesn't feel that he is cheating on his first wife, because he is acting within the letter of the law. Not all women mind being the second woman: the eagerness to get married – and hence gain the status of being a married woman – is often stronger than the desire for monogamy. And the first wife also might not be so eager to get a divorce, for financial reasons – she might end up on the street with nothing.

It is indeed very difficult to comply with the Qur'anic requirement of treating wives equally, as Laila S. Shahd (who studied rural polygamy) found out. In polygamous families, the wife for whom the husband felt the least sexual desire was at the bottom of the wives' hierarchy, and accordingly had a lesser say in the family's daily affairs. The second or the latest of his acquisitions was usually his favourite, because she was usually younger (more sexually gratifying) and stronger (a better worker).[52]

Shahd's study revealed that there are multiple reasons for polygamy. Perhaps the most common incentive for poorer families is agricultural economic reality: the family needs extra workers. So if the first wife is infertile – or she has given birth to too many females (male children are considered to be stronger workers, and they have a bigger inheritance claim for the land), the husband is likely to take another wife.

Yet sometimes sexual urges 'drive' men to take another wife: accidents or the after-effects of having multiple children can make intercourse painful for the wife, and thus reluctant to have sex. Sometimes, it is a wife's bad relations with her in-laws that lead to the husband taking a new wife – the first wife is slighted, while the husband's mother revels in her control. But Shahd argues that sharing a husband is not necessarily the worst option for a rural woman. In fact, a polygamous marriage is often a much safer option than divorce – women retain most of their financial, moral and social security if they stay married, whereas a rural divorcee will attract a poor status.[53]

The majority of Egyptian marriages, however, are monogamous. When the details of a marriage contract have been agreed upon (usually between the families), the fiancé is expected to buy his bride-to-be a golden gift (shabka), which usually means bracelets and necklaces, which the fiancée proudly shows off to the family.

Just in case, families often agree upon a settlement in advance which the wife will receive should the couple go their separate ways. The amount varies from less than €1000 to up to €10000, depending on the size of fiancé's pocket. Yet marriage contract negotiations between families can be derailed over minor details. *Business Monthly* magazine reported cases where disputes over curtains, plastic garbage bins and bathroom decorations meant calling off the wedding.[54]

In an ideal case, after the families agree on the contract details, there then follows the planning stage of the event. All social classes spend huge amounts of money on weddings; poorer families will have saved for years to pay for their children's weddings. Since the 1980s, wealthy Egyptians have chosen five star hotels as their wedding venues, and nowadays Egyptian women's magazines regularly publish pictures from the weddings of the rich and famous. No high society wedding is complete without a singer or two (the latest fad in the weddings of the super rich is to fly in Enrique Iglesias), often accompanied by an oriental dancer. Nor is it enough to have an uncle with a video camera – wealthy weddings have a whole film crew with sound and light technicians.

Once I attended this kind of mega-wedding at what was then the Cairo Meridien hotel, overlooking the Nile. Inji, the bride, and Muataz, the groom, were cousins – a marital situation still common in Egypt. When Inji was 18, her parents told her that she would become the fiancée, and eventually the wife, of her cousin Muataz. Inji confessed to me that at first it was difficult to relate to her cousin as a husband, because since she was a child, she had treated him like a brother. Also Muataz's behaviour towards her changed after they got engaged. For example, he started to pay more attention to the way she dressed. She interpreted this as his way of showing he cared.

Their wedding's opening number was the traditional zaffa, a procession of dancers and singers. Traditionally, the zaffa was performed outdoors, and its purpose is to escort the bride to the groom's house, where the marriage is consummated. An oriental dancer usually swirled around in front of the bride, accompanied by male drummers. Nowadays, however, the zaffa in the wealthy hotel weddings moves from the hotel lobby to the banquet hall, and the groom also takes part in it.[55] A dancer is no longer a must – Inji and Muataz's wedding guests danced without a professional lead.

As the zaffa escorted the couple to the banquet hall, video cameras followed their every move. Wedding guests sat still at the tables, while waiters served juice cocktails. The happy couple sat at their own table, on an elevated platform in the midst of their guests. Dance music blasted out at outrageous levels, to which the only interruptions were live performances by the stars Hakim and Hisham Abbas (Egypt's biggest stars still make most of their income from wedding performances, because concerts are much rarer than in the West). Egyptians love to eat late, and we had to wait until after midnight for the lavish buffet – which started with the must-have prawn cocktail. Altogether, their wedding cost over €16500, not including their honeymoon to Germany and France.

But only a very few can afford this kind of luxury wedding. The financial situation is so dire that many couples simply cannot afford to marry. As a result, the average age for marriage has gone up – it is not unusual for 30-something singletons still to live with their parents. The problem is not merely wedding expenses, but a shortage of affordable housing, coupled to the principle that men are supposed to provide for the family. The idea of a mortgage is still a new concept in Egypt, although the hope is that it will ease the newlyweds' (or would-be-weds') housing distress. Up until now, the down payment on a house was so high that only the very wealthy were able to take out a loan.

Not only are flats expensive in themselves, but so is furnishing them. When the average salary for a government employee is less than €100 per month, it is simply impossible to save the €2000 which is calculated as the average for furnishing a flat. In 2002, 513,000 marriages were registered, 66,000 fewer than the previous year. On the other hand, divorce rates have steadily increased: while in 1970 only 7% of marriages ended in divorce, by 2000, the number had jumped to 40%.[56]

For years Hisham, a friend who worked in tourism, had been frustrated by his inability to marry. Through his work he meets a lot of foreigners, some of them more privately. His engagement to an Italian woman broke off a few years ago, and then his subsequent Czech girlfriend also had second thoughts. He thinks an Egyptian woman is no longer a possibility for him, because he deems them too conservative. And a foreign lady would also be less likely to demand golden jewellery, a ready furnished flat, and her upkeep – something he simply can't afford.

As for many men, the financial side of marriage was a huge headache for him. Until then, he had been living in his father's former office, which he had transformed into a flat – this was the only way he had been able to move out from his parents' house. He once asked me what I thought would be the minimum income to support a European wife. Compared to Europe, living expenses are not high in Egypt, but his €200 monthly salary was simply not big enough to maintain a European lifestyle. He figured if his potential spouse also worked, they might be able to make it. Eventually he got a promotion and a higher salary. And his dream was coming true – he was getting married to an Austrian woman.

Hisham and his fiancée live together, but an Egyptian bride should, in principle, be a virgin. But in reality premarital relations do exist, and in particular, upper-class girls and boys go out together like their peers in the West. Yet these 'wild' years can be concealed once a wedding is around the corner. Some women even resort to hymen restoration operations in order to avoid the shame.

Rumours also circulate about secret *urfi* marriages between university students. *Urfi* is a marriage contract, which is easy to sign – and to break – in a lawyer's office, but it contains no financial obligations. Co-habiting couples might sign such a contract as a proof to their neighbourhood that they lead a respectful life. Yet *urfis* can be dangerous for women, because if they cannot prove that the marriage took place, it is very difficult to verify paternity or apply for alimony.

But such a lack of proof is not insurmountable, as the much-talked about Hind al-Hinnawi case showed. A costume designer, al-Hinnawi was 26 years old when she met up-and-coming actor Ahmed al-Fishawi, two years her junior, on a set of a television film. The couple fell in love. They didn't want to tell their parents, but they didn't want to 'sin' either, so they signed an *urfi* contract, with the idea that they would marry properly later. But things got very complicated two weeks into the *urfi* marriage: al-Hinnawi became pregnant.

"When I learned that I was pregnant, I was very happy. He was the only man to whom I'd given all of this, my body, my love," al-Hinnawi told me, as we sat at a trendy coffee shop in the Maadi suburb of Cairo. She is an intelligent woman with big gentle eyes; her short curly hair was pulled back with a white hair band, a tiny dark-stone stud decorating her nostril – a rare sight in Egypt.

But becoming a father wasn't what al-Fishawi had in mind. He consulted a religious figure, who – much to al-Hinnawi's surprise – was in favour of an abortion.

> At first I thought about an abortion and a hymen restoration operation. And just forget about the whole thing, and leave this chapter of my life behind me. And marry the next man and pretend that I don't know what to do in bed.
>
> But I decided that there was no reason for these kinds of lies. I decided that I won't hide this, because I will suffer psychologically if I get an abortion.

In Egypt, a child needs a father's name on the birth certificate in order legally to exist. Al-Fishawi refused to recognize the unborn child, or to hand over the *urfi* certificate, which would prove that the couple had been legally together. Al-Hinnawi did what few Egyptian women would dare: she decided to have the child and take al-Fishawi to court to prove his paternity. Overnight, the story leaked to the press, not the least because al-Fishawi is a son of well-known actors, and at the time, he was hosting an Islamic talk show for young people.

"In the beginning, no one believed me because he had this Islamic image. So I had to defend myself," al-Hinnawi told me. Her academic, very liberal family was a key part of her 'defence team', supporting her, and even taking part in TV talk shows. This is how her father, Hamdi al-Hinnawi, explained his position to me:

> She was talking about rejecting abortion, and that she will not respect herself if she gets an abortion. And at that moment I understood, that she was alright and she was respecting herself.
>
> I also knew who the father was, and about his attempt to escape and throw all responsibility on her. At that moment I decided not to let her down and I said "OK, I accept your view, don't get the abortion and I will defend you."

At first, al-Fishawi denied even knowing her, and his family attacked al-Hinnawi's, accusing them of just wanting fame. But as soon as his lies started to unfold, public opinion shifted to al-Hinnawi's side. Strangers called her and supported her – in the coffee shop where we sat, the waiter told her that he was proud of her. Even the Grand Mufti, 'Ali Gum'a, stated that al-Fishawi should recognize the child. After two years of court battles, baby Lina finally got her legal status: the court ruled that al-Fishawi was indeed the father.

A woman's honour and virginity are therefore of crucial importance: tarnishing her honour can ruin a woman's chances of marriage. A friend of mine told me the following story: when she was looking for bed linen at her aunt's house, she found a sheet with dried blood in it. When my friend asked what the purpose of the dirty sheet was, her aunt replied: "It is my honour," and folded the sheet back into the drawer. Her aunt had kept the memory of her wedding night with pride, but my friend thought it was a grotesque relic.

The same friend told me how once, while she was still a student, she had returned home a bit later than usual. Her father waited for her, black with fury, and said: "I can do what ever I want with you; I can forbid you from studying, just remember that. Nothing else matters but your honour – it is your only treasure."

Although her father died a few years after that incident – and she therefore gained more freedom of movement – she still takes care how she goes about outside her home. Doormen and other, seemingly idle, bystanders act as a kind of collective father. She doesn't allow 'strange' men to escort her home in the small hours, because the neighbourhood would immediately label her as a prostitute.

Like women in Huda Sha'arawi's time, modern women are freer if they don't have a father figure. Most of the independent women I know, who have their own careers and jobs and who choose their own spouses, have gained their freedom after the death of their fathers. Although these women live with their mothers or grandparents, they have more breathing space than their friends who still live under patriarchy. The latter have to make up lies just to get out of the house, and some marry solely to escape their parents. For some, getting a job can be the only way to have some life outside the home.

If urban women have a little room to manoeuvre, in the countryside a woman's or girl's honour is even more important. Sometimes it is protected by a terrible custom: honour killings. In Egypt, a family's honour is dependent on proper sexual conduct of its female members. Honour killing is a homicide, usually committed by a husband, father or a brother who suspects his wife, daughter or sister of forbidden sexual behaviour. Usually mere suspicion is 'reason' enough.

Although in Egypt honour killings are not as common as for example in Jordan, it's an ingrained habit in the rural south. Yet no one knows how many women are killed in the name of 'honour' – these killings are not categorized separately in murder statistics.

In 2004, together with four women's organizations, the Egyptian authorities launched a campaign to root out this habit. I went to see one of the project coordinators, lawyer Hala 'Abd al-Qadir, who works at the Centre for Women's Legal Assistance (CEWLA). Dressed in a pastel-coloured *higab*, forty-something Abd al-Qadir had toured Upper Egyptian villages, listening to sad stories such as this:

> The girl's period was late and her belly swollen. She was taken to a doctor, who examined her superficially and announced that she was pregnant. On the way home her embarrassed parents drowned her in the Nile. Later her body was found and an autopsy was performed. She hadn't been pregnant after all.

She was yet another unnecessary victim. If they ever went to trial, her parents probably got off scot-free, or received only short sentences: Article 17 of the Egyptian Criminal Law states that the judge can mitigate a punishment if the circumstances require it – a violent crime can be mitigated into a civil offence. This article is very often applied to cases of 'honour killing'. Article 17 leaves a lot to the discretion of an individual judge, because Egyptian criminal law doesn't specifically mention honour crimes.

Although women and men are supposed to be equal before the law, again the reality is different. Most Egyptian judges are male, and often act according to their prejudices or ignorance. "Judges, too, are products of their environment. If he is from the south, he might think that a short, let's say two-year sentence, in an honour crime case is enough," 'Abd al-Qadir states. Because the law is on the side of men, it is 'easy' to commit honour crimes.

Usually the perpetrator is a husband (41%), who suspects his wife of adultery. Fathers (34%) and brothers (18%) kill a daughter or a sister whom they suspect of immoral behaviour. Rape victims are also sometimes killed in the name of honour. These findings can be found in CEWLA statistics, which were gathered by studying 125 homicides reported in Egyptian newspapers between 1998 and 2001.[57]

> The girl was working in the fields, doing agricultural work. The young supervisor raped her and she became pregnant. The girl told her mother what had happened and they went to the police. The man was brought in, and they got married at the police station. [According to a now defunct law, a rapist wouldn't be charged if he married the rape victim.]
>
> This was outwardly normal marriage, they lived together and had a son. But after a year her brother and cousin learned about the rape. Although she was living with this man, they got into her house and killed her. They also killed her husband and their little son. In their mind, the couple lived in sin, as criminals, and that called for revenge.

Usually just a *suspicion* can trigger the murder. This is despite the fact that in Islamic law, the charge of adultery requires four witnesses to actual penetration, which in practice is impossible to present. As 'Abd al-Qadir notes:

> Rumours can ruin a girl's reputation in small communities. A girl can go out with her hair open, or in 'suspicious' clothes, or be late from work — and rumours start to circulate that she is not

honourable. And then someone has a talk with her father or brother…

According to a popular saying, a girl's honour is like a match; it can only be lit once. Women's organizations find it problematic that women's honour is tied to the honour of men and the whole family. The campaign aims also to change people's attitudes such that defining honour isn't tied to a woman's virtue, but to a man's honesty, for example.

Although women's organizations have raised the issue, talking publicly about honour killings is still very difficult. This culture of unspoken violence is deeply embedded in rural society and attitudes. Hala 'Abd al-Qadir told me that initially she was afraid of going to small villages and raising the issue. But she was positively surprised that people *did* want to talk about it.

Both Islamic and Christian religious authorities have denounced honour killings, but social attitudes don't change overnight. In addition to honour killings, the campaign raised the issue of rape and other forms of violence against women. By engaging police and the wider audience via TV ads, the campaign wants to convey the message that all violence against women is wrong, that a woman's honour is not tied to what she has under her skirt, and that even that belongs to her alone.

Another glaring societal shortcoming, and a source of sadness in many marriages, is female genital mutilation (FGM), which is also called female circumcision, usually by its supporters. Although none of my female friends is circumcized, some 97% of Egyptian women are to some extent (from 1995 Population Statistics) The work of NGOs has nonetheless begun to bear fruit: today girls are 10% less likely to be mutilated than their mothers were. The more educated the mother, the less likely her daughter is to undergo FGM.[58]

The International Population and Development Conference held in Cairo 1994 is considered to be a significant milestone in changing Egyptian attitudes towards FGM. An issue which had previously been a taboo was brought into public view, and dozens of NGOs rushed to educate Egyptian women on the physical health hazards, and psychological damage, of genital mutilation.

Yet it is usually mothers who insist on having their daughters 'operated' on, before they are married off, because "all the other girls are cut too". A new and effective system to persuade women of the lack of stigma in not undergoing FGM is the so-called 'positive deviance' idea. This is a woman from the same community, who hasn't been operated upon, who tells the other women how she was able to marry and have children, and that there's nothing wrong with her sexuality.

According to various studies, this custom is so diehard because people believe that it represses a women's sexuality and therefore increases her marriageability. It is a common belief that Islam supports the custom, but the Grand Sheikh of al-Azhar, Muhammad Tantawi, has affirmed that Islam doesn't even mention it. FGM is more a cultural rather than religious phenomenon, and indeed is practised by both Muslims and Christians in Egypt. Similarly, female genital cutting is common in the countries of the Nile valley and other parts of Africa but not to a large extent in other parts of the Middle East.

Girls are usually cut at the time they reach puberty, often together with other sisters or neighbours. It is a transition rite from childhood to adulthood, and usually the girl receives gifts afterwards. In Egypt the most common form of cutting is the so-called *sunna*, which means cutting off the clitoris, or an incision on the clitoris. In Upper Egypt however, a more crude form is practised, *excicio*, which means cutting off some of the labia. In general, the custom is more common in the countryside. This is how a Cairene woman, born in 1950, depicts her operation:

> ...I was six years old [...] when, I was being circumcised. I remember the circumcision clearly, and when the knife hit, it was as if someone had built a fire under me. They then twist a length of clean sheet or gauze which is soaked in disinfectant and sulpha powder and bind the child with it. My heavenly days, it's worse than fire, and you stay in bed, unable to move, with legs apart, for days!
>
> I wouldn't do it to my daughter. I wouldn't want to hurt her. But when they did it to me, I had no choice and no mind of my own. I couldn't discuss or argue or resist.[59]

In 1996, the FGM operation was banned from taking place in Egyptian hospitals. The law was appealed and reinstated in 1999, but it hasn't reduced the practice much. Most of the girls are operated on at home (similarly, 60% of women also give birth at home), often in unhygienic circumstances. The law has a loophole: a girl can be operated on if medical reasons so require – whatever they may be.

What is surprising is that doctors still perform half of these cruel cuts, even though they risk three years imprisonment. Often they are simply motived by money: doctors who barely make a living with their miserably low salaries can make a few extra pounds with this lucrative side-business. And a doctor perfoming the operation can merely certify a 'medical necessity'.

Many doctors are simply ignorant of the health risks, and operate only to get some extra cash. Circumcised women are more at risk of infection and they are more prone to remaining childless. Pregnancy and delivery are more painful for them; the FGM operation always leads to loss of blood – and sometimes even death. The problems don't stop there: painful intercourse leads to sexual reluctancy and therefore it affects both parties.

But if one is to believe Egypt's most famous sexologist, Hiba Qutb, not all hope is lost, even if a woman is circumcised. Qutb is a serious, confident but pleasant veiled woman, who obtained a sexology PhD in the United States, specializing in Islamic sexuality. She is a regular commentator on Arab satellite channel talk-shows and has broken the taboo that a woman can talk about sexuality in public. She also believes that cut women can reach orgasms as well – all they need is a little guidance.

"When a cut woman comes to see me, this suggests to me that the couple doesn't know how to practise foreplay correctly. I believe that a woman doesn't lose everything even if she has been cut: the external organ has been removed, but the nerves are still intact. So all you need is a different foreplay. So I teach the men how this should be done to their wives, so she can reach an orgasm," Qutb told me in her office. Her serious style and religious references (she argues that Islam invented foreplay long before it was discussed in the West) have made her acceptable, even in the most conservative circles. "I talk about sex like other people talk about politics," she explains, smiling. "I'm flattered to be able to do this kind of work, to be the pioneer of sexuality in Egypt."

With figures like Qutb putting "the cut" on the table, attitudes are slowly changing. Studies indicate that the key is educating women, because they are mainly responsible for continuing the custom (sometimes with male approval). Education renders women more receptive to new ideas – but it doesn't reduce the risk of FGM per se. But it is still glaringly apparent that a lack of awareness about the dangers of FGM – and gender issues in general – is alarmingly widespread.

Even as a child, the 'Other Sex' is made dangerously interesting: in state schools, girls and boys are divided into separate classes from 6th grade onwards, but in private schools they continue to be taught in the same classroom. In the last year of junior high school, reproduction and sexual organs are taught quickly and scientifically. Some teachers mention contraception, but many of my friends told me that more often than not, the teacher prefers to skip this topic completely. So youths get their sexual information from smuggled porn magazines – or the internet.

The Minister of Culture, Faruq Husni, wanted to change this, and in February 2001 he suggested that schools should offer more sex education. The Minister of Education disparaged the idea, arguing that these issues are already dealt with in biology, Arabic and religion classes.[60] Religion classes touch slightly on the topic – by emphasizing the importance of marriage and warning against extra-marital relations.

An important opening in this discussion was the film *Girls' Secrets* (*Asrar al-Banat*), which premiered in spring 2001. The film tackled such taboos as underage, premarital sex and teenage pregnancies. Predictably, it got the audiences gasping for breath. Based on a true story, the film presented its message in a novel way: without underlining or judging. Furthermore, it didn't have any superstars or top-of-the-charts background music. The director Magdi Ahmad 'Ali came from a humanitarian background: he had directed documentaries for the Red Cross, and worked in a hospital.

The film starts dramatically: the protagonist, 16-year-old Yasmin, gives birth, standing up, in her aunt's bathroom. Even though it doesn't show any intimate details, it is surprising that the shocking scene passed the censor. Yasmin had managed to conceal her pregnancy from her whole family – she had tied a scarf over her belly and coloured her sanitary pads for the previous nine months.

Her family learns the true face of things when Yasmin is taken to hospital. Her religious family is deeply shocked – her mother curses her to the deepest hell because she has shamed the whole family. That's why the mother lies to the doctor that the girl's husband is travelling. The young doctor doesn't believe this explanation, and without asking anyone, performs female circumcision on Yasmin. "So that she wouldn't repeat the same mistake," the doctor says. His colleague reminds him that the Ministry of Health has forbidden FGM, but he doesn't try to stop him.

Only Yasmin's aunt seems to understand her. The aunt blames the religious, conservative family for their ignorance and backwardness. In a flashback we see how sex education at school went downhill: the girls succeeded in making the male substitute teacher blush so much that he couldn't teach anything. That's why Yasmin didn't know what kissing the boy next door might lead onto. To avoid a bigger shame, Yasmin is forced to marry the boy, but she is anything but happy. Then the baby dies, and the marriage is annulled. Yasmin's father locks her in her room.

After the film, a group of women in the cinema lobby discussed what they had just seen. They thought that more boys should see the film, because they need to carry some kind of responsibility. The secular press widely praised the film, which challenges middle-class values and beliefs – these kind of 'mistakes' are usually thought to happen only to the members of the lower social strata.

The director had stated that the middle class just refuses to admit that all kinds of things happen behind closed walls. In his opinion, the head-on collision between Islamic-Arabic and Western culture has led to a bourgeois identity crisis. For them it's hard to admit that sometimes what happened to Yasmin happens to ordinary girls, even in Egypt.

Thus *Girls' Secrets* dealt with several issues on the silver screen for the first time: youth ignorance on sex education, premarital sex, and FGM. Perhaps a new film could tackle a related issue – the use of contraceptives. It is still very difficult to market condoms for family planning campaigns, because the connotation is that condoms are only used in extramarital affairs and with prostitutes. I couldn't believe my eyes when I saw the first condom advert on the Cairo–Alexandria road in 2003.

Further, while the HIV problem is still relatively small, only about 0.1% prevalence among the adult population, prevention is difficult because many still believe that the virus is an Israeli plot, designed to destroy the Egyptian youth. Because such issues cannot be talked about with their real names, conspiracy theories abound.

A couple of years ago a stubborn rumour circulated in Cairo about a chewing gum which put its users under a spell of uncontrollable sexual urges. However, according to the story, which was reported even in respected papers, the gum's effect was short-lived and dramatic: a moment of ecstasy was followed by impotence and the sexual paralysis of the whole society. And who was rumoured to be behind this devilish product? The Israelis, of course. Because they want to see the Arab populations extinct.[61]

In Egypt, it is probably safe to say that they shouldn't worry about extinction, on the contrary. Egypt's population grows by over a million per year. Over-crowding and population growth are serious problems, which eat away at the benefits of economic growth. Therefore in Egypt, family planning has been a major part of development policies. It was already integrated into government policy in Nasser's time with the establishment of the National Population Council in 1953.

This was a time of optimism about the fruits of the Revolution: economic growth and development would even out the population growth, which was then about 2.45% per year. Nasser, a father of five, probably felt like many army officers, that the size of the population was also a measure of its military might.

But by 1961, Nasser had already revised his family planning plan. He announced that population growth was the biggest hindrance to elevating Egyptians' living standards. Yet it wasn't until after the Yom Kippur war in 1973, that the national population program was integrated into state 10-year plans. As with FGM, the Cairo Population and Development Conference was also a milestone for family planning.

A new consensus was reached that family planning is the key, but not the only, way to curb population growth. Enhancing living standards, equality between the sexes and empowering women were deemed equally important. After the conference Egypt committed itself to following an action plan, which aimed to reduce infant mortality, prevent STDs and unwanted pregnancies.[62]

This commitment has brought tangible results. While in 1960s Egyptian families had an average 6.7 children, by 1999 this number had come down to 3.3 per couple. The target is less than three. According to surveys, most women would like to control how many children they will have, and the majority of married women have heard of contraceptives and know where to get them. Yet only half of them actually use contraception. Therefore sex education is needed, particularly in the countryside where many women believe that taking a pill after intercourse is effective enough.[63]

Although Egyptian women are in many ways worse off than their Western sisters, their mundane, day-to-day worries are often similar. But in Egypt, women perhaps emphasize more the idea that the home should be clean, and that women want to please their husbands by being good chefs and by prettying themselves. Even if veiling is on the rise (see Chapter 3), it doesn't mean that women don't care about their looks. Egyptian women seem to put much more time and effort on grooming than their counterparts in the West.[64]

I was quite astonished to see how many women go to the hairdresser regularly. They have their curls straightened with hot irons, and then curled again in princess locks. For a middle-aged woman, going to a hairdresser is still relatively cheap, and hair salons are also places to meet female friends.

Veiled women also go to a hairdresser; in some places they have their own sections and female hairstylists. A veiled friend once asked where I had coloured my hair. She wanted to know because she had just had highlights done in the same colour – but she couldn't show me hers in the middle of a restaurant. This woman can truly say she adorns for herself only (or for her female friends?) because no men can admire her new coiffure.

While manicures and pedicures are important for Egyptian ladies, the Arabic speciality is *halawwa*, sticky hair removal paste cooked together from sugar, lemon and water. Egyptian women remove all body hair, which often includes pubic hair. *Halawwa* is spread on the skin and removed with a quick pluck, like with wax. It is a painful experience, but Egyptian women just say that they are used to it. The *halawwa* ritual is usually performed at home, in the hands of a special *halawwa* lady, but the paste is also sold in supermarkets.

With grooming come Western beauty ideals. While pale Northern Europeans dream of an even tan, on the south coast of the Mediterranean, paleness is the trump card – many women even resort to skin bleaching creams. In the *Fair and Lovely* cream commercials a girl complains about her dark complexion, and her girlfriend recommends this particular product. Lo and behold: after using the cream she gets a boyfriend or a starring role in a theatre play! Yet bleaching creams are often harmful to skin, so many women endanger their health using dodgy pharmaceutical products.

Admiring slim or skinny model-type figures is also a recent Western influence. Egyptians like to joke that once a foreigner moves to Cairo and eats local food, it doesn't take too long before he or she needs to buy bigger clothes. Egyptian cuisine is heavy: *samna* (clarified butter) being a major ingredient, nor is sugar spared in desserts. These culinary customs come with a price, but health officials have only recently raised the alarm about the growing numbers of clinically obese people: in 2005 over half of Egyptian women were obese (body mass index over 30).[65]

In the TV commercials, fat women cook and serve food, clean and do the laundry, while slim ladies lie on the beach or shop at malls, wear make-up and drive fancy cars. Scholar Iman Basyouny sees this as the new cultural image: obese women are traditional and home-bound, while slim women are achievers, active and desirable. The slim body has come to symbolize beauty, success and style.[66]

More and more women want to look like the achievers in the ads, even though the average Egyptian man still prefers a rounder figure. As a result, even poorer girls take slimming pills, acupuncture needles and crazy diets.[67] Gyms have mushroomed in number, and some Egyptian women seem to live in them. I've seen them praying in the changing room, eating lunch, popping their vitamins and slimming pills, and chatting with their friends.

Losing weight is the hottest topic in the changing room. Having tried many cabbage soup diets, I can't judge anyone, but few of these women seem to get any results, and eating disorders have increased, just as in the West. This new dieting trend may also point a way for lower-class girls to 'climb up the social ladder' – they admire upper- and middle-class women, who have better standards of living, and are therefore slimmer and taller.[68]

Since dieting doesn't always work, slimming clinics and weight loss operations have become increasingly popular. Female customers of diet clinics confessed to Basyouny that a slim body was a tool in trying to get man – and in keeping from losing him to another woman. They all reiterated that women were doomed to suffering throughout their lives.[69]

To question this 'natural' state of affairs (or just for fun), I once dressed up as a man for Halloween. The party was held at the American Embassy in Cairo, and I was disguised as a mercenary, benefitting from an acquaintance's rather dubious wardrobe offerings. I wore camouflage trousers and army boots, with a worn-out olive t-shirt and a wide-brimmed camouflage hat. The piece to crown this hideousness was a thick fake moustache and heavy make-up, which made me look like I'd been through some hard times, and had not been getting much sleep.

My disguise worked like a charm. It was wonderful to walk the streets with no one eyeing me up, or wolf-whistling! What freedom! Even the US Marine who met party guests at the door thought I was a man. "In you go, mate," he said and then took another look at my passport. My costume was most confusing – at least four Egyptian men came and asked if I was a man or a woman. I just grunted.

Although I didn't make cross-dressing a regular habit, I couldn't help remembering how different it was for men to walk the streets, how much easier it is for them. Perhaps a woman wearing the full-body veil, the *niqab*, feels the same.

Notes

1 http://ecwronline.org/images/pub/ssh/sexualHarassmentResearch Results2008English.pdf.

2 http://woundedgirlfromcairo.blogspot.com/.

3 'Egypt first lady plays down women harassment reports', AFP, 14/11/2008.

4 In 1979 parliament had a 30-member quota for women (out of 360 MPs), but this was omitted in the 1986 electoral law.

5 UNDP Human Development Report, 2008.

6 Badran and Cooke, 1990:223.

7 Badran, 1993:129–134; Badran, 1996:8–10, 53–55, 61–65, 142–151.

8 Sources for the Huda Sha'rawi sections are her English memoirs, Shaarawi, 1986; and Badran, 1996; Ahmed, 1992:172–188.

9 The word feminism/feminist wasn't used before 1923, but rather its Arabic substitute nisa'iliyya (women's/feminine). The word feminism/feminist was adopted only during the organizational phase. It was taken from French, which was the lingua franca of the Egyptian upper class.

10 This 'isma agreement meant that the future wife dictated the rules of marriage, for example that it was to remain monogamous. 'Isma was very unusual.

11 Slavery was abolished in Egypt in 1877, but in practice it continued into the early 20th century.

12 The veil remained as an elite accessory up until the overthrow of the monarchy in 1952.

13 Scholar Leila Ahmed has criticized Sha'arawi for her pro-Western views and veil focus, like this: "It was incorrect in its broad assumptions that Muslim women needed to abandon native ways and adopt those of the West to improve their status; obviously Arab and Muslim women need to reject (just as Western women do) the androcentrism and misogyny of whatever culture and tradition they find themselves in, but that is not at all the same as saying they have to adopt Western culture or reject Arab culture and Islam comprehensively. The feminist agenda as defined by Europeans was also incorrect in its particularities, including its focus on the veil. Because of this history of struggle around it, the veil is now pregnant with meanings." Ahmed, 1992:166.

14 Shaarawi, 1986:131.

15 Prostitution was abolished in 1949 by a military decree, Whitaker 2006:132.

16 Badran, 1996:127–135.

17 Hoffman, 1985:234–235.

18 Al-Ghazali, 1994:50–51.
19 Hoffman, 1985:237–250; Badran, 1996:163.
20 Nelson, 1996:226.
21 Nelson, 1996; Ahmed, 1992:202–207; Hafez, 2001, s. 28.
22 El-Saadawi, 1999.
23 El-Saadawi, 1997:6.
24 HRW no. 8, 2004:8.
25 Hafez, 2001:32–33.
26 Ibid., 2001:80.
27 Ahmed, 1992:230–231.
28 Moghadam 1993:107–08.
29 Esposito 1994:94–96.
30 Moghadam 1993:108–110, 148–9.
31 Hoffman-Ladd, 1987:33.
32 Egypt also has four governmental shelters. HRW no. 8, 2004:46.
33 Hoffman-Ladd, 1987:34.
34 UNDP, 2004, 2008.
35 UNDP, 2004, 2008; Rania al Malky: 'Egypt's online teenybobbers expose education fiasco', *The Daily News Egypt*, 29/8/2008.
36 Baker, 2003:25–26.
37 See *Egypt Almanac*, s. 120–121; *Daily News*, 29/8/2008.
38 Zanaty & Way, 2001.
39 Ministerial Decree No. 155 of 2003 from the Ministry of Manpower and Immigration. The decree, issued 19 August 2003, forms part of the executive regulations of the new Labour Law, Law No. 12 of 2003.
40 Yasser Sobhy, 'Economic empowerment', *Al-Ahram Weekly*, 1–7/4/2004, issue 684, Moghadam, 1993:56 Ahmed, 1993:211.
41 Badran, 1996:188.
42 Anonymous judge, quoted in HRW, no. 8, 2004:15.
43 *Nahdit Misr*, 10/6/2004, Vol. 1, issue 62.
44 Sullivan, 1986:86–102.
45 Although only the family law is based on *shari'a*, other laws have to comply with it. All laws are drafted by committees, and then approved by the parliament. After that al-Azhar studies the new laws and issues a statement whether they are *shari'a* compliant or not.
46 Moghadam, 1993:109–110; Karmi, 1996.
47 See HRW, no. 8, 2004:1–4, 7.
48 Reuters, Egypt: 'First Group of Female Judges Appointed', 22/3/2007; IPS, Egypt: 'Female Judge Appointments Stir Controversy', 16/4/2007.
49 This is the case even if the husband was a Muslim. If a Muslim woman wants to marry a non-Muslim, he has to convert to Islam. A Muslim man may however marry a non-Muslim, provided she is one of the Peoples of the Book, or converts.

50 Reem Leila, 'Citizens at last', *Al-Ahram Weekly*, 1–8/7/04, Issue No. 697.
51 *Egypt Today*, 'By the numbers', 11/2004.
52 Shahd, 2001:64–67.
53 Shahd, 2001:19–35, 90–96.
54 Dalia Merzaban, 'The marriage market,' *Business Monthly*, 11/2003.
55 Kent & Franken, 1998.
56 Rania Khallaf, 'Silence is not golden', *Al-Ahram Weekly*, 11–17/3/2004, issue no. 681.
57 CEWLA, 2002.
58 El-Gibaly, Ibrahim, Mensch, Clark, 1999.
59 Atiya, 1984:110–111.
60 Gamal Essam el-Din, 'Sense and sensibility', *Al-Ahram Weekly*, 8–14/2/2001, issue no. 520.
61 Ghoussoub, 2000.
62 Ibrahim & Lethem Ibrahim, 1998.
63 Shahd, 2001:93–94.
64 Ghannam, 2004.
65 WHO statistics, http://www.who.int/infobase/reportviewer.aspx?rptcode =ALL&surveycode=102529c1&dm=5.
66 Basyouny, 1997:5–6. On the other hand, the men in the commercials are obese and eat with great appetite, but women are never shown eating, p. 43.
67 Ghannam, 2004:58–59.
68 Basyouny, 1997:33.
69 Basyouny, 1997:89, 103.

3

Hold on to your veil, Fatima!

— —

In the run up to the Iraq war, a massive demonstration was held in the Cairo Stadium. Speakers from Islamists to Leftist activists affirmed their solidarity with the people of Iraq; the intensity of the inflammatory speeches burned my ears. Tens of thousands of students took part in this government-sponsored mega-event, together with civil servants and peace activists – all, of course, under the omnipresent eye of the security forces.

Journalists were ushered to a lodge where the scholars of al-Azhar (Islamic) University sat in harmonious ranks wearing their burgundy felt *tarboush* hats; in a row above them sat the representatives of the Coptic Church in their black cloaks and long beards. Next to their booth were al-Azhar's female students, sitting decorously in a sea of pastel-coloured veils.

All around, the crowd was shouting "Down, down, George Bush" or "We sacrifice our blood and souls for Iraq" – and the charged atmosphere spread also amongst these young women, some of whom came to talk to the journalists by the booth. "Why do Americans want to kill Muslims? They only want Iraqi oil!" "What about Israel – Palestinians are suffering because America supports Zionists!" the female students shouted, reinforcing their point with vigorous hand gestures.

Most of these students wore the loose *khimar* veil, a garment favoured by the Islamists as it reaches the hips and softens the contours of the body. My attention was drawn to a quiet young lady, whose friends brazenly talked with the members of the press. She wore typical conservative Egyptian clothes: ankle-length skirt and a matching loose blouse. But it was her contrasting veil that made the combination rather strange.

She had draped a black-and-blue leopard pattern chiffon scarf over her face, so that only her eyes could be seen. She was a walking contradiction: a *niqab* veil, intended to make its wearer invisible, in an alluring pattern.

Subsequently, I often bumped into these kinds of wearers of confusing dress combinations. In downtown Cairo a woman passed me by, wearing a body-hugging black skirt and a skin-tight, off-white top, leaving little to the imagination. This curvaceous woman was crowned with a chest-length black *niqab* veil, offering just a hint of her eyes through a small opening.

Traditionally, the *niqab* is worn together with black cloak, the *abaya*, which dulls the shape of the body, giving a sack-like image of the wearer's figure. This dress combination is often worn with gloves, even in the heat of the summer – only eyes are allowed to be seen. But this young woman was promenading hand in hand with her female friend, swinging her hips seductively, deliberately attracting the attention of the men, young and old alike, passing time in downtown Cairo. What are these young women trying to convey? It seems that their message is that they are at once chaste, with a deep-seated religious conviction, but at the same time are desirable, sexy and dedicated followers of fashion. Traditionally, *niqab* wearers are regarded as deeply religious: their wearers want to be invisible, asexual. The full-body veil denotes the extremist reading of the Qur'an that women should cover their whole body. Yet Qur'anic verses on veiling leave room for different interpretations:

> And tell the believing women to lower their gaze and be modest, and to display of their adornment only that which is apparent, and to draw their veils over their bosoms. (24:31)

> O Prophet! Tell thy wives and thy daughters and the women of the believers to draw their cloaks close round them (when they go abroad). That will be better, so that they may be recognised and not annoyed. Allah is ever Forgiving, Merciful. (33:59)

The Qur'an doesn't therefore specify outright what the scarf or veil should be like, however, a widely accepted interpretation holds veiling to be a religious duty for women. From another point of view, the veiling order only applies to the wives of the Prophet, who hold a special status amongst women. In Egypt, the veiling debate surfaces from time to time, opposing views being the conservatives (the veil is obligatory) and modernists (the Qur'an doesn't specifically require women to veil).[1]

Currently, a consensus seems to prevail that the veil is a religious duty, and thus a decent Muslim woman has to wear a scarf. At the same time, the debate over veiling does not attract the same kind of obsession in Egypt as in the West, mainly because veiling is so widespread that no one makes a big issue of it. It is also why women don't much like to talk to foreigners about veiling— it's a personal choice which doesn't need justification.

The requirement to veil derives from a conservative Islamist notion that a woman's body, hair and even her voice are so sexually explosive that they have to be concealed. According to this interpretation, a woman is an active temptress, and a man a passive victim of his desires. Women must be shrouded to protect men and for the sake of functional society.

The late Sheikh Muhammad Mutawalli al-Sha'arawi, an extremely popular TV-preacher and former minister of *Awqaf* (religious affairs), was well-known for his misogynistic opinions. Years after his death, cassettes, videos and books of his sermons continue to sell well. The Sheikh had required compulsory veiling, because otherwise the society wouldn't be able to function properly. This is how he warned about the dangers of non-veiling:

> Society is composed of either married men or youths who have not yet married, because they have not yet provided themselves with the necessities of life – that is, they are still studying, or they have not found work. What will the situation be? Youths in their adolescence are just waiting for something to stimulate their instincts… If a youth sees these girls and sees their *tabarruj* [display of female body] and *zina* [adornment] a [new] factor has come into his behaviour … and he will try to relieve himself in any way. In this way, the society is polluted.[2]

Sha'arawi's society is thus solely comprised of men – the appearance of women is a novelty for him, which creates chaos unless they cover their heads.

A woman's body is therefore simultaneously vulnerable and threatening. Perhaps the wearers of the new *niqab* combination just reflect this contradiction. According to the Egyptian academic Fuad Zakariya, the body of a veiled woman is objectified; it becomes sexual. In other words, he says that the Islamists claim that a woman's body is more significant than her intellect. By this logic, men act completely in accordance with their lust.[3]

Most Egyptian women however consider the *niqab* too rigid, and it is worn mainly in Salafist circles. Nowadays the majority of Egyptian women – of all social classes – wear *higab* veil, which covers the hair and neck and is tied underneath the chin. Although the veil still symbolizes religiosity or belonging to the Islamist movement, there are several different motives for veiling.

When women are asked about veiling, the most common answer is religious motives: a need to be closer to God. Still others speak of a strong faith and see the veil as a religious duty. Some women will tell you that they want to be chaste, proper women. Such self-definition is connected to the illusion of bodily integrity: for example in crowded buses women are often subjected to sexual harassment. They hope that the veil will tell the other passengers: I'm a good Muslim, don't touch me.

In reality, hair cover doesn't give protection: veiled women also get their share of indecent touching or whispered, blunt suggestions. Egyptian author Sonallah Ibrahim describes in his novel *The Committee* the bus-squeezing – the Arab equivalent of Western discos – where this same thing happens, face to face.

But our national substitute fulfils a more complex role than mere release of repressed desires. It is a successful way of fighting the boredom arising from over-crowding and frequent long delays in streets jammed with private cars. Likewise, for me,

it is an important means of releasing tension and one method of
acquiring knowledge.[4]

Nevertheless Cairo has one pinching-free zone: women-
only metro carriages. According to metro officials, women
themselves asked for their own space in the early stages of the
metro, and now the front two cars are reserved for women.
Given the choice, I prefer to travel in the women's car, because
in the packed mixed-car one might be crushed into the orbit
of an uninvited squeezer.

The women's car has a high level of solidarity, although
in the heat of summer the metro is almost unbearable. Sweat
trickles uncomfortably, and plump women in polyester blouses
and cheap deodorant jostle from all sides, trying to keep
their balance despite their shopping bags and children. One
would think that wearing a veil, particularly the *niqab*, is very
impractical. But a veiled woman's answer is often simple: It's
hotter in Hell.[5]

Veiling is essentially about women's role in society.
The Islamist ideal, of a dedicated veiled wife and mother,
placing her family above all is utopian, affordable only by the
wealthiest. Often the West's interpretation of the veil is an
obligation dictated by men, a tool of oppression to bind the
woman to the home, at the mercy of her husband and her
domestic duties.

Sometimes women do take the veil as a result of male
pressure, but more often than not it's the woman's decision.
The veil does not represent "a return to the Dark Ages" – on
the contrary most veiled women work outside the home. It
has been argued that veiling gives the women an opportunity
to function in the public, male-dominated sphere: the veil
communicates that the wearer is a good Muslim, although she
is operating outside the home.[6]

One major reason for veiling is social pressure: when all of your friends wear scarves, few want to be the sole woman without one. Usually the veil is taken in the teens, a period when the opinions of others are very important. A girl who takes the veil is greeted with *"mabruk!"* (Congratulations!) as if it was her birthday. Some mosques even hold *higab* parties for freshly veiled girls – the celebratory programme consists of singing religious songs and the girls get to wear a crown on their heads, much like an American prom queen.[7] This is how a female Islamist preacher describes *higab* party:

> The experience of meeting a girl who is donning the veil for the first time might also become of interest and inspire those girls who are not yet veiled to wear the veil too. The celebration is a lot of fun. We sing special songs and the newly veiled girls wear a crown on their heads like queens, and we all congratulate and honour them. It's a great way to reinforce the importance of the Hijab as Islamic dress.[8]

In Egypt, community is emphasized above individualism and therefore the approval of friends and family is very important. Few dare, or even want, to be different. Egyptian filmmaker Yousri Nasrallah's documentary *On Boys and Girls* (*Subyan wa Banat*, 1995) discusses this phenomenon pointedly.

In a certain vocational school, only one of the teachers doesn't wear the veil. She explains that since everyone knows that she is an honourable woman, she doesn't need a scarf to prove it. Veiled colleagues try to persuade her to change her mind: if you're a good Muslim, it's better to cover your head. A few months pass and the rebellious teacher enters the school veiled. In a slightly resigned voice she tells that this is better, to take the veil was the right decision.

This phenomenon could be compared with the need that young people in the West feel to wear a certain type of jeans in order to feel part of the group. In Egypt, the veil fulfils the same role, although, of course, it doesn't necessarily mean that its wearer is not a convinced member of her own religious community.

A non-veiled, successful, young physician told me that many of her friends have decided to don the veil. "All the time, we non-veiled women feel like the accused; we have to defend the lack of veil constantly. Many women just don't have the strength to argue against self-styled moralists; it's just easier to go with the flow. But no one would admit that this is the real reason for their veiling. I think the whole phenomenon is just pure hypocrisy," she says.

Such hypocrisy has its roots in the Egyptian obsession for emphasizing the outward manifestations of religion: nowadays it is almost a fashion to be publicly religious.[9] Use of all kinds of religious paraphernalia has increased: more and more men can be seen rolling prayers beads between their fingers, murmuring the 99 beautiful names of God. Tapes of Qur'an recital blare out here and there, and almost all taxi drivers keep a Qur'an on their dashboard.

Mosque attendance is on the rise, and every self-respecting city block has at least a prayer room, if not a mosque. The religious stickers which were banned in the 1970s have also made a visible come-back: stickers proclaiming *"La ilaha illa Allah"* (There is no God but God) can be spotted in private cars and even in public transportation. If the marker of religious women is the veil, for men it is a beard, or among young men the *zabiba* ('raisin'), a dark callous on the forehead, which is a sign of frequent prayer. It is formed when the forehead touches a specific praying stone when praying.

With all this emphasis on outward religiosity, hypocrisy often follows. A grotesque story which got a lot of media attention centred on Ragab al-Suwirki, the owner of *Tawhid wa Nur* (Unity and Light) – a chain of shops. Projecting a religious image and long bushy beard, al-Suwirki sold all kinds of items in his shops; the successful chain was like the clothing department of a K-Mart, only with a religious flavour. But al-Suwirki had a weakness: young women.

According to the charges, this Don Juan of Egypt had five official wives (Islam allows a maximum of four at any one time) and 29 additional "wives" of whom some were under age (i.e. under 16). The charges alleged that al-Suwirki was married to these teenagers for a few hours or days, and then gave them money. In other words, he was involved in 'legal' prostitution.[10]

Al-Suwirki was also accused of forging IDs of some of the girls he married, so that they would appear to be legally eligible. The father of one of the girls and officials responsible for registering marriages were also involved in the plot. Al-Suwirki claimed that all of the marriages had been Islamic, and that the charges were just a conspiracy, aimed at destroying his retail empire. He was sentenced to seven years hard labour.[11]

Although superficial religiosity makes headlines, the events of 9/11 and the US-led overreaction that followed have increased genuine religiosity across the Arab world. US military actions in Afghanistan and Iraq (on top of its unfaltering support for Israel) were seen as an attack against all Muslims. The terrorist hunt and what some have called the clash of civilizations, revived the concept of the Islamic community, *umma*: Muslims are one, despite their nationality. As in Western Muslim communities, so in Egypt veiling or growing a beard can be a definition of identity: a means of conveying that the wearer belongs to the sphere of Islamic-Arabic cultural heritage. It can therefore be an anti-Western statement, a desire to 'go back to the roots'.[12]

On the other hand, some women don the veil as a feminist objection to materialism and commercialization of women's bodies; such women usually choose to wear the more voluminous *khimar* scarf. One might think that veiled women would save on expenses as they don't have to groom themselves, but a whole new business has risen dependent on the veil: *muhaggabat* (veiled women) have their own shops where they can buy scarves to match their outfits, and other loose-fitting clothes. Women's magazines offer styling tips for the veiled, and tell them where to find the best patterns. In Cairo, there are even scarves by top fashion designers. *Jumanah* magazine presents 'veiled fashion': even brides have veils to match their wedding gowns.

Yet women, particularly the younger ones, often combine the veil with Western clothing, so its colour has to match the rest of the combination. Nowadays, veils come in all materials, patterns and colours. Some women apply the veiling rule so that as long as limbs and hair are covered, the garments themselves can hug the figure. Often veiled women use a lot of make-up, and curls escape from under the scarf. A woman might still pay regular visits to the hairdresser, even if she wears the veil. Religiosity is hardly the chief motive for these women, but rather it is social pressure. It can be said that for more and more women the veil is just a piece of clothing. It has become the norm for dressing.

In the 1980s, one of the most important motives for veiling was financial. A friend of mine who studied at Cairo University at the time said that, initially, it was only the poorest students who wore the veil – they saved on hairdresser expenses. A higher echelon civil servant gave a similar explanation: "Egyptian women have bad hair and that's why they have to go to the hairdresser. But they can't all afford it, so that's why some wear the veil," he said with a straight face. Whatever the quality of Egyptian women's hair, veiled women definitely save on salon expenses.

It is doubtful that those who wear the face-covering veil *niqab* spend much time at the hairdresser. But they are a minority in Egypt, and the full-body veil is not tolerated everywhere. They are forbidden on university campuses, including at the Islamic al-Azhar University. The decree to that effect issued by the Ministry of Education in 1994 has been explained on "security" grounds: the university has to be able to recognize the students, for example in examinations.

The then Minister for Higher Education was considered to be a liberal, who opposed religious extremism, so it is commonly thought that the *niqab* ban was primarily a message that overtly religious symbols would not be tolerated on campus. It has been said that the state doesn't want to promote religiosity, although most women are now veiled; it fears that the Islamist opposition benefits from a rise in religiosity and that's why the state doesn't want to encourage it.

However, the *niqab* ban is not observed literally (women get away with it), in governmental universities at least. The elite American University in Cairo (AUC) has made several headlines over *niqab* issues – 19-year-old AUC economics major Muna's case was one of them in autumn 2000.

AUC was established in 1919 as the flagship of English-language university education in Egypt; it was also supposed to help Americans understand the Middle East better. Nowadays it hosts some 5000 Egyptian students, who pay thousands of dollars in term fees. "Today, AUC emphasizes liberal education [...] In addition, the university maintains its strong commitment to fostering understanding across world regions, cultures and religions."[13]

It is certainly all that, but most of all it is a strange fortress where rich families' spoiled kids pay more attention to the latest fashion trends than to Derrida's deconstruction theory. When I was working on my MA thesis, I tried to use the AUC library as my reading room. Studying there turned out to be impossible: couples used it as a dating ground, groups of friends as a great place for socializing, and mobile phone users as an ideal place to test ringtones – despite the ban on mobile phones.

AUC students often speak a mixture of English and Arabic, and since many of them got their elementary schooling in the West many never master classical Arabic at all. Fewer than average numbers of girls wear the veil, although headcoverings have gained prominence there lately.

In contrast, Muna was a bit of an exception amongst the mainstream AUC students: a deeply religious young woman. She started off by wearing the *higab*. Muna frequented an Islamic study group, which studied the holy book (the Qur'an) and the Prophet's tradition (*hadith* literature). "From what I was reading, I came to the conclusion that *niqab* was the proper option," a publicity-avoiding Muna told me at the time.

She said that at first she had thought of switching to *niqab* after marriage, but the decision to bring forward the introduction of the full-body veil grew little by little. "Well, at first I was afraid what people would say at university, or among my family and friends," Muna recalled. In the beginning, her parents objected to her radical transformation – often parents oppose a young woman's veiling because it is thought to have a negative effect on her marriage prospects, particularly if the veil is the puritanical, all-covering *niqab*. Gradually the family adjusted to the idea. Muna was allowed to wear the *niqab* for a month in the campus before it was banned.

A media frenzy arose based on the notion that an elite university, which prides itself on a liberal tradition and respect for individual liberty – to a point, that is – did not allow difference. AUC's position was that, ultimately, it is obliged to follow the rulings of Ministry of Higher Education: *niqab* is forbidden. The university sees the matter as one of security, because a student is difficult to recognize just by her eyes; Muna sees it differently, and considered the ban to be a form of discrimination. "I showed my face to the security guards at the gate, and during the exam season to the examiners – this procedure would have been fine with me," she explained.

Muna wasn't allowed to wear *niqab* on campus, and she was required to sign a declaration that she would comply with AUC policy on veiling. Instead of the *niqab*, Muna and her friends opted for a temporary solution: they covered the lower part of their faces with a book or a piece of paper, looking like drivers at Cairo airport holding name plates for arrving passengers.

Other AUC students have complained that these paper-wearers bring an uneasy, fanatic atmosphere onto campus. Although most of the paper-wearers act out of religious conviction, their intentions have not always been pure.

A friend of mine who taught at AUC at the time recalled an event. While serving as a monitor for a test, a few students in the classroom held papers over their faces. But there was one whose paper moved so frantically in front of her face that the examiner decided to check if everything was in order. The young woman had covered the paper with notes; her disposable veil had turned into a handy crib sheet. Yet it is unlikely that she was the only one cheating in that classroom: the skill is learned in elementary school and continues to be cultivated in university – with or without a veil.

In the end, however, AUC had to retreat from its stance. A student from the Islamic al-Azhar University was told not to enter the campus with *niqab*. She took the case to an Administrative Court, which decided that AUC had broken the law. According to the verdict, a student has the right to express herself via the veil. AUC has appealed the verdict, and the court gave its final verdict on June 9th 2007 – ruling in favour of the student.[14] AUC has argued as per the Ministry of Higher Education, that the veil-ban is purely a security matter, which has come to the fore particularly after 9/11. However, the Administrative Court verdict applies only to this particular student's case, and does not set a precedent for the university policy as a whole.[15]

Although a veiled woman is almost the norm, *higab*-wearers have caused problems, mainly for image reasons. The example of Nirin Salim is like a Hollywood film – complete with a happy ending.

Ever since she was a child, Nirin Salim wanted to be a pilot. When her family travelled on holiday, young Nirin's highlight was always the aeroplane experience. Every time she flew, she wanted to visit the cockpit and chat with the captain. While other girls played with their dolls, Nirin flew model aeroplanes. The dream of being a pilot endured, even as she was crowned Miss Egypt in 1989. Unlike many actresses and singers who denounce their past after a religious awakening, Salim doesn't regret her beauty queen era. "That was then, and in my opinion the pageant was in conformity with Islam – even the swimsuit round was held behind closed doors," Salim told me at the time.

After the beauty contest, Salim got a job as an airhostess with Egypt's national carrier, EgyptAir. But instead of handing out plastic trays, she was eager to get hold of aircraft controls. A year later, she gained her pilot's licence at a Californian flying school. Her first appointment was with the now defunct Shorouq Airlines, jointly owned by EgyptAir and Kuwait airlines. She advanced rapidly in her career, and became a so-called "A-class" co-pilot who flew charter flights to Europe.

"For me it wasn't important where I was flying, as long as I could fly," she recalled. She was the only female pilot in the company – although Egypt has about 10 female pilots.

Everything was going smoothly until the holy month of Ramadan in 2000, when she decided to take the veil. "I had thought about it for a long time, and every time I saw veiled women, I admired their courage. Lately I've become closer to God, so I decided to veil," she said to explain her decision. Very often, the decision to don the veil is preceded by a deep thought process.

Salim purchased a blue veil, matching the colour of her uniform, and tied it tight over her hair, under the pilot's cap. While her colleagues seemed to react positively to the novelty, her employer disagreed: she was suspended from flying. She was told straight to her face that she was not allowed to fly if she wore the veil. Salim kept her scarf, but a month later lost her job.

The reason given for her dismissal was alteration of her uniform from that stipulated in her contract. Our heroine didn't think she had altered her uniform (because for her the veil was an integral part of her new identity) and the contract made no specific reference to the veil. She did not think that her almost unnoticeable scarf was a safety risk either, because it impeded neither her vision nor her hearing – although the *niqab* would have been another thing altogether. Shorouq Airlines have refused to comment on the case, but many observers have interpreted that the dismissal had more to do with image. Perhaps after 9/11 a veiled pilot would be seen as a threat in Europe, where Shorouq Airlines was operating.

The attitude of Egypt's tourism sector towards veiling is generally negative: many travel agents' clerks and guides have been told not to come to work veiled. The fear is that tourists might interpret veiled workers as backward or incompetent, when tourism officials want to show the modern face of the country. Therefore many tourism sector employees remove their veils during work hours. But has anyone ever asked tourists what they really make of the veil? Wouldn't it just be an added experience for European tourists, looking for the ultimate Oriental exotica?

Our veiled pilot complained about her treatment to the Employment Tribunal, demanding compensation for lost income. When the issue appeared on the news, she gained a surprising supporter in the form of the Muslim Brotherhood. Although this moderate Islamist group is well known for championing those persecuted for their beliefs, it is also known for its fierce anti-beauty pageant stance.

The Brotherhood argues that beauty pageants are against the Egyptian constitution, and defame women. Muhammad Mursi, the head of the Muslim Brotherhood parliamentary bloc, told me at the time that while he had indeed heard about Salim's pageantry past, now she was suffering discrimination stemming from expressing her religious conviction. "Now she is trying to start a new, more conservative life, may God have mercy on her," he noted.

Salim says she doesn't have any regrets, although the idea that she might never be allowed to fly again saddened her. She is still waiting for the verdict on the compensation, and for a while her prospects for flying again looked gloomy. Finally in 2004 she got a job with Air Memphis, flying charter flights to Europe. "I had proved that the veil didn't interfere with my hearing or vision, and the passengers onboard didn't mind it," Salim told me in spring 2007. Just four months ago, her route was cut and she had to compromise with her new employer Air Cairo. "I'm not allowed to wear the veil with my uniform," she sighed, as if tired of fighting over her headscarf.

Meanwhile, Shorouq Airlines has gone bankrupt, and as at Air Cairo, the attitude towards veiling has become no more tolerated in certain fields. In the Egyptian private sector there are no accepted norms when it comes to veiling. For example, multi-national companies, television, and the tourism sector reflect a negative attitude towards it.[16] Employees who veil are usually assigned back-office roles, particularly in companies dealing with foreigners.

In the autumn of 2003 a group of reporters for Egypt Television sued the company for discrimination. These women had been sidelined to work behind the camera, or their contracts hadn't been renewed as soon as they took the veil. Egyptian television news and current affairs programs don't feature veiled announcers or reporters, because the state doesn't want to encourage religiosity.

Veiling is a sensitive matter; these women were afraid of losing their jobs, and so were unwilling to be interviewed under their real names. I spoke with a few of these young reporters, and to their mind the matter was clear-cut: the veil is an expression of their identity; the employer should not interfere. "If my employer doesn't want my contribution the way I am, I'll go somewhere else," one of them said.[17] A growing number of veiled reporters have started to freelance for Saudi Arabian religious channels, where a diametrically opposite veil policy is in place: you *have to* wear a veil on-screen.

Like the pilot Nirin Salim, many women don the veil during the month of fasting, Ramadan. During the holy month, believers are not allowed to eat, drink, smoke or have sex from sunrise until sunset. They should also read the Qur'an and spend time with their family. Most Egyptians keep Ramadan, even if they aren't normally religious.

Following the Prophet Muhammad's example, Ramadan should be a time of physical and mental striving, of abstinence.

Yet in reality, this is the time when people truly indulge in food. In Egypt, the consumption of meat and sugar increases enormously: housewives prepare delicacies for *iftar* (breakfast), ending the daily fast, while many people cram their stomachs just before sunrise with *suhur* (dinner).

By the second week of Ramadan, Egyptians start to lose their nerve. Despite the commercialization of Ramadan, and the side-effects of daylight fasting (crankiness and a decline in productivity), the holy month is a time of togetherness and composure. During Ramadan, Muslims spend more time pondering religious questions, visiting mosques and reading the Qur'an. This is the time when many decide to become better Muslims, and for women this decision is often manifested by taking the veil.

Famous actresses, singers and belly-dancers pose re-pentantly in glossy magazines, revealing their new-found faith; how they left behind a life of sin, and now perform only for charity. Some celebrities continue working in television – as religious programme hostesses or as preachers, although according to persistent rumours, Islamists or Saudis have paid these women to take the veil, renounce their "immoral" profession, and stay at home.[18]

Quite a few of these starlets have become convinced of the necessity of *higab* after hearing the sermons of celebrity preacher 42-year-old Amr Khaled. Labelled as a preacher of "modern Islam", Amr Khaled was catapulted into the lime-light as an upper-class preacher – he is from a well-to-do family. Good contacts with the elite guaranteed this former Muslim Brotherhood member access to private 'Islamic salons', and eventually (via satellite channels, cassettes, computer programs and DVDs) to ordinary Egyptian homes.

Swapping accountancy for preaching, Khaled started his new career in the middle-class neighbourhood of Muhandisin, next to the Shooting Club. This establishment was a regular hangout for the nouveau riche who had made their fortunes in the Persian Gulf oil countries, as well as being a place where secularists and Islamists fought over power. From the Shooting Club, Khaled's path led to bigger and bigger mosques, filled to the utmost limit with eager listeners. However, citing traffic jams, the authorities forbade him from preaching in the centre of Cairo; he had to retreat to suburban mosques, further from the city centre: Amr Khaled had become too popular.

Smartly but casually dressed, Khaled's demeanour was in tune with the times; unlike traditional preachers, he spoke like his target audience, in colloquial Arabic, and about mundane issues. He didn't try to portray himself as a theologian; in soft tones, he talked about God's love and forgiveness rather than about hellfire and damnation. His basic message was: 'it's ok to be rich, as long as you act according to Islam'. As an example, he reminded his audience of the importance of modesty and respect for Islamic principles during the summer holidays, when temptations are known to run wild at Egypt's most expensive resorts. Khaled has been compared to American televangelists, who combine faith and fun in their emotionally charged message.

Khaled's target audience was not just the rich young; it was women. Although his ministry might be outwardly modern, he is nonetheless conservative in his opinion of gender roles. He argues that veiling is a religious duty, because unveiled women are promoters of sin. (According to the modern interpretation of Islam, veiling is a right not an obligation.) This doctrine should not be questioned, even if one doesn't fully understand it, Khaled argues. In such thinking, Khaled shows the influence of his mentor, Umar 'Abd al-Kafi, who supported gender segregation and objected to women working outside the home.[19]

This is how Amr Khaled describes the importance of veiling in his website:

> If I ask you sister a question: If you have something precious, will you protect it? If a woman has a pearl, for instance, will she put it in a safe place away from danger? I do believe every woman will. The more this pearl is precious, the more the woman will keep it aloof of others. She will keep it away from any treacherous eyesight. A pearl is preserved in an oyster, which is not beautiful at all. Nevertheless, the oyster is badly needed for the protection of the pearl. The same applies to hijab, which is indispensable for women's protection. What is the most precious possession of a woman? Isn't it her modesty? Doesn't that deserve even higher protection?[20]

Sociologists tend to agree that celebrities' taking the veil is a chain-reaction. Although Khaled's message offers little new (besides tailoring it to the problems of the rich), he represents a new trend which has been called Active Piety. Sociologist Asef Bayat terms Khaled a post-Islamist: his message is simultaneously conservative and moralizing – like the traditional Islamists – and modern because it is connected with the material problems of the upper class. Bayat argues that a paradigm shift is occurring: away from mass Islamist movements, towards personal piety and conduct. The fundamental goal is personal salvation.[21]

'Salvation seekers' were numerous, and Khaled attracted such a huge following that the government became worried. Khaled was banished from Egypt on the eve of Ramadan 2002 – although the official version explained that the preacher had left for PhD studies in Wales. Despite his physical absence, his tapes and CDs sold like hotcakes throughout Egypt and beyond; he has been the best-selling author at the Cairo book fair for several years now. His website gets almost

30 million hits annually, and in 2007 *Time Magazine* named him number 13 of the world's most influential people. Khaled was allowed to return to Cairo in late 2005, where he set up an office in the Muhandisin neighbourhood. He was still keeping a low profile, and because the office didn't have any signs at the front, it was a bit tricky to find. Several people sat in the reception area, waiting silently for the superstar. Wearing a blue pinstriped suit, orange tie and a TAGHeuer watch on his left wrist, he greeted us with a warm smile. He speaks fluent English, but wanted to conduct the interview in Arabic, the language of his original message.

Indeed, he spoke like the preacher I had seen on television, his voice rising when he wanted to say something intense, and quickly lowering again to almost a whisper. He would occasionally close his eyes, as if being moved by a divine force. He performed this act very well, with an intensity that seemed genuine.

"Faith pushes development, and moves this development. I can tell you that we started with thousands, then tens of thousands and I don't think I'm exaggerating if I say that hundreds of thousands of young men and women are working with us," he said. He had recently started his Life Makers program, which encourages young people to be active: take care of their health (he had a non-smoking campaign) or try to generate jobs (cultivating tomatoes on rooftops).

"My goal in life, and my message is participation, in the events of this rebirth (*nahda*) in this part of the world. It's not important if I won't live to see it, but we have to plant the first seeds of this renaissance," he declared. But of course I had to ask him about veiling, since he is responsible for so many women taking it.

> *Higab* is a religious duty (*fard*) for us; we cannot say this isn't
> so. We cannot remove this truth. But on the other hand, Amr
> Khaled's personal opinion is co-operation with women, respect for
> all the women and there is no preference if someone is veiled
> or not. Never.

When we finished the TV interview, I've never seen the
Egyptian camera crew so excited. The cameraman and soundman were full of awe and respect for Mr Khaled. And we all
ended up taking pictures, posing next to the preacher.

Yet there are girls and women who wish not to wear
the veil, or have unveiled. For them non-veiling is a protest
against mainstream Islam or against Islamism, but they may
be no less religious than their veiled sisters. They just feel that
Islam doesn't require a veil. For a woman to reveal her hair
might also be a sign of a secular or westernized worldview, or
simply a manifestation of wealth and social freedom to go
about without a veil. It may also be a feminist statement: the
veil is seen as an instrument of inequality because it separates
women from men, yet at the same time, no comparable
modesty is required of men. Nevertheless, non-veiled women
often feel the need to emphasize their equal piety through
their demur conduct or choice of clothing.[22]

Hadil is a writer for a culture magazine in her late
20s, who doesn't want to put a scarf on her head. "I think that
more important than the outer sign is inner faith, morals and
ethical principles," Hadil says. She is a decent, if serious, family
girl, who lives at home with her middle-aged, middle-class
parents. She doesn't drink alcohol, doesn't have a boyfriend,
prays periodically and keeps Ramadan. At work, she is in
regular contact with the opposite sex, and like many successful
women she has an unforced approach towards friendly
male-female interaction. She does not think the veil is needed
as a proof of high morals.

Hadil's mother took the veil after she turned 30, when her brother died suddenly. "I thought a lot of about death, and what leading a good life entails. I became convinced that I should try to be a better Muslim and so I donned the veil," the mother recalls. As a young woman she prided herself on her fabulous hairstyles, but now the maths teacher wears a bonnet, which is more like a decorated knitted cap than a scarf.

Their family album illustrates how times have changed. The photos from the 1960s could be from anywhere in the world: backcombed hair, heavy eye-liner and miniskirts were a part of the Cairo street scene, as much as veils are today. Little by little, moving to the 1970s, the pictures document the rise of the Islamist trend, and more veils appear on female relatives, until we get to the early 1990s and the mother's *hajj* (pilgrimage) photos. Posing in her pilgrim's white garb, she looks happier than in all the other photographs.

But she hasn't completely burned the bridges to her past. Her husband, a retired lawyer, joined our discussion. "Yes, but tell me why do you still go to the hairdresser every week, even when no one can see your hair?" The mother smiled flirtatiously, and answered: "For you, of course!" Hadil burst into laughter and her father also had a hard time believing this theory. It was difficult to say whether the mother's reply meant that old habits die hard, or that she really wanted to look nice for her husband. For many Egyptian women it is a matter of pride to beautify themselves for their husbands – and they leave the veil on the coat rack at the front door.

A much smaller group are those women who've had second thoughts and taken the veil off. For them the topic is sensitive, and they don't really want to dwell on the subject. They feel that their society finds it difficult to understand why they de-veiled – there must be something wrong with a woman who does so.

Hadil's friend Karima*, in her early 30s, took off the veil for practical reasons. She works at a travel agency, and the environment doesn't favour veiling. Taking off the veil wasn't hard for her, even if talking about it is. She just wanted to adjust to the circumstances, and didn't think that her employer's request was unreasonable. "I'm still the same person, I have the same values and I haven't forsaken my faith," she said.

Hala* is in her thirties, single, lives with her parents and is currently working on her political science Master's thesis. Like many of her friends, she took the veil as a teenager. "At that age one becomes more religious, and the veil is a way of showing that to others," she says. Hala visited a mosque with her friends every Friday, where she attended Qur'an reading classes after the afternoon prayer. These classes consist of explaining the Qur'an, and pupils can ask advice on how to be a better Muslim.[23] Hala says the veiling was a chain-reaction: when one friend took it, others congratulated her and so others followed suit.

But Hala's family didn't approve of her decision to veil, even though her mother was veiled. "It's a normal reaction; my parents told me that it would be better if I didn't take the veil," she explains. Her parents' reaction might be compared to how their Western counterparts would feel about piercings or tattoos – it is a radical, irreversible act. But her family got used to it. Seven years passed, and Hala had a change of heart. "I was just about to graduate from university and, in hindsight, I guess I was thinking that I was starting something new, I wasn't a student anymore. The veil just didn't feel like me anymore," Hala recalls. "I didn't feel like it was 100% a religious symbol. When you're a teenager, everything is so black-and-white and it was easy to believe in it," she says.

---

* the names have been changed

Her family and friends were rather surprised by her decision, but no one condemned her. "It was the same reaction as if one of my friends had suddenly started wearing contact lenses instead of glasses. Some see that the friend's appearances have changed, some don't even notice, but the difference is not drastic," she downplays the effect. However, some religious friends tried to convince Hala that this was just a phase, she would return to veiling.

When she was studying for her BA, she says, half of Cairo University students were veiled – and it was more common among students who came from outside Cairo. "Now there are more veils, but at the same time you see a lot of clothes that would have been banned when I was studying!" Hala says. By this she is referring to the Western fashion: short skirts, hipster jeans, figure-hugging and transparent clothes, popular especially among first- and second-year students, much as with the AUC students. Two parallel trends are apparent: while the number of veiled women has grown, so too has the number of those who wear skin-tight clothing – not just between four walls but on the streets as well.

In Hala's view, the veil is not the mark of a good person; rather it denotes a person's conduct towards others. "Anyone can wear the veil, but it doesn't mean that the wearer is a genuine, believing Muslim," she says. Urban legends tell stories about prostitutes who wear the veil to hide their profession.

So why has the veil become such a contradictory, two-faced piece of clothing? The veiling debate masks a huge question which is never discussed, at least in Egypt. If women feel the need to veil in order to protect themselves from the leers and gropes of loutish men, why is there no discussion of the need to teach manners to men? Or of the equal requirement for male modesty and decency? The Qur'an advises men similarly:

> Tell the believing men to lower their gaze and be modest. That is
> purer for them. Lo! Allah is aware of what they do. (24:30)

Perhaps the gender roles are seen as so different that women
don't even remember to demand better behaviour of men.
In spring 2003, I was covering this parallel phenomenon of
increased veiling with the Westernization of Egyptian fashion
for YLE news. In the same Muhandisin neighbourhood
where Amr Khaled started his career, I talked to a young,
veiled shopkeeper.

She showed me a sleeveless light-blue top. I asked her if
she wanted to wear one like it. "Of course!" she replied and
told me that she wears revealing outfits at girls-only parties, at
home. She wouldn't dare to wear it on the street, because she
would be harassed. "If it wasn't for the men, women could
wear what they want!" she declared, laughing. So what should
be done about the men, I asked. "You can't do anything about
them!" She giggled at the impossibility of the suggestion.

Maybe women could launch a counter-attack: if the
majority of women wear the veil, and the veil is the marker of
a proper Muslim, then aren't all Egyptian women virtuous? If
we decide that they are all virtuous, then they might as well
take the veil off? We shall remain waiting for the next wave,
the return of those who follow Huda Sha'arawi's example.

Notes

--

1 See for example Iqbal Baraka, *al-Hijab. Al-Ru'iya 'asriyya*, 2004.
2 Hoffman-Ladd, 1987:31, translations for *tabarruj* and *zina* added by S.N.
3 Hoffman-Ladd, 1987:28–29; Zuhur, 1992:101–2.
4 Ibrahim, 2002:144.
5 Zuhur, 1992:75.
6 See for example Abu-Lughod, 1998.
7 *Al-Hayat*, no. 619, 8/12/2003, *al-Wasat* weekly supplement.
8 Hafez, 2001:67.
9 See for example Amin, 2002.
10 This is more of a Shi'ite than a Sunni custom, the main branch of Islam practised in Egypt.
11 'The cost of marriage', *Al-Ahram Weekly*, 24–30/1/2002, Issue No. 570; Dalia Dabbous, 'The man who loved too much', *The Cairo Times*, 30/8–5/9/2001, Vol. 5, Issue 25.
12 cp. Zuhur, 1998:104–5.
13 http://www.aucegypt.edu/aboutauc/HistoryandMission/Pages/history.aspx.
14 EIPR press release, 9/6/2007.
15 Mahmoud Tawfiq, 'Veiled threats?', *The Cairo Times*, 13–19/12/2001, Vol. 5, Issue 40.
16 Most female diplomats are un-veiled, nor do men have beards, because it could be interpreted as denoting Islamist sympathies.
17 The Court ruled in their favour, but Egyptian Television didn't comply.
18 Abu-Lughod, 1998:249; Yomna Kamel and Sara Mashour, 'Jumping on the bandwagon', *Cairo Times*, 14–20/11/2002, Vol. 6, Issue 36.
19 Issandr El Amrani, 'A sheikh for modern living', *Cairo Times*, 14–20/11/2002, Vol. 6, Issue 36.
20 http://www.amrkhaled.net/articles/articles498.html.
21 Asef Bayat, 'From Amr Diab to Amr Khaled', *al-Ahram Weekly*, 22–28/5/2003, Issue No. 639.
22 See Zuhur, 1998:115–117.
23 See Wickham, 2002:133–134. Particularly in Islamist-dominated mosques, the (male) instructor sits behind a curtain, and the women write their questions on paper which they pass to him, because a woman's voice is *awra*, "a physical adornment or attraction capable of arousing male desire".

4

The General's garden

She said to him: "You are no longer with me."

He said, and he was talking to himself: "The cleverness of the ape is the root of all misfortune. He learned how to walk on two legs, and his hands were free."

"That means that I should leave."

"And he came down from the apes' paradise in the trees to the forest floor..."

"One last question before I go: Do you have a plan for the future, if things get difficult?"

"...And they said to him: 'Come back to the trees, or the beasts will get you.'"

"Do you have the right to a pension if – God forbid – you are actually dismissed?"

"...But he took a branch in one hand and a stone in the other and set off cautiously, looking away down a road that had no end."[1]

This description is from the pen of the Arab world's only Nobel Laureate, the late Naguib Mahfouz. *Adrift on the Nile*, published in 1966, depicts nightly marijuana-infested gatherings of a miscellaneous group of friends on a houseboat on the Nile. After smoking a water-pipe of hashish, the protagonist Anis Zaki sinks into the depths of most exquisite hallucinations, and the conversations among his friends transform into overlapping monologues. Only one of the group members, a young journalist concerned over the future of the protagonist, doesn't indulge in drug abuse. In the end, a tragedy breaks up the group, but the protagonist cannot kick his habit.

The houseboats floating on the Left Bank of the Nile have not been treated as solely literary symbols of sin but they've also witnessed rip-roaring times in real life. Originally houseboats were called *dahabiya* (from the word *dahab* – gold), as at the beginning of the 20th century their edifices had to be painted gold. Houseboats existed long before this: Queen Cleopatra was reputed to receive guests in a luxurious houseboat, while Napoleon and his soldiers also enjoyed staying in the floating homes after their invasion of Egypt at the end of the 18th century.

At first, houseboats were a sole prerogative of the rich, where the elite went to escape the scorching summer sun and receive guests, and hold parties. Little by little, houseboats lost their luxury status, and the requirement to paint them golden lapsed. Then, after electricity and sewerage was extended to reach the houseboats, ordinary Egyptians began to move into them year round. Coffee shops, clubs and even a floating health centre sprang up to cater for the inhabitants.[2]

During WWII, the houseboats were subjected to different kind of demand: all of a sudden hundreds of thousands of soldiers needed housing. Most were in transit, on their way to

North Africa to fight first the Italians attacking from Libya, and later the Germans under Rommel. Others, particularly high-ranking British officers, were interested in renting out houseboats, from Cairenes struggling to make ends meet. It was in this era that the tales of the houseboats as bordellos and covert double-agent meeting places began to circulate.[3]

The film *Days of Sadat* (*Ayyam al-Sadat*), screened in spring 2001, depicted one such encounter: young Anwar al-Sadat (at this stage merely a rebellious officer) meets belly-dancer and spy Hikmat Fahmi and two German spies on a houseboat. One of the spies was the Hungarian Laszlo Almasy (also depicted in the story *The English Patient*), the other was German spy John Eppler.

The scene in the film was shot on my friend's houseboat. Australian photographer Bill had to evacuate his home for a week while the film crew refurbished the upper floor of the boat, while downstairs resident, blond Canadian journalist Neil was recruited to play the German spy. He landed a full speaking part, having to speak Arabic with a German accent. *Days of Sadat* did well at the box office: it was the second best selling movie of 2001, netting LE11 million.[4]

As *Days of Sadat* and the official annals recount, before the 1952 Revolution, houseboats were dens of vice and depravity, where lovers met in secret, and gambling and prostitution flourished. The obese profligate former King Faruq was a habitué of the Nileside cabarets.

The physical location of the houseboats shifted several times, washing up beside Kit Kat Square (named after Faruq's favourite dancehall), on the west bank of the Nile, across from affluent Zamalek island. After the Revolution, the Square was levelled to the ground, and a mosque was erected in its place, although most pious Muslims have forgotten that the mosque carries the same name as the previous nest of vice.

Islam forbids drug abuse, although drugs are not specifically mentioned in the Qur'an. There is, however, consensus that the Sura warning about the dangers of alcohol also refer to drugs:

> They question thee about strong drink and games of chance. Say: in both is great sin, and (some) utility for men; but the sin of them is greater than their usefulness. (2:219)

> O ye who believe! Strong drink and games of chance and idols and divining arrows are only an infamy of Satan's handiwork. Leave it aside in order that ye may succeed. (5:90)

Everyone interprets the prohibition in his / her own way – and alcohol and drugs are used across all Egyptian social classes. Some consider smoking *bango* (Egyptian for marijuana) as completely acceptable but never touch alcohol.

Young religious Muslims, in particular, feel guilty about drinking. One man in his thirties, from a well-to-do family, confessed to me how, as a teenager he and his friends would drink booze on Thursdays, and then go the mosque to pray on Fridays. "We knew it was wrong to drink, and we felt guilty. But we considered partying and praying as completely separate." He still drinks and prays, but never keeps alcohol at home and swears he will stop drinking 'one day'.

Most Egyptians never drink in front of their family, or try to hide their habit. But when upper-class friends get together, usually alcohol is served. Some weddings even have an open bar, depending on how conservative the host family is.

The Copts, Egypt's Christians, don't have to worry about a guilty conscience because they are allowed to drink. In the old Christian quarter of Mar Girgis, tourists can buy beer from a normal kiosk, but during Ramadan the ban on alcohol includes them too: with an Egyptian passport you cannot get a beer even if you are a Copt.

Egyptian parties are somewhat different to those of northern Europe. Once, I was invited to a dinner party hosted by a young, successful marketing director. Together with a Canadian colleague we hoped that this party would be a good chance to practise our networking skills.

The invitation was for 8 p.m. When we reached the house it was only a quarter past eight, and my companion panicked: a quarter past eight in Egypt meant that we were way ahead of our time. But it was too late to escape, because the host had seen us from the window. We just hoped we were not the first ones to arrive.

However, it was not to be! Obviously the host hadn't prepared himself for such an early arrival. So we sat stolidly and stared at the living-room decorations, which signalled that someone in this household was very fond of ivory. Carved, life-sized phallic objects abounded, even on the table masquerading as fruits. On enquiry, we discovered that our host's father was a retired ambassador, and had spent quite a bit of time in African countries.

A waiter brought us juice on a silver tray, while our host tried hard to conceal his discomfort, and soon disappeared to the other room to talk on his mobile. We started to plot our escape. It was obvious that this was going to be a 'dry' party, so we decided to go out for a beer for a couple of hours, and return once more people showed up. As an excuse, we told the host that we'd go to pick up my colleague's wife, who had promised to meet us in a bar and act as our saviour.

But then our host insisted incessantly that we take his driver, and would not take no for an answer. In the end, it was easier to get rid off the driver, who didn't even ask why we were headed towards the Beirut   the hotel where most of the local drinking scene could be found. After our second beer, we toyed with the idea of making a hoax call to the party to hear if there were party noises in the background. But eventually we decided to take the bull by its horns and go back to the party, whether there were people there or not. It was 10 o'clock.

Back at the party, only a handful of people had shown up – so much for networking then! After our beery breather, it was easier to endure listening to the firm's girls giggling and the host's clumsy attempts at flirting. In the end, people dispersed and the only ones left were the host and a girl who said she loved the Celine Dion songs playing in the background. Our host confessed that he was crazy about all love songs. By mutual consent, I and my colleague decided to leave at once, even if this meant missing out on the cheesecake. Once outside, my colleague wondered whether this was an issue of cultural differences, but a party without booze to lubricate the conversation is depressing. So we proceeded immediately to another bar.

Although our host had chosen a sober lifestyle, Egypt has a millennia-old tradition of drinking beer and wine – ancient Egyptians even took them to the afterlife. For example the pyramid builders washed down their daily meal – dried fish and bread – with beer. Wine pots were found from the Pharaoh Tutankhamun's tomb, from which some might conclude that Egypt has a flourishing, traditional brewing industry. Alas no, although now it has recovered a drinkable level after hitting rock bottom.

Stella Beer has been an Egyptian icon since 1897. Sold in green half-litre bottles, it is now the choice of an Egyptian patriot. Yet up until ten years ago (before the state monopoly al-Ahram Beverages Company (ABC) was privatized in 1997) drinking Stella was something of a gamble.

Ash regularly covered the bottom of the bottle, while the wildest urban legends told of cockroaches and other extra

spices that escaped the careless brewery workers' sieve. It thus
became customary to sample the beer while at the bar, so that
you could get a replacement if necessary. ABC is no longer
in Egyptian hands, it's owned by Heineken, and the quality
has improved such that Stella is competing with noteworthy
foreign brands.

Egypt also had a thriving wine industry at the beginning
of the 20th century – Egyptian wine was formerly world class
– and the red wine *Omar Khayyam* won prizes in several
French wine competitions. After nationalization in the 1960s,
the quality of the wine started to sink, hitting rock bottom in
1980s. By the 90s only the rosé was remotely drinkable – the
white wine tasted like vinegar, and a British tourist went into
a coma after a couple of glasses of the red.

Egyptian wines earned nicknames like Chateau Migraine
from their horrifying after-effects. Smart people used them
only for cooking. The bad quality may explain why Egyptians
don't drink much wine – 85% of wine produced is sold to
unsuspecting tourists. Some believe that beer-drinking comes
from the British occupation and their habits: 81% of beer goes
into quenching local Egyptian thirst.[5]

ABC recruited a French oenologist to work a miracle
and save the grapes of Gianaclis village. Located in the Nile
delta, Gianaclis's vineyards were in miserable state, as was the
machinery. The staff had to be retrained and the quality has
indeed seen some improvement year on year. By 1999, *Omar
Khayyam* was again drinkable. It's still disproportionately
expensive, because the state adds a luxury surtax on top of the
price. Yet that's what you have to settle for because you can buy
imported wines only in the best restaurants – attracting 300%
luxury tax unless you know where to buy it under the counter.

Beer and wine are sold in small off-licences, or from the
new ABC outlets called Drinkie's. One can also order alcohol

as home delivery, which is very convenient if you don't want others to know that you drink. But the marketing department of Drinkie's shops has adopted a rather pushy technique: when weekend approached, the shop would call and ask if I wanted to place an order. The first time I was so dumbfounded that I almost slammed the phone down on him: were they hinting that I was an alcoholic? But these calls continued on a regular basis, and often they tried to sell me new items like Egyptian vodka or whisky. The latest marketing campaign was a text message from the booze dealer: "Drinkie's is happy to announce the birth of Auld Stag, ID vodka, Gin & Chill. New premium members of an impressive portfolio! Call us now!" How on earth did they get my mobile number?

Based on this information one might think that half of Cairo is happily quaffing locally brewed liquors. Yet under the burgeoning Islamist trend, drinking is considered immoral, but perhaps the younger generation is habituated to alcohol through these vodka cocktails. Economically and socially, the elite can afford to ignore what the masses think of them, although no one rages drunk on the streets of Cairo.

Drinking parties are common in Cairo, although one can find dozens of bars and restaurants serving alcohol. Stella is particularly popular in the small 'speak-easies' of downtown Cairo, where women are a rare sight. *Al-Hurriyya* (Freedom) coffee shop is a downtown Cairo landmark, adorned with a huge Stella advert. There, local men play backgammon or chess by day, sipping Turkish coffee, or tea spiked with mint, and inhale the fumes of the *shisha*, the hubbly-bubbly water-pipe exuding smoke with apple or honey scent. Such a scene has been immortalized by numerous local visual artists across the ages.

As dusk falls, the beer drinkers crawl in: leftist intellectuals, artists, poets and other characters swimming against the stream.

Amongst them, you can spot a few tourists or ex-pats. The waiter brings the beer to the table, accompanied by a salty bean snack called *termis* (white lupin). At the end of the evening, the waiter simply counts the bottles on the table to determine the bill; someone orders *arak*, cheap aniseed liquor which turns milky when mixed with water; peddlers scurry between the customers, selling napkins and wrist watches, or offering a shoe shine.

Despite the male predominance, *Al-Hurriyya* is a fairly female-friendly place, where the male inhabitants settle for a few curious glances from their tables, although a woman has to ask the cashier for the key if she wants to use the toilet. Its hygienic condition leaves much to be desired, and there is no point hoping to find paper in the loo – they don't hawk those napkins outside for nothing!

Until the mid-1990s, with the exception of these male hangouts or hotel bars, Cairo had only a handful of drinking establishments where one could enjoy an alcoholic beverage. As students, we mainly frequented a disco called *Casanova* in the basement of the shabby al-Burg Hotel beside the Nile. There we danced *Macarena* with local gay boys, while Sudanese prostitutes plied their trade with ex-pat men.

With its tasteless décor and tackiness, *Casanova* was a somewhat surreal place, but in a fascinating way it was a morality-free zone. It was fun to drink beer inside the cellar and mull on how far away the world outside was. Of course, that kind of sinful theatre couldn't last forever, and the place was closed down because of the constant brawls.

In 1995, Cairo nightlife experienced a revival when the *Tabasco* restaurant opened. By law, all drinking establishments must also offer food, meaning that they nominally must be restaurants, but *Tabasco* felt like a real bar. It was youthful, trendy, cosy and inexpensive. Soon it became the meeting spot of upper-middle-class Egyptians (the only people who can afford to go out) and Cairene expats.

Several other bars opened in *Tabasco*'s wake, and by the beginning of 2000, Cairo nightlife had revolutionized: there was a whole lot more to choose from. Wealthy, Westernized youngsters wanted to have the same lifestyle as their European or American peers, of which going out to bars and clubs is an integral part. Local women started to frequent bars, showing up in sexy outfits, which would cause a riot if they walked down the street in daylight. But you never saw local women drunk, or a local man staggering along the street: Egyptian drinking has well-defined limits.

If you stick to the local offerings, going out is relatively cheap (certainly when compared to European prices). Hotel bars and discos are still expensive, but they are usually the most popular hangouts. Because imported alcohol is so expensive, Egyptians often bring their own bottle to restaurants, usually a bottle of expensive whisky – Johnny Walker Black Label is a long time favourite. Once I counted the row of Black Label bottles at *Rithmo*, a trendy hotel bar: 19 bottles, each with a name tag. The customer pays only a corkage charge and can sip from their own bottle when they want.

The driving force behind this wave of new bars is an Egyptian-Croatian entrepreneur called Nicha. He is an unpretentious man, whose family belonged to the former Egyptian court. You can spot him in one of the many restaurants he launched, a cigarette in one hand and drink glass in the other. His touch is evident in nearly all Cairene hot spots, from *L'Aubergine* or *Rio de Cairo,* to the provocatively named *Latex* nightclub, where you can catch a sight of young people wildly dancing to techno.

Of course, not everyone approves of this kind of immoral behaviour. In spring 2004, the Number One National

Morality Police – the Muslim Brotherhood – proposed a ban on selling, possessing and drinking alcohol. As a punishment they advocated a sentence of 40 lashes, although Egypt's legislation doesn't have these physical *hudud* punishments. This is not a new topic – indeed the Brotherhood makes similar proposals every year – but this time, several MPs from the ruling NDP party supported the proposal. Human rights organizations expressed concern over the suggested floggings, while political commentators believed it would never pass into law because of the likely harm to tourism and investments by foreign breweries.[6] The proposal was quietly shelved.

Although statistics are not readily available, probably more common than drinking is the consumption of mild drugs. Cannabis, or *bango* as it's called in Egypt, is the most common drug, used by all social classes. If in Europe drink-driving is a problem, in Egypt the problem is 'high' taxi drivers. Most noticeably by night, I've come across taxi drivers with no concept of right or left, let alone street names. Their movements are as if from a slow-motion film, and when the driver slowly steers into the oncoming traffic, it's time to catch another ride.

Cannabis (and to a lesser extent opium) is grown in rough terrain, mainly in southern Egypt and the Sinai peninsula, where it is difficult for the police to monitor. From time to time the Ministry of Interior conducts high-profile drug busts accompanied by media fanfare, in which air-strike planes drop herbicide on the Bedouins' precious cultivations. Mysteriously, a small portion always survives, ending up abroad, or on the local market.

The inclusion of cannabis in the League of Nation's list of banned drugs in 1925 is actually thanks to Egypt. An Egyptian diplomat successfully lobbied for a ban by presenting a connection between cannabis use and insanity.[7] Yet up until

the 1980s, Egypt had very lenient drug laws. Islamic Cairo
was a well-known market place, where cannabis was sold openly
over the counter, while Cairene Police stations apparently
resembled drugstores, as corrupt police officers sold confiscated
hash caches.

The situation changed with the dawn of the Mubarak
era, when legislation was enhanced by more severe punishments:
producing, buying, selling or possessing drugs now attracts a
life-sentence or death penalty, in addition to a fine of up to
LE500,000. Not too long ago, a creepy sign greeted visitors
to Egypt at the airport passport control: foreigners who dealt
in drugs would be punished according to the law – "Death by
hanging", it read. Welcome to Egypt indeed. Despite such a
stark warning, some foreigners involved themselves in the
drug trade, and languish in Egyptian prisons still.

While the author Naguib Mahfouz's description of
floating drug dens is still partially alive, normal houseboats
have become more bourgeois. Nowadays, some 30 different
houseboats remain, each a two-storey box construction with a
balcony and patio or a garden on the bank side.

Living in a houseboat is no longer cheap, as Cairene
landlords cottoned on to a steady demand among ex-pats.
Boat owners may live on the upper deck, or (as in one case)
just use it as a locale for rendezvousing with his mistress. After
all, houseboats offer a unique Nile-view and many residents
argue that the air along one of the world's longest river is
cleaner, and life more peaceful, than elsewhere in Cairo.

There are, of course, downsides, as most of the boats are
in rather bad shape. Waste 'management' very often means
that you'll notice your garbage bag floating past the boat two
days after you gave them to the *zabbal*, or rubbish collector.

Security is another problem. Each boat has its own
doorman, who often lives in a small hut in the houseboat

garden or patch. But the doorman can only secure the shore side; a friend's bicycle was stolen from his balcony, probably taken to a fishing boat on the Nile. Fire safety is another concern: in December 2003, four houseboats burned to the ground, among them a restaurant.

I experienced living on a houseboat when holidaying as a guest in my Norwegian friend Andreas's floating flat in 1996. My room was a windowless, gloomy, brown wallpapered cabin, with only a bed and rock hard mattress as furniture. Otherwise the flat was very cosy and in the afternoon, we would we sip gin and tonics on a tiny balcony, enjoying the bleak January sun.

In addition to rent, Andreas' landlord, a retired army general, demanded that all guests staying downstairs should pay a courtesy visit to him upstairs. The General was in a habit of boasting about his army rank to Andreas and used to tell a story about how he was sent to military academy in Moscow during the Soviet era. He became fluent in Russian and allegedly befriended some Egyptian officers who are rather high ranking today.

Despite being in his 70s, he hadn't given up his love of flirting. Because Andreas' TV showed the same satellite programs as the General was watching, Andreas knew that every Thursday and Friday evening his landlord indulged in watching Polish porn films. Andreas thought it best to warn me about the General's potential advances.

We climbed the squeaky wooden stairs to his balcony, garnished with a haphazard collection of pots and pans and metal scrap. A slim, quite short old man with alert grey-green eyes appeared at the door; as a young man he probably had been okay looking, although he couldn't boast about broad shoulders. Andreas introduced me to the General, who seemed be making up his own mind about me. We made two minutes of small talk while he checked me over from head to toe. In the end, he politely asked me to come say goodbye before I finished my vacation.

I kept my promise. The night before I left, I climbed those worn stairs again. Having heard more stories about the General's molestations, I decided to take a British male friend as my chaperone. The general opened the door in a good mood, but his smile faded when he saw that I hadn't come alone. I introduced my friend, and when the General heard the word 'British', his smile vanished completely, to be replaced by a suspicious expression, recalling painful memories perhaps. "He must have been at the Suez," my friend whispered as we entered.

The Suez crisis in 1956 sealed the exit of British troops from Egyptian soil. This was the Cold War era, when both the Soviet Union and the United States competed to gain a foothold in the Middle East sphere of interest, while the United Kingdom and France clung to the remnants of colonialism. Together with Indonesia's Sukarno, Yugoslavia's Tito and India's Nehru, Egypt's president Gamal Abdel Nasser had just become personified as one of the leaders of the Non-Aligned Movement, at the Rangoon summit of 1955. Already popular at home, now Nasser became one the leading figures of the Third World fight against imperialism.

Although Egypt was formally independent, the Suez Canal (which links the Mediterranean to the Red Sea) and the French company managing the canal (the Suez Canal Company) were still guarded by thousands of British troops.[8]

Egypt and Great Britain had signed an Anglo-Egyptian agreement in 1936, formally concluding the 64-year British occupation of Egypt – but not including the Suez Canal. According to the agreement, Canal security was supposed to be a joint matter, but in reality Egyptians had no business in Suez without permission from the British authorities. The canal had been administered by the British since 1869 when Egypt's regent, Khedive Isma'il, in a state of acute bankruptcy sold his 'golden shares' to the British.

The presence of the British troops was a real thorn in the side for Egyptians. Egyptian corvée labour had paid dearly to dig the Canal; farmers with inadequate tools and insufficient nutrition had died in their droves: 100,000 men died over the ten-year project. For the post-WWII British and French, the Canal was a crucial oil transport route; for the Egyptians it was a potentially inexhaustible source of income, held by foreigners. The 1948 war after the declaration of the state of Israel offered the Egyptian resistance an opportunity to attack British troops, but minor attacks didn't force the British to withdraw.[9]

After the Free Officers' coup in 1952, withdrawal negotiations were put on the agenda. The cost of maintaining the Canal, and the constant guerrilla attacks were a burden for the British and therefore in 1954 the two parties signed an evacuation agreement: the British would leave Egypt for good by June 1956. This scenario didn't please the Israelis, who would rather have seen the British stay manning the buffer zone between the two neighbours.[10]

Around the same time, Nasser got the idea of building the Aswan dam. This massive project was to double Egypt's cultivable land area and generate electricity for the industrial sector. Egypt had applied for a loan from the World Bank to fund this, but the loan was blocked by a US objection. Just before this, Egypt had announced that it had bought arms from Czechoslovakia (in reality from the Soviet Union) and this thrust Egypt into the Eastern camp. In return for funding the dam project, the Americans tried to pressure Egypt to drop the arms deal, and to sign a peace agreement with Israel. As a counterstroke, on the 1956 anniversary of the Revolution, Nasser announced that he would nationalize the Suez Canal.

Egyptians celebrated the decision; after all, the Canal was like a state within the state, a symbol of oppression. The British has started to consider the Canal as their own property, and its nationalization threatened to cut the lucrative maritime trade, causing huge financial losses. The British suspected that Nasser had concealed the nationalization plan when the evacuation plan was on the table. The French were also furious because the Canal management company was French-owned, and the Canal had been designed and built by a Frenchman, Ferdinand de Lesseps. Adding fuel to the French fury was Egypt's support for Algerian freedom fighters. The ingredients of the crisis were readily apparent.

France, Great Britain and Israel signed a secret agreement to attack Egypt. On 29th October, Israel sent paratroopers to the western side of Sinai. Egyptian troops dug in on the other side of the Canal. And perhaps somewhere there was our houseboat general, waiting for a battle call.

On the next day, before Israeli troops had reached the Suez Canal, France and the United Kingdom demanded that both parties withdraw from the Canal. Israel obeyed in accordance with the secret agreement; Egypt refused to withdraw and so France and the United Kingdom attacked, destroying Egypt's modest air force directly on the ground in the airbases. Nasser found it difficult to believe that the British had concocted this campaign with Egypt's arch enemy, Israel.[11]

The Soviet Union and the United States intervened, and demanded an end to the fighting. An armistice was signed in November at the United Nations, demanding foreign troops' withdrawal from Egypt, and the UN sent its Emergency Forces to the Egyptian–Israeli border. Sunken shipping was recovered, and the following year the Suez Canal was operated completely by Egyptian hands.

The Egyptians considered the war as their victory, and Nasser immediately became a Third World hero, who had taught a lesson to former colonialists. Together with the 1952 Revolution, the nationalization of the Canal was to become the most significant event in Egypt's contemporary history. The war is still commemorated with pride as an occasion when plucky little Egypt beat Great Britain.

So my British friend felt like a defendant when the General asked us in. The scent and thick smoke of cannabis lingered in the living-room. "We're just smoking here with some friends," the General said, as if it was the most natural pastime in the world. I exchanged a 'I wonder what will happen' look with my friend. The General told us proudly that he cultivates the narcotics himself, and took us to the balcony to admire the home gardener's crop: on a side table of the balcony sat a bushy *cannabis sativa* plant in a flower pot, clearly the product of tender loving care.

The General escorted us back into the living room where we were confronted with a sight straight from the pages of Mahfouz's novel: five men of varying ages sat on a sofa, taking great pleasure from the offerings. "What would you like to have? We have hash, grass and then that pipe," the General offered.

In a neat row on the table were hand-patted, single dose hash balls, the size of finger tips. Next to them was the much advertised marijuana, in ready rolled joints. But by far the most impressive intoxication device was an enormous bamboo pipe. The bamboo cane, over a metre-long, acted as a pipe, and was being smoked by a plump, white-haired man, of roughly the General's age. Coals, which had been heated in an iron helmet on the floor, topped the bowl.

After marvelling at the contraptions, the General decided to introduce the men puffing away around the table. The white-haired man was a retired sports coach. Next to him sat

two middle-aged men, whom the General described as
businessmen.

On the corner of the sofa sat a man much younger
than the others. He was probably in his thirties, and talked
incessantly into his bulky Nokia. In those days, mobile
phones were a rarity and he had obviously become a cellular
addict. "That's my son, a police officer," the General said. The
man momentarily took his eyes from the window and nodded
at us, continuing his phone conversation.

Our host had decorated one of the living room walls
with A5 size photos of himself, his friends and high-ranking
former colleagues. Also among the photographs were wedding
pictures of a Spanish couple who had lived downstairs. The
wake from passing police patrol boats, and the loud Arabic
pop-playing, neon-flashing smaller boats rocked the boat
every once in a while, producing an uncomfortable churning
sensation in the pit of the stomach. To the General and his
friends the unhurried, drug-hazed moment among friends
was commonplace – to us it was yet another unexpected
Cairo experience.

My friend and I were anxious to compare notes, so we
started to look for a quick exit from the General's unusual
herb garden. Eventually, we just decided to leave the General
and his friend in their smoky embrace. As we were leaving,
the General wanted to give us yet another sample of the
famous Egyptian generosity: he gave me a tape of a famous
Egyptian singer of the 1960s and claimed that he had written
lyrics for her. I never found out whether he really was
an unpublished poet, or whether his claim was influenced by
illegal herb-infused hallucinations, like those of Mahfouz's
protagonist.

Notes

—–—

1 Mahfouz, 2001:167.
2 Samir Rafat, 'The Nile Dahabieh', *The Cairo Times*, 24/7/1997, Vol. 1.
3 Cooper, 1989:123 (Kit Kat club); al-Sayyid Marsot, 1985:99–101.
4 *Egypt Almanac*, 2003:75.
5 *Egypt Almanac*, 2003:218.
6 Magdy Samaan, 'Prohibition Blues', *The Cairo Times*, 13–19/5/2004, Vol. 8, issue 11.
7 Roger Owen, 'Banning blue smoke', *al-Ahram Weekly*, 9–15/12/2004, issue no. 720.
8 Gordon, 1996:158; Heikal, 1973:49. According to Gordon, in 1951 Suez had 38,000 soldiers, Heikal says in 1956 it was 80,000 men.
9 Al-Sayyid Marsot, 1985:66–70, 96–98, 110–112.
10 Shlaim, 2000:110–112.
11 Heikal, 1973:63–71, 93; Al-Sayyed Marsot, 1985:112–113; Shlaim, 2000:162–185.

5

Followers of St Mark

——

A soldier in a guard post opposite the church saw her first. Palms upwards, dressed in blue-and-white garb, the Virgin Mary appeared above the St Marcus Church bell towers, encircled by lights. This first sighting was in August 2000, in the southern Egyptian town of Asyut. Soon others witnessed apparitions of Mary: flocks of doves between the church towers, and strange lights around the church.

The local police investigated the matter, but couldn't figure out where the lights originated from, so the unofficial explanation was a heavenly miracle. Asyut, which had been a hotbed of militant Islamists and a major locus of sectarian strife just a few years before, now started receiving a flood of pilgrims from all over the country.

My (now ex-) husband Steve became obsessed with these lights, so off we went to Asyut. But as soon as we stepped off the train, we received a reminder of the violent years. A police officer in civilian clothes greeted us at the platform and followed us everywhere during our stay. "For your safety," he explained.

Asyut is a rather uninteresting Upper Egyptian rural town, although it has a pleasant Nile Corniche. The city has a significant Coptic Christian minority – southern Egypt has comparatively more Copts than other parts of the country. The thought that these streets had seen fierce fighting between Islamists and Copts, as well as between Islamists and the police, made the city interesting in a sinister kind of way. Today Asyutis take security seriously, and they want foreigners to feel protected. After all, tourists had also been Islamists' target.

But no sooner had we arrived than it seemed that we might have to leave Asyut without a story. As we checked into the hotel, we were told that we had arrived a day late. "Yesterday, the lights were very strong," the hotel staff reported. It was Sunday, and we had somehow assumed that it would be a safe bet to expect them at a weekend. But no, we were told that the lights were really strong on Thursdays and Saturdays. And weaker on the other days.

Nonetheless, we decided to stay put in the churchyard, just in case lights – or even better, the Virgin Mary – appeared after all. The youngish parish priest, Father Zakka, told us excitedly how hundreds of people had made their way to the church, and seen Mary with shining white doves, fluttering above the church. Father Zakka wore the black priestly gown of the Coptic Church, and like many of his colleagues he sported a thick, unkempt salt and pepper beard, and held a wooden cross between his palms. He insisted on offering us tea and biscuits, which was a nice gesture in the cooling evening, mosquitoes feasting on us in return.

Father Zakka told us that a few years earlier, he had had a very mundane job. Before his call, he had been a food and beverages manager at a hotel in Aqaba, Jordan. "At that time a lot of Finnish tourists came to Aqaba. I think I can still remember a few words… hmm… härkä (beef)!" he reminisced, and looked into the horizon, smiling. His story is not unusual; it is quite common for Coptic priests to join the church in mature years, after worldly careers.

Father Zakka believed that the lights and the Mary apparitions could be interpreted in two ways. It could either be a warning that the sinful ways of the world must come to an end, or a sign of hope that life will improve. Collectively, Coptic Church officials took the latter opinion because the relations between Copts and Muslims had been so volatile. Islamists had killed Christians and robbed their shops during the violent years of the 1990s.

While we were talking, a group of believers who had been signing hymns at the churchyard, suddenly rushed to the corner by the door. Someone had spotted Mary, and now everyone had their eyes fixed on the bell tower. While the group saw a dimly lit Virgin Mary, all I could see was the beam above the bell. No matter how hard I tried, I couldn't see anything but that.

Lights didn't come that night either. A photographer friend told us later that the lights looked like flashlights, but it was difficult to tell where they originated from. Their source remained a mystery, but the million pilgrims who visited Asyut were convinced of their divine origin. Later the Coptic Church officially confirmed the apparition.

Usually the Coptic Church interprets light apparitions as manifestation of God's blessings. Light can emanate from a saint, a church or from icons. Copts believe that in a mystic way icons represent the virtues and characteristics of those saints depicted in them. Miracles are also said to have occurred in monasteries, where oil lamps have apparently started to burn on their own.

Yet the church light phenomena have been reported all over Egypt. Arguably the best-known Virgin Mary apparition is the one that was witnessed in 1968, in the Church of the Holy Virgin in the Cairo suburb of Zaytun. The Coptic Church investigated the apparition, and declared that Mary had indeed been seen several times, and that this apparition had revived the faith of many, and healed the sick. The apparition was also taken as sign that God was still on the side of the Egyptians, although the country had suffered a crushing defeat by Israel in the preceding year's war.[1]

Egyptian Copts are the largest Christian minority in the Middle East – they form roughly 10% of the population. Egypt has also a tiny – and diminishing – Jewish community, an uncounted number of Shiite Muslims, small numbers of other denominations such as Catholics and Protestants, as well as a small Bahai community.[2]

The word Copt is derived from the Greek word for ancient Egypt, *aigyptos,* and Copts often emphasize that they are the original Egyptians, descendants of the Pharaohs. Indeed, the Coptic Church is one of Christendom's oldest churches. According to Coptic tradition, the church was established by the evangelist Mark in the first century AD. The Coptic Church split from the Byzantine Church after the Council of Chalcedon in AD 451, due to an argument over Jesus's nature: Copts believe that Christ had a solely divine nature, whereas Byzantines believed in both divine and human nature.

After the Muslim conquest (AD 639) of Egypt, Copts and Jews legally became *dhimmis*, under the protection of the ruler. They paid the personal tax *jizya*, and they were exempted from military service.[3] In return, they were allowed to practise their religions and live according to their own customary laws. Although at times Copts were persecuted, or rulers tried to convert them, Egypt never became wholly Muslim. The Copts even managed to keep their own Coptic language – although it hasn't been spoken since the 11th century, it is still the language of liturgy and monastic church services.[4]

The era between Muhammed 'Ali Pasha (1805) until the British occupation (1882) was beneficial for the Copts. The majority of civil servants were Christian, although they were still the same 10% minority. Their skills in trade and languages also put them in a favourable position with foreign investors.[5] Copts were also highly visible in politics, particularly in the ranks of the *Wafd* party, which spearheaded the national movement before independence.

Milad Hanna is an acknowledged Coptic commentator, member of the leftist Tagammu' Party and a former MP, so he was my first reference on the Coptic issue. The first thing a visitor to his house sees is a sturdy display cabinet. Hanna eagerly shows his numerous awards, always by starting the sentence with: "I'm a humble man, but I was awarded such and such…" The decoration granted by the Swedish King Carl Gustav XVI seemed to be his favourite.

Although the constitution of 1923 stated that the official religion was Islam, Copts have been able to practise their religion freely – within the confines of the Church that is – proselytising is not allowed. "The years 1923–1952 were the best for Copts when it comes to representation in the parliament and cultural life. Copts were affluent and well-educated: 25% of university professors, diplomats and judges were Copts," Hanna told me.

But during the Nasser era, Copts – indeed the citizenry

in general – withdrew from politics, because Nasser's one-party system didn't allow independent views. "The Free Officers didn't have any Copts among them, so Christians kept a low profile. In the 1956 elections, not a single Copt was elected, so Nasser became worried. It was his idea to nominate 10 Coptic members," Hanna reflected.

Copts have therefore concentrated more on the world of finance, and would rather act as private entrepreneurs than work for the government. Nasser nationalized a raft of private companies, causing huge losses to businessmen and women – Copts in particular. This is when a large number of Copts left the country and established churches in the West. Nasser also tried to nationalize religion – al-Azhar became subjucated to the state, but the Coptic Church kept its independence.

The constitution of 1971, which stated that *shari'a* is one of the sources of legislation, doesn't specifically mention Copts. They are allowed to follow their own rulings where *shari'a* might contradict their customs, such as issues related to family law. For example, the Coptic Church doesn't recognize divorce, but can grant it in special circumstances. If one of the spouses has been unfaithful, or develops a mental illness, or if the spouse has vanished for more than seven years (for example, working in the Gulf) the marriage can be annulled. Lately there's been talk of granting a divorce if the husband is violent – if the wife's life is at risk.

But what is the position of women among Copts? Does it differ from the surrounding Muslim society? I asked this of Laila Iskandar, a short, stylish woman, who works with the most downtrodden Copts of all, the Cairo garbage collectors. She thinks it's difficult to evaluate women's position – level of education and financial realities define a woman's position in marriage:

> Perhaps the position of a Coptic woman is better in the sense that her marriage is more stable because divorce doesn't exist – she doesn't have to worry about being cast off, like Muslim women do. A woman can therefore use more of her assets for raising her children and educating them, since she doesn't have to think about having to save for a rainy day.

Some Coptic women participate in politics (see Chapter 8), but overall Copts have played a minor role in the higher echelons of politics. A veritable 'mass exodus' from politics took place during Sadat's rule, as the president addressed the nation with progressively more and more Islamic references. "In the 1960s and '70s politics moved to universities. This was also the time when the Islamic movement grew stronger – this was a channel for the Muslim youth. The Copts saw the churches as a channel for activity, maybe by giving donations, but not politically," says Rafiq Habib, a well-known Coptic author.

Copts tend to regard Sadat's era as the darkest for the Christian minority. The bearish middle-aged Coptic scholar called Samir Morcos argues that Sadat practically split the nation. "Historically speaking, during the times when *ahl al-dhimma* references [Christians and Jews under Muslim protection] have surfaced, Copts have sought refuge within the Church." Under Sadat, religion surpassed nationality as the main marker of identity, and this made Copts feel like second-class citizens.

But because Copts had withdrawn from politics and were more active within the church, by default the church became more politicized. Since 1971, the Coptic Church has been under the pontificate of Nazir Gayyid, Pope Shenuda III, a former monk and a teacher at Sunday school, and lecturer at theological college. As soon as he took up his new position, he started to activate and renew the church, paying special attention to youth education and ecumenical activities. Shenuda increased the number of dioceses, and established Coptic Churches in the United States and in several African countries. A former monk, he also channelled resources to renovate medieval monasteries. Indeed, monastic life is experiencing a renaissance thanks to the active Pope.[6]

Today thousands of pilgrims and tourists visit Egypt's many monasteries (18 for monks, 6 for nuns). Among the most popular is one named after one of the first adherents of monastic life, Saint Anthony. This oldest inhabited Christian monastery in the world is located in the desert, near the Red Sea coast. According to legend, St Anthony was the son of a wealthy merchant in the late 3rd century, who discarded his worldly possessions, and started to wander the desert in search of God. The reputation of this wise hermit spread, and people started flocking to see him, and to be healed. But St Anthony had gone to the desert in search of solitude, and so he secluded himself in a cave 300m up a mountainside, where he spent 30 years praying and meditating.

His followers moved to different corners of Egypt, and hence spread monasticism. St Anthony's monastic rules are still obeyed today. "The four main columns of monastic life are obedience, poverty, chastity and solitude," Father Anthony Ruways told our four-member group. These days the monastery's over 100 monks are not entirely alone – a steady flow of pilgrims and tourists keeps them busy. And in the middle of his explanation, Father Ruways' mobile phone rang. He took it out of the pocket of his habit looking a bit embarrassed – monks are not supposed to carry such devices.

Even though interest in monastic life has increased, Father Ruways told us that it is not so easy to become a devotee of God.

There are five steps to be a monk or a nun. Number one: finishing education. You know if someone is a failure in studies, has many problems, he is escaping, lazy, didn't find a girl to marry... [We have] No place for such people.

Most of us are graduates of universities, some have MA, PhD, very few are not educated but have very strong spiritual life in their hearts. Number two: they have to finish their military service, which is obligatory in Egypt.

Thirdly: recommendation from priest of his church that he is good. Fourthly: he has to come frequently to visit the monastery, many, many times: so we tell him: "not now, come back again, we have no room". We want to check if he still wants to be a monk. And he can decide to do it or not.

The last step is very important. He has to be a novice for up to three years, under training, under observation... we put him under the microscope. It is very secretive: if he is good, decent, obedient, working seriously, if he is happy, if everybody is recommending him, he is not troublemaker... Then he can be ordained to be a monk and have a beard, a sign of consecration.

These were the characteristics Pope Shenuda was made of. He was bold, although his political manoeuvres were bound to get him into a confrontation with the President. Sadat was furious when, in 1972, the Pope encouraged a priest to hold a service in the village of al-Khanka, where an illegally built church had been burned to the ground. During Nasser's time, a quota had been set on how many churches could be built annually. However, this was no longer in line with Coptic population growth – more churches were needed to serve everyone. That was why Sunday school buildings were sometimes illegally converted into churches, even though Sadat doubled the annual quota of new churches from 25 to 50.[7]

Whether he intended it or not, Pope Shenuda had become the political leader of the Copts. He made a visit to the United States, where he met President Carter, among others. Carter introduced this oriental Pope to the media as 'the leader of seven million Egyptians' – although the recent census had put the figure at two million. For Sadat, the Pope's activities were too independent, and they ate away at his image as the 'father of the nation', his favourite epithet.

Shenuda was in the Wadi Natrun monastery when 170 church officials were seized in a mass arrest in September 1981. He was already expecting some kind of punishment, because in addition to his other 'misbehaviour' he had refused to receive government representatives at the Easter reception, and had ordered the bishops into the desert to pray for 'liberation from oppression'.

In this tense political climate, it didn't come as a huge surprise when Sadat dismissed Shenuda. The Papacy was entrusted to an administrative committee set up by Sadat. Shenuda was held under house-arrest in the monastery, and Amnesty International adopted him as a prisoner of conscience. The Pope made his return to public life four years later, after the new President Mubarak revoked his predecessor's dismissal decree. To many observers, the Pope seemed more diplomatic – a sign of this new attitude was an *iftar* (Ramadan breaking the fast meal) dinner which he hosted, attended by the top Islamic authorities and policy makers.[8]

But worse times yet lay ahead. The relationship between Christians and Muslims reached their lowest point when radical Islamists launched their campaign of violence in the early 1990s, accusing Copts of being infidels (see Chapter 1). In the south, Islamists robbed Christian shops, demanded protection money and killed individual Copts – even monks. Some of the killings, however, might actually have been motivated by blood feuds between clans (*tar*) a common occurrence in the south.

Copts felt that the government wasn't making a big enough effort to protect them, or arresting the militants terrorizing the countryside. Indeed, the violence of the 1990s and Muslims' silent approval – as Copts feel it – is still a bone of contention between the Copts and the Muslims. This is why many unhealed wounds from this era resurface from time to time.

Milad Hanna reminisces of the time when Egyptian Islam was beautiful, "it had a Sunnite face, Shiite blood, Coptic heart and Pharaonic bones," as he puts it. Hanna is not the only one to notice that the Wahhabi trend brought back from Saudi Arabia by Egyptian migrant workers changed the characteristics of the faith – it became more intolerant. After those years of violence, the Copts have also developed suspicion towards the state: they question whether the government really wants to solve the underlying problem, or just want to sweep them under the carpet.

In 1994, Cairo was supposed to host a minorities conference, with the question of the Coptic minority on the agenda. One of the Egyptian delegates was the renowned sociologist Saad Eddin Ibrahim, Director of the Ibn Khaldun centre, which specializes in enhancing democracy and dialogue (see Chapter 6). Among its activities, it had published reports on Coptic–Muslim relations. The conference took place at the time of the fiercest Islamist–government fighting, but the Egyptian media slammed the meeting, and it had to be transferred to Cyprus.

For many Copts – including Pope Shenuda – the title of the conference was a major issue. They didn't accept terming the Copts a 'minority'. "We do not accept being distinguished from other Egyptians. We do not accept the term 'minority' as if such meaning of claiming political rights or foreign help. We are Egyptians, part of Egypt, of the same nation," Shenuda said.[9]

Samir Morcos was one of the main opponents of the conference. "I wrote articles against Ibrahim. My message was: don't approach the Coptic question from a 'minority' point of view, but on the basis of citizenship. If you talk about a minority, you are indirectly supporting the Islamists, who only see Islam and non-Islam," he says.

Rafiq Habib also finds the minority definition problematic. "We're not a minority; we are all Egyptians – we have the same heritage, culture, and lifestyle. A different religion doesn't mean we have other differences, but unity. Minority means somehow that you're not native." Habib considers this unity as something so self-evident, that he doesn't see a contradiction in joining a project with moderate Islamists in the al-Wasat party (see Chapter 8).

> Al-Wasat is a culture project. Our culture and heritage is the same, one *umma*. It is labelled Islamic, but it is the continuum of ancient Egyptian and Coptic culture, based on religion. Both Muslim and Coptic cultures are very religious, and in Egypt they both convey the same values, meaning that the core of the culture is similar. Al-Wasat is therefore a political project, which expresses our set of values, which is one. But the party focuses on politics, not religion.

Yet the notion of ancestry has been raised several times lately, particularly after the horrendous al-Kosheh case gained international attention. In 1998, two truck drivers were found dead at a school yard in the Upper Egyptian town of al-Kosheh, a town with about 70% Coptic majority. The fighting between Islamists and Copts had calmed down by then (and al-Kosheh had been calm until then), so the government was eager to put a lid on even a minor disturbance which might otherwise have been labelled as sectarian. Perhaps that's why the police decided that the perpetrator must have been a Copt, although they had no idea who was guilty.

Because the Egyptian police are generally not properly trained in criminal investigation methods, they resorted to torture in order to get a confession. For three weeks, hundreds of villagers – possibly including children – were summoned to the police station or the nearby hills, where they were tortured physically and mentally, so severely that 14 villagers were hospitalized.

According to the Egyptian Organization for Human Rights (EOHR), 500 people in total were subjected to torture. Torturing a suspect's relatives and acquaintances is common all over Egypt, and is inflicted on both Muslims and Christians. Although the torturers in al-Kosheh were Muslims, few considered this case as having sectarian motives, but rather as a flagrant abuse by the police.

However, the case took a different twist when it leaked to the international media. The *Daily Telegraph* wrote that Egyptian Christians had been crucified, teenage girls raped and babies brutally beaten in the police-led raid against the Copts, the 'ancient inhabitants of Egypt'. According to the article, Copts have been living for centuries in the midst of hostile Muslim conquerors, and are persecuted for their faith.[10]

Due to this fault-ridden article, 29 US congress members sent a petition to Mubarak, asking him to stop torture. The US Congress had just passed the *Freedom from Religious Persecution Act*, to a large extent thanks to the lobbying of Copts living in the United States. The most extreme measures of the law allow the United States to impose economic sanctions against any state which practises widespread religious persecution. Critics of the law see it as directed against Arab and Muslim majority countries.[11]

Mubarak retorted that this was an internal matter. Security officials tried to play it down, and claimed that the torture marks were old, or that they were scars of skin diseases. The files of the investigation weren't published, and officials tried to brush the whole case under the carpet. EOHR however published a report on their findings. This caused an international uproar, and embarrassed the Egyptian government. EOHR was made a scapegoat – its director Hafiz Abu Sa'ada was accused of illegally receiving foreign funding, and therefore further tarnishing Egypt's reputation abroad. Abu Sa'ada was detained for six days.

Eventually, the government declared it would conduct a thorough investigation, but it still took two years to find the murder suspect, and none of the police officers who participated in the alleged torture were convicted. Whether it was a way to alleviate guilt or not, nonetheless the government made some concessions to improve the position of Copts. Some confiscated church land was returned, and church building regulations were relaxed a little – now building permission for each church is granted by the district mayor, not the national President.

Although the al-Kosheh case wasn't regarded in Egypt as sectarian strife, it turned into one in January 2000. A dispute between a Christian merchant and a Muslim customer led to rioting and the death of 19 Copts and two Muslims, and dozens were injured. This was the worst Coptic–Muslim confrontation in 30 years. This time, the government seemed to have learned a lesson, and about 90 villagers were quickly arrested. This so-called "al-Kosheh II" prompted the local press to orate about the necessity of stability and harmony between religions, as a way to blur the sectarian issue. Al-Kosheh village's name was changed to al-Salam (Peace).[12]

Yet the verdicts for rioting didn't please everyone – one Muslim was convicted of manslaughter and possession of unregistered weapons; another one was convicted of manslaughter; and two were convicted of vandalism. Pope Shenuda declared that he rejected the verdicts, but a retrial in 2003 only altered the sentences slightly. Copts argued that the trial was sloppy and lacked evidence. The Court of Cassation upheld the convictions.[13]

Many people think that an "al-Kosheh III" is possible. One of them is Yussef Sidhom, the editor of Coptic weekly *Watani* (My Homeland). A clock depicting Jesus suffering with a crown of thorns decorates his office wall, as do pictures of saints. "As long as the security apparatus is infiltrated by Islamists, and as long as there is discrimination between Copts and Muslims, there will always be the danger that al-Kosheh III will happen somewhere in Egypt," Sidhom told me. But he also thinks that the situation of Copts differs greatly between the cities and the countryside.

> In larger cities Copts are mixed with Muslims, and they see their problems as touching all Egyptians: lack of democracy and human rights. In smaller rural communities, however, the Copts are more aligned with their church rather than with the rest of the society – this is why hatred is spreading.

Not only violence, but sex has also chafed Coptic–Muslim relations. In the summer of 2001 emotions ran high when an Egyptian tabloid published pictures of a Coptic monk frolicking in bed with a woman who was allegedly married.[14]

"Monastery turned brothel" was the *al-Nabaa* headline in the 17th June issue. The three-page photo essay relied heavily on pictures taken from a videotape of the cell of a monk in the Asyut monastery. Although the pictures were blurred so that certain shapes were out of focus, it was obvious that he wasn't practising penance. This particular *al-Nabaa* issue sold like hot falafels, because the Egyptian press rarely publishes such risqué pictures. Eventually black-marketeers were selling it at ten times the original price.

On the same evening, some 4000 outraged Copts gathered by the Cairo cathedral. This meeting turned into a riot – six police officers were injured when the angry mob threw stones at them. To calm things down, Pope Shenuda was called in. He told the crowd that the paper had been sued for defamation. The demonstrators demanded that the whole paper be closed down.

The church issued a statement, which said that the monk in question had been deposed from the monastery five years previously because he had abandoned the church teachings and monastic rules. The Pope emphasized that the ex-monk's misdeeds had taken place outside the monastery. It later turned out that the video was filmed in the defrocked monk's mother's apartment. After the riots, *al-Nabaa* and its sister publication were temporarily closed, and the editor of *al-Nabaa* was sentenced to three years imprisonment for defamation of religion.[15]

A smaller storm in a teacup occurred in winter 2003, when the local press started to pay attention to the so-called "fish sticker" dispute.[16] In recent years, Copts have placed fish stickers on car bumpers, as a symbol of Christianity. The stickers come typically in two designs, either with simple streamlined fish, or ones with 'Jesus' written inside. The fish is an ancient Christian symbol, which was already used in Roman times as a secret sign of the Christian faith. The symbol is a pictograph of the Greek word for fish – *ichthys,* whose letters spell 'Jesus Christ, Son of God, Saviour.' Nowadays the fish symbol decorates Coptic Church altar clothes and other religious items.

For some reason, Muslims responded to the fish sticker trend by gluing shark stickers on their cars. They also come in two designs, simple sharks, or ones with the Muslim pronunciation of faith, *La ilaha illa Allah* (There is no God but God) written in them. In this rather childish sticker match, the shark is supposed to show that it can eat the smaller fish. Some Muslims have even said that a shark bumper sticker means that Muslims are stronger.

The shark stickers angered many a Copt – they had just wanted to express their Christianity, but Muslims had taken this as challenge. Analysts explained in the press that they perceive the sticker phenomenon as Copts' willingness to express their religion more openly.

Christians can often be recognized by their tattoos; a cross on their wrists, or crucifixes, or their names (although many names are used by both denominations), but the stickers are a more public pronunciation of religion. Egyptians are religious people, and are not shy talking about their faith. For example, Coptic taxis tend to have pictures of the Virgin Mary or saints, whereas Muslim drivers decorate their cars with stickers of Qur'anic verses, or other Islamic paraphernalia.

Conversions between the two faiths are rare and problematic – sometimes so controversial that the Pope himself has to intervene. In December 2004, a private matter escalated into such a scandal – causing Pope Shenuda to retreat into Wadi Natrun again. Wafaa Konstantin, the wife of a Coptic priest, had taken refuge in a police station, claiming to have converted to Islam. She demanded police protection against fellow Copts, fearing that they wouldn't accept her conversion, which seemed to be motivated less by religious conviction, and more by an unhappy marriage and the Coptic ban on divorce. Copts protested in huge numbers and accused the state of interference. So heated did the issue become, that it prompted Shenuda to retreat into the monastery. He declared that wouldn't come out until the issue was settled. Within weeks, Konstantin's conversion to Islam was declared null and void.[17]

But the issue of conversions was not put to rest. In the midst of the 2005 parliamentary elections, a tape of a banned theatrical play resurfaced in the city of Alexandria. *I was Blind but Now I Can See* was a Coptic play about a young man who is persuaded to convert to Islam, but then reverts to Christianity. The play had been banned, but the Pope refused to condemn or apologize for it.

The Muslim Brotherhood has a broad support base in Alexandria, but it wasn't immediately evident who was stirring this stew. Thousands of Muslims marched to the church which was rumoured to have distributed the tape, leaving three protesters dead and over 140 injured. Again, the state tried to solve the issue by heavy-handed application of the security apparatus, leaving Alexandria residents – and particularly the Coptic community – perplexed and scared.[18]

No wonder, then, that another incident took place in the Mediterranean city. In April 2006, what the state media labelled as a 'lone lunatic' stabbed several people (one of them lethally) in two different churches. We arrived at the scene in St Mark's Church that afternoon. Blood could still be seen on the ground, the trail leading to the adjacent hospital. The atmosphere was both tense and sad at the same time – a group of men had gathered outside to protest. "This is not the first time! Why is this still happening?" one protestor said.

Inside the hospital, a young man called Michael Bisada lay in bed. "When I stepped out of the church, a man with two knives attacked me, one hitting my arm, all the way to the bone," he explained, visibly in pain. He claimed that the police saw the attack, but didn't interfere. This is a common complaint from the Copts: since Copts are underrepresented in the police force, they feel discriminated against. The discrimination extends even to hospitals – in summer 2008, the Egyptian Doctor's Union ruled that organ transplants between the two creeds are forbidden.[19]

In the light of these events, Copts feel more and more cornered. It is little wonder, then, that their participation in societal decision-making has been circumspect. Usually their representatives in parliamentary elections don't exceed 2%. Parties are simply reluctant to nominate Coptic candidates, because the parties don't believe in the Copts' chances. In the last parliamentary elections of 2005, only one Copt (the all-time lowest showing since 1956), the former Minister of Finance Yusif Boutros Ghali, got through and Mubarak nominated another five.

Former MP Milad Hanna sees the policy of Presidential nomination as problematic. "Overall, Coptic performance in the parliament has been weak, possibly because the president only nominates weak personalities and pretenders. They are there just to say that 'Copts are satisfied', so that they can secure re-election." As a housing specialist, he was one of the nominees in 1984. "Because I spoke my mind, I was forced to resign. I was told that I was giving up paradise and that I would never be elected again," he recalls. The system of quotas and nominations is favoured only by a few, loud Copts, and particularly the Coptic groups abroad.

Coptic candidates usually portray themselves as representatives of the whole nation, and avoid religious issues. Yet religion keeps on surfacing. Christian candidates sometimes have to tackle the Islamic concept of *wilaya*, which means that a non-Muslim shouldn't be a Muslim's 'protector' or 'guardian'. Some politically incorrect opponents (usually from the Muslim Brotherhood) have raised the issue of *wilaya* particularly on the eve of elections, as a campaign tool to render their Coptic opponents as 'unqualified'. In the election year of 2000 the Grand Mufti of al-Azhar issued an important fatwa, stating that Muslims can vote for whichever candidate they deem as most qualified, regardless of their religion. Copts have therefore concentrated their efforts on private enterprise, like minorities the world over. For example, MobiNil – a mobile phone operator, and the flagship of the Cairo bourse – is owned by the Coptic Sawiris family. Their family empire runs from construction companies to holiday resorts. Copts have indeed become prominent in the fields of tourism, car manufacturing, pharmacy and consulting. However, perhaps the most downtrodden of all Egyptians – the *zabbalin* (garbage collectors) – are also Copts.

Cairo has some 60,000 garbage collectors, who make a living from recycling the garbage they collect. Every day, they collect 200,000 kilos of waste, which accounts for roughly a third of Cairo's garbage. The largest *zabbalin* community, the Muqattam hill, is a miserable place. The sickly sweet smell of rotting garbage envelops the place, the unpaved roads are muddy, and here and there goats root through the garbage.

Women and children sort the waste outside their homes – without protective gloves. Hospital waste comes with the ordinary garbage, so it is little wonder that this work is life threatening. Hepatitis and other diseases are common, not to mention parasites. The bulk of their income comes from recycling (selling plastic, metal, etc.), but some also comes from fees collected from their customers. Until 2009 they also earned money by raising pigs – the Muslim ban on eating pork doesn't include them – however, in 2009, the government culled all pigs as an overreaction to swine flu.

Yet their valuable, if inhuman, recycling work has not been appreciated. In 2003, the Cairo sanitation department decided to privatize waste collection, and three foreign companies won the contract. The sanitation department had become concerned that 20% of Cairo waste remains uncollected – the poorest neighbourhoods cannot afford to pay waste collection fees. In these areas, garbage is usually burned, which, of course, worsens the air quality. This privatization caused many a *zabbal* to lose his job; instead, they have become 'scavengers' as *zabbalin* rights defender Laila Iskander puts it. "Also the income from recycling has diminished, because there is less garbage to recycle – most of it ends up in the dump yard."

Despite the many obvious problems the Coptic community is facing, or maybe because of it, the Coptic Church is experiencing a renaissance of sorts. Monastic life has become popular, and church attendance is on the rise. Secular thinker Hanna sees this activism, promoted by the Pope, as misguided:

> Shenuda is in favour of Coptic Christian fundamentalism. It is first of all based on monastic life and convent Christianity, which means living in harsh conditions and the acceptance of suffering for the Christ. They live more for the afterlife than today. These are not the components of a healthy society.
>
> Culturally speaking, the Egyptian Coptic community is not healthy, and that is why they accept the current situation: as second-class citizens. Copts are not promoted, they don't get high official positions in the government or ministries … and they accept this! Instead, they focus on business, which creates a warped community. Business without politics can be easily erased; it is naïve to expect that concentrating on private enterprise is safer. After all, we live in dictatorship.

Watani magazine editor Sidhom argues along the same lines as Hanna:

> It is a positive development that during the last 40 years the Coptic Church has truly become an international church. Studying the Coptic language and preserving it is extremely important for research.

But the negative aspect is that the Church has spread an umbrella, under which the Christians stand – this harms their citizenship. Some Copts even say that they should speak Coptic amongst themselves in daily life! When Copts are fighting for their rights, the Church has become an important power-broker, which harms the question of citizenship. I would like to see the day when the Church separates the spiritual from the political. I don't think that the Church should trespass its spiritual role.

Sidhom argues that discrimination still runs deep, at the highest levels in diplomacy, judiciary, army, police, universities and banks. But he sees a significant change which has taken place during the past couple of years in both the school curriculum and the media. "When I went to school, we read about Coptic history. But with the Islamist influence in the 1960s and '70s, references to Coptic history were reduced to a minimum," he says. Copts have complained that school history lessons start from the Arabic conquest, as if Copts didn't exist.

Sidhom praises Saad Eddin Ibrahim, who pushed the textbook issue with the Minister of Education. Sidhom was a member of the committee which selected texts for new books, those currently in use. "Radio and television don't have programs which bad-mouth Christians anymore, but newspapers and magazines still publish these kinds of articles."

However, Milad Hanna thinks that the government's way of handling the Coptic issue is wrong. He argues that nurturing the relationship between Copts and Muslims is far too important to be left in the hands of security officials, as has been the case until now. He has suggested establishing a national unity council, which would consist of politically aware personalities and security officials. "The other option would be to change the mandate of the Ministry of *Awqaf* (responsible for religious affairs) so that it would include Coptic affairs," Hanna suggests.

Although many Copts talk about discrimination, it is often difficult to understand this conflict because it is not readily visible on the Cairo streets. At the same time, people are wary of talking about problems, and deny that there is a conflict. But how important is religion in the day-to-day dealings between people? The majority of Copts and Muslims live together in harmony; many have friends from both denominations and they participate in each other's religious feasts. Inter-marriages, however, are still rare, and frowned upon. "Perhaps religious issues are a problem in the new urban slums, which were established during the worst time of Islamist influence – they are places which don't have a communal feeling," Laila Iskander assesses.

Yet the relationship between Copts and Muslims has worsened over the last few years. Copts were appalled and frightened by the Muslim Brotherhood's electoral gains in 2005. Rafiq Habib argues that until then Copts had held the view that the state would stem the tide of the Islamist trend.

> This makes the Copts always support the regime. Even the attitude of the Copts in the [Israeli] war against Gaza [2009] was not good: the Church thanked Mubarak for his stance, and so most Muslims were angry with the Church's statement. Now we have an additional problem: somehow the Muslim masses think that Copts stand with the regime, with Israel and America. This will deepen the problems.

The majority Muslims often see Copts as a 'spoiled' minority backed by the West. Therefore the government is reluctant to give them any concessions (such as church building permissions, etc.) because such an act could be interpreted as favouring Copts. The general mood of protests, strikes, and civil rights demonstrations of the mid-2000s prompted some Egyptians to think that Copts were better off.

As a result, increasing criminality is often played out in sectarian terms.

This in turn has energized Coptic groups outside of Egypt, spreading information on mistreatment via the internet and satellite channels. Mutual mistrust remains within Egypt, and without active state involvement (beyond a security point of view) the situation is likely to escalate even further. In this situation many Copts consider emigration – their exodus is already higher than Muslims.

Lack of information and ignorance of the other is often the reason for suspicion or violence. In summer 2004 a rare event occurred: a film called *Bahib al-Sima* (I Love Films) went on national release, a film about a Coptic community. The film tells a story of a family living under the rule of fundamentalist Coptic father. Films about Copts are rarities amidst the action films and cheap entertainment. Initially, the Egyptian censors were worried that the film might offend the Coptic Church. Prior to its release, it was shown to Coptic intellectuals and academics, who were reported to be happy with its contents.

The film's director Usama Fawzi has said it is a protest against oppression and extremism. The film's narrator returns to his childhood in 1966 Cairo. The father scares his children with warnings of hellfire, fasts 200 days a year, and considers films, dance, singing and even conjugal sex to be sinful. The son is a diehard movie fan, who is forbidden to go to the cinema. The mother longs hopelessly for her husband's love. She rediscovers her passion for nude painting, and gets a taste of passion outside the marriage.

The film's narrative turns to oppression. The father discovers widespread corruption at his work in a school, and falls out with his employer. He is taken to a police station in the middle of the night where he is tortured, and accused of being a communist. Around the same time that he is diagnosed with a heart condition, the movie-fan son is also diagnosed with a chronic illness. The father ends up in a bar, a broken man, admitting his inadequacy and fear. The son gets a television.

After the film had been showing for a few weeks, the protests began. Angry Coptic masses gathered in front of the cathedral, and demanded that the film be withdrawn. They felt that the movie denigrated Copts – for example, it shows a fight in a church. A group of priests sued the film-makers and demanded that the film be banned.[20] The film remained in the cinemas, and even did relatively well in the box office, although it wasn't a major hit.

But *Bahib al Sima* brought the reality of Coptic life to the wider Egyptian audience. The Coptic issue was no longer something to be talked about only in whispers. One of the signs of better relations between the state and Copts is the revival of Coptic feasts. Coptic Christmas (December 7th) is now a public holiday. This decision was praised, but Copts wish that their most important holiday, Easter, would get the same status.

Also, the fact that Copts can celebrate their non-religious feasts has revived the Church. In 1990, at the request of the Ministry of Tourism, Pope Shenuda listed all the sites that the Holy Family is believed to have visited when they fled into Egypt. There is no archaeological evidence of the Holy Family's visit, but the Coptic Church deems the visit as historical truth.

At the end of January 2004, I participated in one of these pilgrimages along the "Holy Family trail", in the Mallawi crossing the Nile Festival. With me was Dana, my American camerawoman, and we were filming a cultural story about the Copts' social position and in particular this feast, which is purely of popular origin. Our tour leader was Kees Hulsman, a middle-aged Dutch Coptic covert and an expert on Coptic affairs. He admitted that no one seems to know how far back this feast can be traced; it has just been passed on from one bishop to the next. In any case, crossing the Nile is the only public feast celebrating the Holy Family's journey in Egypt.

Our entourage consisted of a mixture of journalists and pilgrims, including an American and a German priest and elderly Coptic sisters with amusing hair nets which made their hair look like pointy cones. Our first station was the Blessed Virgin Church on a hill in the village of Gabal al-Tir, surrounded by lush fields. Outside the church, a group of villagers gathered to wonder at the foreigners, and to ask for money. Inside the church, an Egyptian tour group was listening to the priest's explanation of the church's history.

I sat on a bench inside the church and guarded the camera bag. Curious villagers wanted to be part of our report, and they pushed in front of me a little boy dressed in a man's suit, with the word *Friends* embroidered on his breast pocket. They wanted to know what I thought of their church, and what was it like to live in Cairo. They found it strange that I was living in Egypt all by myself – I guess they thought I was much younger. Next to the church was a souvenir shop selling Jesus paraphernalia. Hulsman had advertised their home-made Communion wine – which I of course had to try out.

Our journey then took us to Deir Abu Hinnis, one of the few Coptic-only villages in Egypt. Local nuns served us a vegetarian dinner, before we headed to our main destination, Mallawi. On the city streets, young girls walked arm-in-arm in front of groups of boys. Hulsman told us that during the Islamist fighting in the mid 1990s, the whole city had looked like a battlefield. "The streets were guarded by tanks and soldiers, and we couldn't move anywhere without police escort," he recalled.

In the evening we interviewed the Bishop of Mallawi, Demetrios, who greeted us holding a wooden cross in his palm. Copts either kiss the cross, the hand holding it, or both. The Bishop picked his words very carefully when I asked him about the position of Copts. He emphasized the importance of being able to have a public celebration after the violent years. "Now we have a reason to celebrate, we have hope for better times ahead," he said. He also pointed out that Copts were given permission more often to renovate churches, and build Sunday schools.

After the interview, two American, thirty-something, idealistic-looking men came into the Bishop's office. One of them, a bespectacled, prematurely balding man greeted the Bishop in colloquial Egyptian Arabic, *Izzayyak*, which translates to "How are you doing?" (Hulsman had instructed me to address him as "Your Grace".)

The Bishop was not put off by this overly informal greeting, but invited the men to the next day's celebration. The duo had participated in the festival once before, and last year the Bishop had given them a gift. "Thank you so much for that beautiful fabric you gave me, great colours, the red, white and black," the speaker praised. "Those are the colours of the Egyptian flag," the Bishop noted curtly. The visitor's face turned embarrassed and confused – instead of the church, he had been bowing before the state, it seemed.

Our night's lodging was a building reminiscent of a summer camp: long rooms with high ceilings, filled with rows of bunk beds, colourful sheets, uncomfortable pillows and a pervasive mild scent of mould. Dana and I thought that it would be a good idea to taste the Communion wine. It was sickly sweet, but with a bit of imagination, it could pass as port wine. It wasn't good enough for Dana, though, and she took out her hipflask of whisky. Sleep arrived.

The next morning, at 7.30 a.m., the Bishop was supposed cross the Nile in a sailing boat. We were exhausted from the journey, the late interview and the early awakening – but still the Bishop's entourage was nowhere to be seen. While we waited, a steady stream of festival goers crossed the river. Most were choir-boys in white gowns, holding crosses and banners. In the Bishop's boat, the choristers turned on their loud speakers and sang hymns. The air was buzzing with the excitement of a great popular feast.

After two hours of waiting, the Bishop finally arrived. He climbed into the sailing boat, which was powered by a huge sail decorated with a painting of the Holy Family. On the far bank of the Nile, a cheering crowd received him, which slowly advanced towards Kum Maria hill, the centre stage of the festivities. The villagers had gathered along the road and they sung and applauded the passing procession. At the foot of the hill stood a festival tent, where the Coptic representatives, Muslim leaders and local dignitaries sat in harmony on a dais. A girl choir was singing, and a couple dressed as Mary and Joseph, with baby Jesus on donkey-back, came to greet the Bishop.

The true popular festivities took place outside the tent; it was a joyful day for the kids. They wanted to practise their English and every so often asked us: "What's the time? What's your name? What is your nationality?" Another highlight occurred around midday, when a rather peculiar trail of cars came around the tent. On the first one stood a trio in Pharaonic costumes and heavy make-up. They were followed by a group of enormous mock Holy Family members; plaster-Joseph's arm swung in the air, the car jerking slowly forward.

It was hot, dusty and we were tired – no matter that we were attending a happy occasion. Dana's next suggestion was telling of our mood: Kum Maria hill is supposed to enhance fertility, and so she suggested that I should do my TV stand-up by rolling down the hill. This sight would have probably attracted too much attention away from the motorcade (and I didn't want to risk the belief actually working on me), so this rolling was never recorded for Finnish TV posterity.

Notes

—-—

1 Meinardus, 1999:113–118; Al-Sayyid Marsot, 1985:126.

2 Egypt recognizes five religious minorities: Copts, Protestants, Catholics, Seven Day Adventists and Jews, see *Egypt Today*, 4/2004.

3 *Jizya* was abolished in 1815, Meinardus, 1999:66.

4 Perho, 1998:131; Diana Digges, 'Strongholds of Orthodoxy', *The Cairo Times*, 4–17/2/1999, Vol. 2, Issue 25. The Bible was translated into Arabic at the end of 11th century.

5 Solihin, 1991:17; Wakin, 2000:10–11.

6 Meinardus, 1999:3–7. For a fascinating depiction of monastic life, see Dalrymple, 1998.

7 Heikal, 1983:173.

8 Digges, 1999; Heikal, 1983:170–174, 248–249; Meinardus, 1999:8.

9 Meinardus, 1999:85.

10 Christina Lamb, 'Hundreds of Christians Raped, Beaten and Tortured by Police', *The Daily Telegraph*, 27/10/1998,

11 Khaled Elgindy, 'Diaspora troublemakers', *The Cairo Times*, Vol. 2, Issue 25, 4/2/1999; Steve Negus, 'Village of fear', *The Cairo Times*, 1/10/1998, Vol. 2, Issue 16.

12 Norbert Schiller, 'Kosheh investigations begin', *The Cairo Times*, 13–19/1/2000, Vol. 3, Issue 24.

13 Hossam Bahgat, 'Making it go away', *The Cairo Times*, 8–14/2/2001, Volume 4, Issue 47; Mostafa Hashish, 'Another Kosheh verdict', *The Cairo Times*, 6–12/3/2003, Volume 7, Issue 1.

14 Coptic monks are celibate, but Coptic priests may marry.

15 Ashraf Khalil, '*Al Nabaa* fans the flames', *The Cairo Times*, 21–27/6/2001, Volume 5, Issue 16; Tariq Hassan-Gordon, 'Al Nabaa editor gets three years for defaming Coptic community', *Middle East Times*, 21/9/2001.

16 See for example: 'Fish vs. sharks, A religious battle', *Associated Press*, 29/11/2003.

17 Issandr El Amrani, 'The Emergence of a "Coptic Question" in Egypt', *Middle East Report*, April 28th 2006.

18 Soon after, Mubarak nominated the first Coptic governor in decades, to Qina in Upper Egypt, see ibid.

19 Dina Ezzat, 'Blessed be the people of Egypt', *Al-Ahram Weekly*, 8–14/1/2009, Issue No. 929.
20 *al-Sharq al-Awsat*, Vol. 27, Issue 9354; Yasmine El-Rashidi, 'They don't love this movie', *Al-Ahram Weekly*, 15–21/7/04, Issue 699.

6

States of emergency

— —

The *Queen Boat's* disco reeked of sin. Dark crimson velvet chairs lined the walls of this dim dance den, and the mirror-ball hanging from the ceiling gave the place a faded, tacky ambiance. One could barely make out the dark, nocturnal river through the windows – the *Queen Boat* was anchored on the west bank of the Nile, opposite the five-star Marriott Hotel. Sporting skin-tight jeans, a group of young gay men danced together in the middle of the dance floor, with the enthusiasm of a shared secret. Sudanese prostitutes eyed the incoming customers and proceeded to slow, almost reluctant, business negotiations with foreigners who ventured in. That night I was probably the only professional woman there whose work interest in the floating disco was legal.

The venue, the *Queen Boat*, was Fred's latest acquisition in his long list of hotbeds of vice. With glasses thick as bottle bottoms balanced on his nose, Fred might have looked like any harmless pensioner, but he was rumoured to have been born in a Berlin brothel. Or perhaps that was just a marketing gimmick, because the 'restaurants' he hosted in Cairo were notorious for similar activities. Not necessarily under his direction, but at least under his permissive, blurry eyes.

Some time after my visit, the humid night of 10th May 2001 was turning into the morning of 11th May – the *Queen Boat* normally started to get busy after midnight – and a group of men danced together under the mirrored ball, just as on any weekend. Suddenly, the carefree merrymaking came to an abrupt end, as tens of police officers in civilian clothes stormed in. Heavy-handedly, they selected over 30 Egyptian men and led them away. Dismayed foreign men and all the women were left wondering what had just happened.

Ashraf al-Zanati, a teacher at the British Council, had spent the evening with his colleagues at a restaurant in the Marriott Hotel opposite. As he stepped out of the hotel, policemen grabbed him and took him away. Both Ashraf and his colleagues were dumbfounded, and no reason was given for his arrest. That night the police arrested 17 other men on the streets of Cairo – they had probably been followed for weeks.

"We were taken to Abdin police station, which is the headquarters of the vice squad," Ashraf said, recalling the events as we sat in Cairo's *Harris* café a year later. Ashraf sipped his cappuccino, the expression on his face still one of bitter disbelief, as he recalled his nightmare.

Two days after their arrest, the men were taken before a prosecutor, who asked them all if they knew a person called Shirif Farahat. No one admitted to knowing him. Then they were taken to Cairo's central prison, Tora. Only there, from reading the newspapers, did the men get to know why they had been arrested: "At Tora I learnt that I'm supposed to be a member of a group – led by Farahat – and that I don't believe in revealed religions. And that one of the rituals of this group is having sex with men," Ashraf told me. He didn't know any of the other detainees.

At first, these men were accused of defamation of religion. It wasn't the first time that the *Queen Boat* had been raided, but due to the severity of these charges, the case was taken before the state security court, against whose verdicts there is no right of appeal. Later, the prosecutor issued a statement, claiming that the men had engaged in 'strange rituals and organized group sex parties and other abnormal acts'. The case wasn't, however, about a new religious sect; rather, these men had been arrested purely because of their sexual orientation.

Because homosexuality is not criminal in Egypt *per se*, the legal system resorts to those decrees which forbid public indecency and immorality. According to Human Rights Watch (HRW), an American human rights organization, a law which was originally used against prostitution has been modified so that nowadays it is deemed to mean voluntary, non-commercial homosexual behaviour, termed 'debauchery', or *fujur*. Law 10/61 criminalizes 'habitual' debauchery (sex with more than one man, more than once within the last three years) and *di'ara* (applied to female prostitutes). These offences can result in up to three years imprisonment and/or large fines. Usually only the 'passive' partner, *luty*, is prosecuted – he is considered to have lost his masculinity.[1]

Immediately after the prosecutor's statement, the state-owned press and, of course, the tabloids grabbed the news eagerly. Even the flagship *al-Ahram* published the story in its crime pages, with sensationalist wording. According to the newspaper, the detainees were a group who specialized in satanic worship. Other papers declared that the group organized weekly wedding ceremonies for male couples – the last one being on the night of the arrests. The worst part, however, was the fact that some newspapers published the detainees' pictures, together with their names and jobs, therefore tarring them forever. Only a few opposition papers criticized the raids.

Homosexuality is a taboo subject in Egypt, a conservative, Muslim-majority country. The average Egyptian was horrified by the stories of the 'perverts' as the Egyptian press labelled them. Many people think that homosexuality is a Western imported vice, if not a disease, which has no place in Egypt. Yet in reality, homosexuality is as prevalent as in any society, but not openly. It has been argued that Arab society is more concerned with sexual acts and roles than sexual identities.[2] Therefore someone engaging in a homosexual act wouldn't necessarily label himself as gay. But Western gay circles have for years regarded Egypt in particular (and to a lesser extent Tunisia) as good tourist destinations, where holiday 'companions' are easy to find – often for a fee.

Yet the existence of this subculture could hardly have come as a surprise to the authorities: a couple of years before the *Queen Boat* incident, a gay Dutchman – who was presumably on a sex holiday – was killed in downtown Cairo. Hundreds of people were rounded up, as usual.[3]

Among those arrested was the husband of an American friend, whom I'll call Jane. Her husband made his living as a 'hustler', chatting up and trying to lure tourists into downtown souvenir shops. This wasn't the first or the last time he had been arrested – he took detentions as one of the many downsides of his trade.

Jane visited him in the police station and brought him money (to bribe the guards so that he could squat near the cell door, the only place with a hint of breeze), food and sleeping pills (it was impossible to sleep otherwise in the crowded cell). When the police officers heard the couple talking in English, they asked to see Jane in their office.

"Can you translate these documents?" they asked, and showed her the dead Dutchman's diary, and a gay traveller's guidebook. She consented, on the condition that her husband be released. They agreed – yet the police seemed to be so anxious to solve the murder that they overlooked an important conflict of interest: they were being assisted in their murder investigation by a stranger, a foreign woman whose husband was a suspect in a murder case, now being allowed to roam free.

As agreed, Jane visited the police station and translated the diary and travel guide. The deceased had systematically written down the names of every single man and boy he had met – the murderer's name was therefore most probably in the list. But translating the travel guide turned out to be a somewhat harder task to accomplish. "Do foreigners really think that Egypt is like this?" the policemen asked her, referring to the description of the ease of getting gay sex. The policemen simply couldn't fathom that someone would advertise Egypt as a gay paradise – it's not like that here! Jane made futile attempts to explain that she was only translating the text, not taking moral stances.

As this story indicates, the Egyptian police's investigative methods are not the most sophisticated. In the *Queen Boat* case, the murky circumstances opened the door to guessing over the motives. Was it perhaps an attempt to divert attention away from domestic politics and economic hardship? The smear campaign wasn't unique, in the sense that they appear from time to time, and this time the target just happened to be gays.

For many, the case brought to mind the 1997 'Satanists' arrest campaign, much celebrated in the government press.

Then the target was young, long-haired, heavy metal fans. They were arrested on the pretext that they had established a cult which encouraged Devil worship. In reality, they just organized underground concerts and listened to music. Eventually, all 78 detainees were released without charges. But their two-month ordeal had greatly frightened them, and the heavy metal concert scene pretty much died out.

Hussam Bahgat, a journalist and human rights activist who investigated the *Queen Boat* case, told me when it happened that similar arrests of gays had occurred since 1996, roughly once a year, but usually on a smaller scale. He believed that the *Queen Boat* case was designed to divert attention away from economic problems, and that the government wanted to portray itself as the moralist, using the state press. "It wants to show that it's protecting the people from enemies of Islam, be they Israeli spies, Islamists, radical film-makers – or gays."

One possible explanation for the arrests is linked with the establishment of internet police within the Egyptian Ministry of Interior.[4] Egypt doesn't censor the internet, but the net-police monitor certain Egyptian sites and their users for sexually or politically dubious (in the eyes of the government) content. Bahgat recollected:

> In the late 1990s when the internet started to become more accessible, it was such a relief for young Egyptians. Particularly for gays, because for the first time it opened a forum for sharing ideas with like-minded people. You could find countless number of clubs, sites for Egyptian gays, dating columns and chat rooms. Many believe that the Interior Ministry was shocked over the number of the sites, because this meant that gays exist, and that there are a lot of them.

A Human Rights Watch (HRW) report of 2004 records at least 179 alleged 'debauchery' cases since 2001 – 46 of the people involved were caught via internet. After the *Queen Boat* case, gays in Cairo lived in constant fear and didn't dare to set up dates through the net. The popular www.gayegypt.com site posted a warning about police officers who pretended to be gay, but instead of a romantic rendezvous, they would handcuff the hapless date. In addition, the site urged its readers to boycott Egypt as a holiday destination due to the persecution of gays.

According to HRW, the police resort to informers, and detainees' testimonies reveal that the police are under the impression that (passive) gays can be distinguished by their colourful underwear, tattoos and long hair.[5] The police do not spare crude language when describing gay raids:

> We received information that some young perverts frequent the Taverne bar in the Nile Hilton to hunt pleasure-seekers to practice perversion with them. Today, as we were inside the bar to observe the status of public morality ... we saw a person walking around the tables and acting in a way to draw attention, and walking in a female way, touching men inside the bar. We saw him walking outside the bar and walking in the corridors of the hotel, trying to touch men. Then we saw him whispering to a man and they both walked out together. Secret investigations showed that the first person who was being watched is a sexual pervert who practices debauchery with men with no discrimination, and so does the second. The first is a passive whereas the second is active. So we approached them and revealed our identity. They were both escorted to the headquarters.[6]

For his part, Ashraf al-Zanati believed that the reason for the *Queen Boat* arrests lies in Shirif Farahat's (the main accused) love for photography, as well as the prosecutor office's eagerness to lift their profile.

> The whole mess happened because of Shirif. A couple of years before the arrests Shirif came under the scrutiny of the security

forces because of his photography hobby. He had to surrender all his pictures to the prosecutor – among them were pictures of naked boys. The prosecutor had said to Shirif's father: Your son is gay, take him to a psychiatrist and that'll be all.

But Shirif wanted his pictures back, and kept on calling the prosecutor's office, not getting the right person. Then one day someone told him to come over and get the photos. And Shirif fell for the trap. The prosecutor's office wanted to seize the men in the pictures, but this was difficult, because Shirif had mainly taken the shots on the streets, and didn't know their names. I believe that the authorities wanted to catch the men quickly and therefore resorted to a raid on the *Queen Boat*.

The HRW report supports al-Zanati's theory. According to the report, Farahat was a well-to-do businessman, who was arrested on 24th April 2001 and his apartment was thoroughly searched. But the main reason for his future downfall was probably the fact that, for some reason, he recounted a confusing dream he had experienced 15 years previously.

In Shirif's dream, the Prophet Muhammad was visited by a blond boy. The Prophet explained that the boy was a Kurd, who would escape into the mountains after a Turkish attack. Then he would return to take revenge on the whole world, but in particular on the Jews, Christians and Muslims because they didn't stop the Turkish attack against the Kurds.

The state prosecutors decided that Farahat was gay, but this accusation wasn't serious enough to take the case to the state security court. So they added a new charge: disseminating a blasphemous cult. This made it possible to charge him with 'Contempt for Heavenly Religions', article 98.[7]

The *Queen Boat* trial started on 15th June 2001. The detainees were brought into the court room dressed in white prisoners' outfits, and most of them covered their faces, so as to avoid any additional shame. The main defendants Shirif

Farahat and Mahmud Ahmad Allam were charged with 'abusing Islam in order to spread heresy' and 'practising homosexuality as a part of the group's rituals'. The other 50 were charged with 'habitual practice of debauchery'.[8]

According to HRW, some defendants were abused verbally and physically (beatings, solitary confinement). Ashraf wasn't subjected to torture, but for him the most humiliating part of the ordeal was the medical 'examination'. Its purpose was to determine whether the defendants had engaged in anal sex. "The doctors didn't even examine me, but decided that I've had practised anal sex!" he told me, shaking his head in disbelief. The doctors declared that 14 of the defendants had had anal intercourse, although HRW argues that their examination methods were outdated and completely unreliable.

The verdicts were read on 21st March 2002, at the Cairo Security Court. Farahat was handed down the longest sentence: five years of hard labour. Ashraf al-Zanati was among those 21 who got two years' imprisonment. "When I heard the verdict, I just couldn't believe it. The sentences were totally random and the judge didn't even listen to the defence or witnesses," Ashraf recounted, recalling the darkest day of his life.

In prison, al-Zanati and the rest of the convicts were placed in the same wing as Muslim Brotherhood small-timers. Initially the atmosphere was of mutual suspicion – Islamists tend to regard gays as the worst kind of perverts – but soon the inmates started to pull together. Ashraf's most crucial survival strategy was to continue his work as an English teacher in prison.

Ashraf was one of three inmates (out of a total of 22) in his cell who were quite well-off. He shared his cell with Shirif Farahat – who would talk only with Ashraf, because the rest of them openly accused him of being responsible for their fate. The three better-off inmates tried to make do with what they could under the circumstances. The time in prison was a huge lifestyle change for Ashraf, a well-dressed man with an appreciation for life's little pleasures.

"The three of us shared a fridge and a television and often we gave some of our food to the poorer ones. The guards would put the food on the floor and cats ate from it. Who wants to eat it after that? So we had to bribe the guards for every little thing," Ashraf told me. No wonder that his imprisonment ate away all his savings.

Information on the circumstances inside the prison leaked out and the sentences were harshly criticized. Celebrities such as Elton John, Emma Thompson and Sir Ian McKellen signed a petition demanding the release of all the prisoners. Demonstrations were held in front of Egyptian embassies from San Francisco to Stockholm. As a counter-measure, the Egyptian authorities tried to explain that the case wasn't about persecution of gays. They repeated over and over again the mantra that homosexuality is not a crime in Egypt, and that heterosexuals would also have been arrested, had they been engaging in similar acts of debauchery as was claimed to have happened on the *Queen Boat*.

Then, out of the blue, just before a state visit to the United States in the summer of 2002, President Mubarak ordered all but the two main defendants freed, and their charges quashed. The official explanation was that debauchery cases shouldn't have been taken to the state security court in the first place. The unofficial version was that the Egypt–USA free-trade agreement might have been axed if the gays weren't released.

After his release, Ashraf took a taxi home. "I gave a big hug to my sister who opened the door. I took a bath. Then I went to my workplace to meet my colleagues, and received a bouquet of flowers as a welcoming gift," Ashraf recalled. But that was as far as the good treatment went: he lost his job, because his annual contract wasn't renewed. And that wasn't the end of it: his nightmare began again when the prosecutor ordered a retrial – including those against whom charges had been dropped. This time the trial was to take place in a civilian court.

In the meantime, arrests of individual gays in various Egyptian towns continued, albeit on a smaller scale. HRW argues that gay arrests have become a permanent phenomenon. "In Cairo, police had routinely carried out campaigns against various populations whose public presence detracted from the capital's preferred self-image. Street hawkers, street children and sex workers recurred as victims. (...) men having sex with men joined such groups by the late 1990s."[9]

The excellent HRW report also recounts stories of horrendous torture both during detention and imprisonment. Sometimes torture was applied to get confessions, sometimes merely as a punishment. Verbal humiliation in these 'debauchery' cases has always been present, and the shame upon the families is immense. Many lost their jobs, friends, and health solely because of their sexual orientation.

Ashraf al-Zanati was able to prepare for his new trial as a free man, but it was a small consolation for someone unemployed and living in constant uncertainty. "They took 13 months of my life and all of my savings. I often get very frustrated when I can't get answers to my questions: where is the evidence, why me?" Ashraf said and looked straight into my eyes. "Sexual orientation doesn't belong to the state. It's a fundamental human right."[10]

This chapter was the hardest one to write, because it's such a dark segment of Egyptian reality. Human rights reports, studies, articles and testimonies of those who have been tortured, mistreated or abused are so hopelessly sad that one cannot help feeling powerless.

It is incomprehensible how unpredictably and arbitrarily the Egyptian state treats its own citizens, guided by the military dictatorship's culture of violence. The only positive aspect of Egypt's human rights situation is the people, those few brave activists who work hard to make things better, despite the fear of being harassed or arrested. The Cairo Spring in early 2000 brought some hope for activists in all spheres – only to be crushed by 2006 (which I will discuss further in the final Chapter).

Despite the harsh measures, the government hasn't been able to paralyze citizens' activities. Egypt has about 20,000 NGOs, almost 50 professional trade unions and syndicates, and 5000 co-operatives. Most of the NGOs concentrate on charity and offering various services, and they don't deal with political issues. Politically active organizations on the other hand have given the state a headache, because their activities penetrate the area of state sovereignty. Most of the human rights organizations engage in activities which can be labelled political.[11]

Yet it is quite difficult to measure the volume of the activities, because exact statistics don't exist. What we do know is that their activities are limited. The current NGO Law came into effect in 2002, to loud protest. Probably the most problematic clause was that organizations had to apply for registration permission from the Ministry of Social Affairs – a simple announcement wasn't enough, as it had been before. Many organizations decided to register themselves as companies instead.

The Ministry of Social Affairs was also empowered to dismantle any organization it deemed suspect, and to monitor foreign donations more closely. Religious associations receive most of their funding from domestic sources; some organizations make do with membership fees or government subsidies. But human rights groups in particular have been dependent on foreign funding, mainly from the United States, the Netherlands, Canada and Denmark.

Human Rights organizations took their first steps in Egypt during the mid 1980s, and one of the leading figures was a sociologist called Saad Eddin Ibrahim. In the 1990s Nasserists and Leftists joined the human rights bandwagon, and that's also when the first organization self-identifying as working for human rights, the Egyptian Organization for Human Rights (EOHR), was established. The scope of work broadened, and new organizations were established to advance such issues as women's and workers' rights. By the end of the 1990s and early 2000, a new genre of organizations had emerged. These new associations are more thematically oriented.

One of the new organizations is the brainchild of twenty-something Hussam Bahgat's: the Egyptian Initiative for Personal Rights (EIPR). He has been a human rights advocate for years, but he fell out with the older guard. Bahgat's English is flawless and he is a true gem as an interviewee – when he speaks, one perfect quote or sound-bite follows another. It's clear that he has a promising future ahead of him – in 2003 he received Amnesty International's 'Young Human Rights Defender in MENA region' award.

EIPR didn't get permission to register as an NGO, so it is registered as a law firm, and it is therefore a for-profit company – on paper if not in practice. This is how he explained his motives for establishing the organization:

> A young person who doesn't have a political platform and wants to work with human rights faces a dilemma, because the human

rights field is split in two. On one side you have those who are too close to the government and therefore not militant. And then you have the militant types, who are ready to take risks, and support delicate issues, but are too political because their ultimate goal is the change of regime. [For me] it's very difficult to identify with either of these groups.

EIPR wanted to offer a forum for young people who feel a part of the international human rights movement. We want to challenge the government in public and bring out human rights violations, but we are also ready for a dialogue, we want to affect policy change. This is the challenge for me and my colleagues.

Human Rights organizations agree that their biggest problem is the Emergency Law, which has been in effect since the assassination of President Anwar Sadat in 1981 (in fact, since 1967, with a break in 1980).[12] This law, renewable every three years, effectively suspends the constitution, and restricts Egyptians' right to meet, move, reside and express themselves. It allows arrests, searches and confiscation of property without the protection of criminal law. In addition, it grants the state powers to establish special courts, where military judges may be employed – violating the principles of Egypt's constitution and international edicts on the separation of powers and independence of the judiciary.

Furthermore, the Emergency Law grants the President extraordinary powers, such as the right to veto a trial before it is presented in court. The President also has to confirm state security court verdicts, which is a further violation of the principle of separation of powers, and of the independence of the judiciary. In addition, the President can transfer any case within the sphere of criminal or other law to a military court. This particular clause has been used against Islamists.

Given these convenient powers, human rights organizations regard the Emergency Law more as a tool for political control, than as means for averting various threats to the Egyptian society, as the state would have it. EOHR argues that the Law restricts civil and political rights so profoundly that it obstructs effective governance of the country: indeed, it is also used against peaceful, would-be democratic political parties. In sum: it grants the government a carte blanche to violate human rights.

The right to personal freedom and security are the most violated laws in Egypt. A pre-trial detention period can be extended up to six months – which verges on being a punishment in its own right. The detention can be extended even if there are enough guarantors for a bail. It is also very problematic that the police have the right to arrest anyone if they deem there to be enough evidence.[13]

The government defends the continued application of the Emergency Law by saying that it is fighting against terrorism. Much to the dismay of human rights groups, the post-9/11 Sinai bombings and the overall global, Bush-era 'let's fight terrorism' sentiment have strengthened the government's argument for the maintenance of the Emergency Law.

To know more about the government's side on this issue, I went to see Taha 'Abd al-Alim, who was at the time (2004) the Chairman of State Information Services, which functioned under the Ministry of Information. 'Abd al-Alim was previously the vice-president of Al-Ahram Centre for Political and Strategic Studies, but his current role was essentially the government's spokesman.

His office was located near a conference centre, on the road leading to Cairo airport. The walls of his office were lined with glossy coffee table books on Egyptology, and fresh flowers were arranged on the side-table. 'Abd al-Alim puffed away at a cigarette, although he somehow didn't look like a smoker. The academic in him surfaced many times during our discussion, wanting to explain the root causes of issues. He often compared Egypt's situation to other countries:

> The Emergency Law is not as dangerous as say, the Patriot Act in the United States. If we had a law against terrorism, it would make Emergency Law redundant. I believe that the Emergency Law will be abolished in the next few years.

Indeed, since the presidential elections of 2005, there has been talk about changing it into an anti-terrorism law. However, the anti-terrorism law has the potential to be even more repressive than the Emergency Law, because it would grant the security apparatus even more impunity. And even worse, by passing this law it would mean that these oppressive measures would be written into the constitution, giving it a legal blessing.

Often the government's oppression and restriction of human rights has been explained as stemming from the conflict between the Islamists and the state (although the Emergency Law was in force even before Egypt's own war on terror). One of its outcomes has been the trial of civilians in military courts, starting in 1992, when 48 people were convicted of 'terrorist acts, anti-constitutional activities' or belonging to illegal political groups. By 1997, the number of civilian defendants had risen to 214, with a corresponding rise in death sentences and executions.[14] Islamists in particular (both jihadi groups and the Muslim Brotherhood) were taken before military courts, because – according to the official line – the government considered them a threat to public safety.

In October 2001, I was able to follow one of these military trials, in the so-called *Wa'd* (Promise) case. The accused were 94 Islamists who were charged with belonging to illegal organizations, planning armed attacks and conspiracy to cause explosions. While most of the accused were Egyptians, there were also a couple of Dagestanis and a Yemeni. Because it was the first 'civilians in military courts' case in two years, a few curious journalists showed up.

The infamous Haykstep military court is literally in the back of beyond, on the outskirts of Cairo so that security measures can be kept tight. Some unwitting entrepreneur had built a water park on the other side of the road, with the entry gate passing through an enormous jolly clown face. A colleague admitted to having visited the park, totally unaware that the next door neighbours didn't hand out candy floss, but death sentences. He mentioned that the water slides had been quite good.

Within the compound, the courthouse was flanked by a sandy parking lot and a miserable coffee shop. Journalists were not allowed to take in recorders, nor even mobile phones. We were then herded to a waiting minibus, in front of the defendants' anxious relatives. The bus drove past a fenced area, which looked like a training ground for a counter-terrorist strike force: a dusty aeroplane waited for hijacking practices, and a scramble net covered a windowless apartment building.

Although I had seen pictures of military trials before – with the defendants caged like animals – seeing it with my own eyes was still a shock. On the left side of the court room was a huge black metal cage, where white-clad defendants prowled about restlessly. It was like a human zoo, where the defendants seemed like they had already been sentenced. I wondered how anyone could keep their human dignity in such circumstances. The detainees had spoken aloud about torture in detention cells – as usual.

The majority of the defendants sported long beards, which is usually a sign of Islamist sympathies. Quite a few of their female relatives wore the all-enveloping *niqab* veils, and they tried to talk to their fathers, husbands and brothers through the cage, apathetic guards standing in between. Flies buzzed around the stuffy room, and the desert wind whined in the windows. At last, the judge and three jurors in military uniforms walked in. They took their seats behind elevated desks: the symbolism of the power relations was graphically clear.

That day was dedicated to introducing the evidence. The judge pulled out shabby envelopes and cardboard boxes, filled with confiscated books and flyers. Also among the confiscated items were an air rifle and a baseball bat, which the judge dismissed as evidence; the relatives applauded and cheered this decision. The whole process seemed arbitrary: in Egypt one can never be sure if someone has actually committed a crime, or indeed if the evidence really belonged to the accused.

At the end of the session, the relatives stayed with the caged defendants – or at least, they were granted a little precious time to talk. We journalists were quickly hurried out, and the courtroom clerks tried to forbid us from talking to anyone. At the parking lot, we were greeted with an unpleasant surprise: all the confiscated mobile phone SIM cards were locked. Our taxi driver told us that the soldiers had tried to open them, and that to pass the time, they had been listening to old interview tapes left in our recorders.[15]

Resorting to the military courts for those detained for political reasons increased enormously in the 1990s. According to the Ibn Khaldun Centre, in 1992 around 8000 individuals were tried in military courts, but the next year this jumped to 17,191. It went down to 3993 in 1996. To this day, some 18,000 administrative detainees (most of whom are political prisoners, i.e. Islamists) still languish in Egyptian prisons. They are not all necessarily serving a sentence, and some of them have never even been prosecuted.[16]

Handing out Islamist leaflets has been reason enough for an extended arrest.

Yet probably the biggest stain on Egypt's reputation in the field of human rights violations is torture. Human rights organizations agree that it is still common and systematic. In 2007, EOHR verified 226 torture cases between 2000 to 2007, with as many as 40 cases occurring in 2007, making it the worst year. During this period, 93 cases of torture led to death. Torture and other forms of abuse have become a routine element of criminal investigations. This is despite the fact that Egypt is a signatory to the UN anti-torture convention, and was until 2005 a member of the UN anti-torture panel.[17]

Although the Egyptian authorities deny the existence of systematic torture and other human rights violations, ordinary citizens are afraid of the police and detention. Many have heard stories of a friend of a friend who disappeared for a long time into the jungle of detention centres and prisons, before finally, after months of waiting, being released without charges, or even an explanation. Similar stories abound about police stations, where confessions are extracted with electric shocks and beating the soles of the feet. It makes many Egyptians wary of their words and deeds. It explains why, very often when I've interviewed 'the men and women of the street' they wanted to make sure that the story would air abroad, not in the Egyptian media. They didn't want to be caught criticizing the regime and ending up in the dungeons.

Despite state denials, torture is common in police stations, as the case of minibus driver Imad al-Kabir case illuminates. The 21-year-old had been arrested in January 2005 on the grounds of 'resisting the authorities'; more accurately, he had been trying to intervene in an argument between his cousin and some police officers. As a result, he was taken to Bulaq al-Dakrur police station where the officers beat him, tied him by his wrists and ankles, and sodomized him with a stick. The officers made fun of him – and filmed the ordeal on a mobile phone. The purpose of filming the torture was to humiliate him by showing the footage to other bus drivers in his neighbourhood, as a grotesque lesson not to mess with the police.[18]

Egypt's criminal law article 126 sets the punishment for torture at 3–10 years imprisonment, and if the victim dies the punishment is the same as for a premeditated murder. Article 129 of the criminal law, on the other hand, orders a maximum of one year's imprisonment for a public servant who has, using his position, caused physical pain, or harmed the victim's reputation. In other words, torturers usually receive very lenient sentences, on the rare occasions when they are brought to justice.[19]

The Egyptian authorities systematically deny that torture is systematic. The government has even claimed that some of the reported cases of death in detention were suicides.[20] The former State Information Services Chairman 'Abd al-Alim put it this way:

> When you have tens of human rights organizations which defend the citizens, talk about torture, are against it – we are on the right path. The constitution forbids torture, and this kind of crime cannot be forgiven. I cannot claim that everything is well, no, that wouldn't be a human society but a society of angels! But we have to go forward and create a culture, a human rights culture. The balance between freedom and security has to be taken into consideration everywhere in the world.

Eventually, the brutal mobile video footage of the sodomized driver, Imad al-Kabir, ended up on the internet, thanks to an Egyptian blogger by the name of Wa'il 'Abbas. From then on, the story spread like wildfire, first on the internet and then in the local press. The case shocked Egyptians, but also embarrassed the government. Eventually al-Kabir's torturers, Islam Nabih and Rida Fathi, each received three-year sentences.[21]

The new generation of bloggers has become the spearhead in exposing police brutality and other cases of abuse in Egypt. Internet penetration in Egypt is the highest in Africa – about 20% of population have access. The blogger phenomenon is one of the major civil society events in the last few years, enabling thousands of Egyptians to voice their opinions freely and openly on the internet. But not always without consequences.

'Abbas, 34, has had his share of intimidation. He's a pleasant looking man with a round face, goatee and sideburns, and an infectious grin. After posting several videos of torture, harassment of women (see Chapter 2) and vote rigging, State Security Officers paid him a visit. He lost his job as a journalist, and his YouTube and Yahoo accounts were temporarily blocked – but he kept on blogging at his site Misr Digital. In 2007, he was the first blogger to receive the Knight International Journalism Award, and he was also named CNN Middle East Person of the Year, 2007. "The government always blames young people for everything, calling them drug abusers and only interested in materialism, instead of encouraging them. But the bloggers have proved the government wrong," he attested.

'Abbas's blog has a petition for the release of a fellow online poster, Karim Amir ('Abd al-Karim Nabil Sulayman), who is now 24 years old. He was sentenced to four years in prison in February 2007, for 'damaging the country's reputation', 'incitement to hate Islam' and for 'defaming the President of the Republic'.

Despite growing up in a religious home in Alexandria, Amir had become disillusioned with al-Azhar, where he studied law. When his superiors found about his secular-minded blog (where he harshly criticized the attacks against Copts in his native town) he was expelled. Amir didn't deny his writings or being an atheist, and went on to call al-Azhar a racist university because it only allows Muslim students and separates male and female students.[22] He had no idea where his determination to use his freedom of speech would land him. This is what he wrote in his last blog:

> I joined al-Azhar to study in accordance with my parents' desires. In spite of my complete rejection of al-Azhar and religious thought (at a subsequent time), and despite my writings that strongly criticize religion's infiltration into the public life, its control over human beings' behaviour and dealings with each other, and its directing them in conduct, getting rid of these fetters in the form of my (formerly) being a student at Al-Azhar University, was not something easy or trivial as I had envisioned it would be. […]
>
> I'm not afraid at all. My happiness that the enemies of free thought deal with me by employing such methods – which only the intellectually bankrupt excel at – make me more confident of myself, more steadfast in my principles, and on readiness to face anything for the sake of expressing my free opinion.[23]

Amir has been able to communicate a bit from his prison cell, reporting about torture and abuse inside prison. Before the era of web videos and blogs, Egyptian human rights organizations had been documenting torture and other abuses. They used to be vilified by the local press, labelled as fifth columnists working 'to advance foreign interests'. But in the last few years, the media's attitude has changed completely: human rights organizations are now taken seriously. But this couldn't have happened without a profound change in the civil society and a brief – now closed – window of freedom that got its spark from the second Palestinian *Intifada* (uprising), in 2000, and the subsequent invasion of Iraq in 2003.

According to the Emergency Law, meetings and demonstrations in public areas are forbidden in principle. They are only allowed in 'non-public' places, such as inside professional syndicates or political party headquarters, or university campuses. In practice, organizing demonstrations even in these locales has for the most part been prevented.[24]

The law of 14/1923 stipulates that public gatherings must be announced three days in advance. The authorities can forbid the gathering if it is expected to lead into disturbance of public order. The similar law of 10/1914 dates to the British mandate era. It forbids assemblies of more than five people which can 'threaten the public peace'. If this threatening group doesn't obey dispersal orders, they face up to six months in jail and a fine of LE20.[25]

The second Palestinian *Intifada* marked a whole new chapter of activism in Egypt: students, leftist activists, nationalists and Islamists organized demonstrations together and separately. The demonstrations in support of the *Intifada* also planted the seed for the anti-regime protest movement, *Kifaya* (Enough!), which came together in the summer of 2004.

Support for the *Intifada* could be seen and heard everywhere: kiosks sold Abu Ammar (Yasser Arafat's *nom de guerre*) cheese puffs (which tasted like Styrofoam); radio stations blasted the hit song *I hate Israel and love Amr Musa* time and again – even middle-class ladies wore the chequered Palestinian *kaffiya* scarves on their shoulders. To ease the Palestinians' plight, Egyptians donated money, food and clothes – and their own blood. With no means to transport the blood to Gaza, the Ministry of Health had to close the door on blood banks, literally flooding with donated blood.[26]

Egyptians participated eagerly in the boycott of Israeli goods (Ariel washing detergent was among them, perhaps in the absence of more obvious examples of Zionist-looking products) and American goods as well. Fast-food restaurants reported losses, and resorted to advertising campaigns explaining that the staff and ingredients were 100% Egyptian. This boycott was a golden moment for local fast-food joints, particularly a chain called *Mo'men* (Believer). But soon the lure of American hamburgers proved too hard to resist, and Cairenes started ordering meals furtively, by home delivery. Almost every day, I would find myself sharing my apartment building's lift with a grinning McDonald's deliveryman.

But the activist demonstrators took the boycott seriously. Usually they assembled at Cairo University, or after Friday prayers in the heart of Islamic Cairo, by al-Azhar Mosque. Demonstrations became a regular event – and a meeting place for journalists. The same faces dragged themselves out, just in case 'something happens', meaning if the situation turns violent. But the omni-present riot police always far outnumbered the demonstrators. For someone looking at it from the outside it was a bizarre scene: a tiny knot of colourful people shouting and singing, surrounded by thousands of black-clad young recruits with helmets and shields, batons under their belts.

Very rarely did the situation get hairy – usually we just witnessed the cacophony of different groups: the Muslim Brotherhood, as usual, shouting Islamic slogans and demanding solidarity among Muslims. But then the Nasserists, leftists and students started to criticize their own government and the President even more harshly.

Hussam al-Hamalawi who studied at the American University of Cairo (AUC) was one of the activists who could usually be spotted at demonstrations. Energetic and active, he was either voicing his criticism towards the government, or later reporting on the demonstrations as a journalist. He says that the *Intifada* demonstrations were particularly crucial in the awakening of activism.

> AUC students used to be seen as pampered kids, who got beaten up outside the campus. In the mid 1990s, the situation started to change and students became more active. My father was leftist and interested in politics so I got interested in activism that way. But political parties didn't offer the right forum, so I concentrated on the AUC leftist movement. The activists were people like me, the off-spring of educated middle-class parents, not the filthy-rich families' kids.

Opposing Israel's actions and supporting the Palestinian cause was a 'safe' form of protest in the eyes of the Egyptian government: youngsters could vent their frustrations, in tune with Egypt's official line which condemned Israeli policy. But very soon, the demonstrations tried to break out from the campuses and onto the streets. Their slogans criticized the Egyptian regime more and more boldly, and the almost untouchable President. Hussam received a warning via a distinguished colleague of his late father. Someone had called him and said that Hussam had better stay away from the campus.

But, with the arrogance of a young radical, he defied this advice. A couple of days later, state security officials in civilian clothes stopped his car, blind-folded him with his own *kaffiyah*, and pushed him into the back seat of their car. No one told him where they were taking him, but Hussam could guess the destination from the stories other activists had told him. The car entered Lazughly, headquarters of the notorious State Security Investigations, in the heart of Cairo.

> I was still blindfolded, my arms handcuffed behind my back. I was taken up and down the stairs. I knew that it was meant to

disorient me. I thought I was on the second floor – the worst atrocities took place on the fourth floor. Then I was taken for interrogation. They wanted to know the names of the other activists, but I repeated that I wasn't going to tell them anything without the presence of the prosecutor or my attorney. I was taken to another room, and I had no idea what was going to happen next.

The first hit was a shock – after that I started to fear what might follow. There were probably three guys beating me, fists kept on bounding all over my body. They left the room occasionally, and all I could hear was this horrid clanking of metal. I just listened to it, frightened stiff, and wondered what would happen next – anything but electricity! The torturers came back to beat me up, making threats and then they disappeared again.

This went on for about half an hour, an hour, it was difficult to estimate. Then they threatened me with electric shocks and took off my shoes, but I still wouldn't say anything. One of the police officers smacked me with my shoes, but luckily that was it – no electricity. They stripped me and threatened that they would bring a gay officer who would rape me. But nothing happened, and eventually I was able to put my clothes on.

The next scene was the 'good cop' part – I was taken to a room where a police officer scolded my torturers and chatted in a friendly way, asked me to sit down. All this time I was blindfolded. When I refused to talk to him either, I was taken away and the beating continued. I had to stand in one position, hands tied up and they kept me awake all night.

Next day Hussam was taken to the prosecutor's office. It was swarming with Islamists in their white garbs – Hussam stood out from the crowd with his jeans and Reebok trainers. The prosecutor read a long list of charges, among them inciting the masses, and disturbing public order. He repeated his words in front of the prosecutor: he would not say another word without his attorney. He was hurried back to the van carrying detainees, and again no one told him where they were headed.

I had hoped they would have given me 15 days of porridge at Tora – anything but back to Lazughly! The worst thing there was that you never knew what was going to happen next, and then you hear all those stories about what can happen... I was frightened. When I saw from the van window that we crossed the Nile bridge, I fell into despair: we were going back to Lazughly.

Hussam was blindfolded and handcuffed again, but there was no more torture. He was finally allowed to sleep – in a bare corridor. He spent two days there, before being taken to the prosecutor again. He was released on bail of LE1000, only after the prosecutor had given him an educational speech about the dangers of the 'wrong kind' of activism. In the prosecutor's opinion, it wasn't worthwhile to support the Palestinians, nor criticize the government. Still, Hussam had to spend one more night at Lazughly, in a basement cell with *al-Jihad* members. Among them were radicals who had languished in jail for 10 years: they had already completed their sentences, but were still detained.

Hussam returned once more to Lazughly as a detainee, and for the third time with a Human Rights Watch delegation in 2004. The treatment couldn't have been more different.

We weren't even searched! The police officers chatted with me on the lines of 'foreign delegates are here as guests...' Of course they wouldn't give any information, but at least they received us and they actually gave us a written reply to our questions. But the best thing was to be in Lazughly for the first time without blindfolds!

But AUC had not only students whom the government found irritating, but also rather high profile professors, such as sociologist and human rights activist Saad Eddin Ibrahim. In 2000, Ibrahim was arrested at his home in the middle of the night. In the same vein, 27 staff members of his Ibn Khaldun

Centre were arrested. This pro-democracy centre provided information on citizens' rights, wrote reports on the condition of the Copts, and had monitored elections. It also ran a rehabilitation centre for Islamists convicted of armed assaults. Ibrahim and his colleagues were accused of bribing authorities (TV officials for advertising his work), disseminating false information about Egypt (talking about vote rigging and religious persecution), forging election cards and accepting $250,000 illegally (from the EU). The Ibn Khaldun Centre had received a grant from the European Commission to produce a short film with the aim of encouraging Egyptians to vote in the parliamentary elections. The Centre was chosen because it had monitored elections in the past, although it did not receive permission to observe the 2000 parliamentary elections. The EU did not at any stage accuse Ibrahim or the Centre of embezzlement.

The arrest came as a complete shock for the human rights movement: if Ibrahim, a respected, internationally known human rights activist could be arrested in the middle of the night, then anyone could be the next target. The arrest in December 1998 of Hafiz Abu Sa'ada, the EOHR Secretary General, was still fresh in everyone's minds. He too had been accused of receiving foreign funding without permission, in this case $25,000 from the UK government to help fund a women's legal aid project. The real reason, however, was most probably the EOHR report on the al-Kosheh case (see Chapter 5). Abu Sa'ada was released after a couple of days, and the changes were dropped, probably due to international pressure.

Because human rights organizations are often forced to refuse foreign funding, they rely upon volunteering. Foreign funds are often earmarked for democracy projects or supporting women's rights, which the government regards as trespassing on its sovereignty. As a result, groups like EOHR are chronically burdened with financial worries. Human rights organizations have very few active supporters, so they cannot fund the activities by membership fees alone; domestic donors have wanted anonymity, which the organizations cannot afford to grant as it would increase accusations of furtiveness. Since they don't receive government funding, the operation is run on contributions from the board members.

Since EOHR wasn't allowed to register as an NGO, their unofficial status meant that they couldn't draw foreign donations without clearance from the Ministry of Social Affairs. Had they touched such funds, they could be charged under the military degree of 4/1992, which prohibits use of foreign funds. This offence is punishable by 7 to 15 years imprisonment, and there is no appeal. Although the military decree was issued with Islamist organizations in mind (they received funds for social projects and building their networks in the 1990s from Islamic countries), it has been used against NGOs. Abu Sa'ada was charged on the basis of this decree.[27]

A much worse fate awaited Ibrahim, who was initially released on bail after two months in detention. But during his detention, the government press launched an unrelenting smear campaign, accusing him of financial corruption, of accepting funds for a campaign to tarnish Egypt's reputation abroad, and of being a US agent (he was, after all, a dual American citizen, and taught sociology at the *American* University in Cairo.) This ranting continued throughout the preparation for his upcoming trial at the state security court, armed with top lawyers and high profile character witnesses.

The court finally delivered its verdict in May 2001. It was an enormous shock: Ibrahim was sentenced to seven years imprisonment. His staff's sentences ranged from one year to six months, although some received only suspended sentences.

Ibrahim himself was taken at once to Tora prison. The trial was widely and roundly condemned as unfair, and both the charges and verdict politically motivated. The common belief was that the case had the blessing of Mubarak. The President had told *Newsweek* magazine in March that the court case was getting too much attention, and he remarked that some people saw Ibrahim as a traitor.[28]

State security court verdicts cannot be appealed, but Ibrahim took his case to Court of Cassation, which can annul an earlier conviction. The case – and in particular, the disproportionate sentence – had clearly turned world opinion against Egypt. Appeals for his release flooded in from all corners of the world, and news started to arrive of his deteriorating health in prison (Ibrahim suffers from a degenerating disease of his nervous system, which affects his coordination.) In February 2002, a retrial was ordered, and Ibrahim was released, allowing him to prepare for the next trial.

Soon after his release, I went to see him at his home in the Ma'adi suburb. Fifteen minutes drive from central Cairo, Ma'adi is a green neighbourhood, popular with well-to-do Egyptians and foreigners. The streets are narrow, the cars parked by the curbs expensive, and the villas behind fences grand. Ibrahim and his American wife Barbara lived in an apartment, decorated in Oriental, yet simplified style.

It was clear that Ibrahim's health really had deteriorated in prison: his walk was unsteady, and his eyes drooped occasionally like a drunkard's. Despite this, he had been denied permission to travel abroad to receive medical care. Before we got into the details of his ordeal, we looked at pictures taken outside the prison on the day he was released. Joy and relief shone on everyone's face. Ibrahim told me that he was convinced that the verdict was politically motivated.

There was nothing criminal in my case: the fact that I had spoken about vote rigging and discrimination of minorities was something of which the state said – in front of court – that this tarnishes Egypt's reputation abroad! They don't want anyone talking about these issues.

Maybe at some stage, while practising this fundamental right of expression, I stepped on some toes, I crossed some red lines. But I never knew what was green, what was orange and what was red! But I'm not someone who is wary of his words, or practises self-censorship. Now only my family censors me!

I asked him what he thought of the fears in the human rights movement, that now anyone could be arrested.

This shouldn't discourage those who strongly believe in human rights, in the civil society and that this part of the world deserves to join the third wave of democracy. I don't, of course, want everyone to become martyrs, or people who have lesser tolerance to sacrifice themselves.

But I think that our region is under the microscope, and what ever you say about our leaders, they might be smart enough to realize that they cannot crush human rights defenders anymore. Because this is not about human rights as such, but about those who defend them.

Ibrahim wasn't allowed to enjoy his freedom for long. In July that year, he was convicted – and sentenced – again on the same charges. Only at his third trial, in March 2003, was he cleared of all charges. Relieved, he flew to the United States for medical treatment. The Ibn Khaldun Centre was able to re-open its doors in June.[29]

Eight days after Ibrahim's acquittal, the Iraq war began. On the eve of war, 20th March 2003, around 10,000 people gathered in central Cairo to demonstrate. Until then, demonstrations had been the bread and butter for a couple of hundred activists. But on that day, the air was thick with rebellion and excitement. For many Egyptians, that day brought back the memories of student demonstrations of the 1970s. The sheer number of people and amount of activity was something totally unprecedented for all of us there. 'What courage!' we thought.

The demonstration went on for about 12 hours. It was an unparalleled show of civil disobedience. The masses took over the main square of Cairo, Tahrir (Liberation) Square, the locale for the monstrous *Mugamma* administration centre for the Interior Ministry, and a burial ground for dusty memos; the American University of Cairo, the Arab League, the American and British Embassies, all were within earshot. The crowd tried to march on the American Embassy, but the street had been closed to traffic months earlier. Near the embassy, the masses faced a roadblock, but they tried to break through. That's when the situation turned volatile: stones started flying towards the police and back again.

In the midst of this confusion, I was crouching with my colleague Nagwa, trying to keep away from the stones that the crowd was pelting at the riot police. "I'm frightened; I'm not used to this!" Nagwa said, eyes wide with fright, but she seemed to be in control. "Me neither," I replied and tried to predict where the stones were coming from. We decided to move further away for safety, off to a main street. Then the situation calmed down again, and the masses surged back towards Tahrir Square, slowly dispersing.

The next day, the demonstrators marched from the al-Azhar mosque in Islamic Cairo back to the town centre. This time the demonstration was more anarchic – in Tahrir Square a fire-truck was set on fire, private cars were damaged and the flags of the Nile Hilton hotel (right next to the Arab League building) were burnt. The riot police and regular police in civilian clothes beat the demonstrators, but also bystanders.

Elsewhere, police also used unnecessary violence, beating up peaceful demonstrators near the Lawyers' Syndicate. During the demonstrations and the days that followed, the human rights organizations reported that police arrested about 800 people (the Ministry of Interior didn't publicize figures), among them minors and two MPs, who should have enjoyed parliamentary immunity. The detainees have reported being tortured and mistreated, and some of them complained to Human Rights Watch that they weren't allowed to see a doctor while in detention. Most of them were released within 24 hours, but over 60 were kept in for further investigations – they were accused of damaging public property, inciting unrest and failing to obey a dispersal order.[30]

The serried ranks of riot police and armoured trucks remained, becoming part of the Cairo scenery. Although the demonstrators consciously took a risk of arrest, police brutality raised a storm of protest in Egypt and beyond. Another proof of civil disobedience was a petition to the public prosecutor signed by 37 prominent members of society, urging him to sue the President and Minister of Interior for unlawful treatment of the activists.

Aida Sayf al-Dawla, Chairwoman of the Nadim Centre (a support organization for victims of torture) was one of the signatories. Al-Dawla, who teaches psychology at Cairo University, epitomizes the leftist intellectual, with her shortish hair, ornate Arabic jewellery and glasses. She speaks with a very soft and quiet voice, but with the efficiency of a professional speaker. "I don't believe that the President will be prosecuted, but it is important to show who obeys the law and who doesn't," she told me, referring to the petition. "If the government feels so weak that they cannot take this (the demonstrations), then it should be changed. If it's not weak, let people vent their anger!"

The Nadim Centre was established in 1993 in Cairo, and focuses on helping victims of torture, as well as investigating the cases and registering them. It is organizations like Nadim that paved the way for public discussion on the issue of torture. The Nadim Centre's work has also been appreciated abroad – HRW awarded Aida Sayf al-Dawla their highest recognition for her anti-torture work, and as a defender of women's rights. Nothing directly happened as a result of the petition, of course, but the government did take notice that it had to do something to control the human rights field.

To loud media fanfare, the National Commission for Human Rights was inaugurated in January 2004. In the same operation, state emergency courts and sentences involving hard labour were abolished. The Commission was tasked to publish an annual report on human rights violations, handle victim complaints, and advise the government on human rights issues.

Local organizations' initial reaction was sceptic; this was, after all, a governmental committee, which was to investigate its own human rights violations. The 27-member Commission went operational in the summer of 2004, headed by former UN Secretary General Boutros Boutros-Ghali.

The critics pointed out that the Commission was an attempt to put forward a better face for Egypt abroad, with a respectable figurehead who also happened to represent a minority grouping – the Copts. In his Opinion piece for the *Washington Post*, Boutros-Ghali pointed out that externally imposed solutions for respecting human rights don't take into consideration the fact that the concept of human rights is not alien to the Middle East.

I am fully aware of the gap that exists between concept and action, and there is still much work to be done to consolidate the Egyptian human rights movement. But I also acknowledge that, in light of fundamentalist terrorism that we are all now familiar with, security problems at times take precedence over the protection of civil liberties.[31]

Some human rights activists raised fears that the Commission would undermine the work of other human rights organizations and subvert their role. Hussam Bahgat is one of the few activists who considered the establishment of the Commission a positive development:

It's a step in the right direction that the government has realized that it needs its own body for handling human rights. I don't see any confusion on who does what – NGOs and the Committee. They cannot do more than they are doing now. But it has a mandate to contact the Ministry of Interior on behalf of a victim – I don't know where this will lead but (the door is open). They are holding monthly meetings with the Interior, Foreign and Justice Ministries, as well as with the public prosecutor – this is the first time that these institutions talk about human rights together.

Yet I don't think that the government has changed its human rights policy. It gives positive signals abroad, while it leaves the statue quo as it is. I don't think that the situation here will change under the current regime.

But the protest movement which had kicked off at the start of the new millennium gathered wind in summer 2004. The opposition press, spearheaded by the Nasserist Party's flagship newspaper *al-'Arabi*, started criticizing the government and the President personally in increasingly harsh terms, accusing the regime of supporting the United States. Just a few years before this opening up, it would have been unheard of for the press to criticize the President and his inner circle.

But *al-'Arabi*'s editor, the firebrand 'Abd al-Halim Qandil, learned the hard way where the limits of the opposition's critique of the regime are drawn. He was abducted from his home in November 2004, blindfolded, pushed into a car, beaten up, and threatened with death unless he stopped talking about 'people in high places'. His ordeal ended with him being robbed, and left naked in the desert on the outskirts of Cairo. The Journalists Syndicate condemned the reprehensible attack, and demanded an investigation.[32]

Qandil was also a leading light of what came to be known as *Kifaya* (Enough!), the Movement for Change. This protest movement had started to gather strength that summer of 2004, particularly after a government re-shuffle brought the clique of Gamal Mubarak – the President's son – into the government. This seemed to confirm the suspicion that the President was grooming his son for the 'throne'. The plebiscite for the Presidency was due the next year, and this protest movement decided that 23 years of Mubarak rule was enough – hence the name. In December 2004, the left-leaning movement held its first demonstration on the steps of the High Court, with their logo, red *Kifaya* written on yellow stickers. It was the first of many anti-Mubarak demonstrations – something unimaginable just a few years before. (More in Chapter 8.)

A year earlier, two independent newspapers, *Nahdit Misr* and *al-Masry al-Youm*, had received a much coveted printing licence – the first time one had been issued in 40 years. This was taken as another sign of the regime's wider tolerance for opposition voices. The press was nationalized by Nasser in the 1960s, and Egyptians got used to reading what the government wanted them to read – people still treat the press with scepticism. The government has eight publishing houses printing a variety of dailies and magazines – in Arabic, English and French. The Opposition press came about simultaneously with the establishment of new parties during Sadat's rule, but their days of freedom came to an abrupt end with the mass arrests just before Sadat's assassination in 1981.

Of the Egyptian newspapers, the most widely read is *al-Ahram* (the Pyramids) which was established in 1875, making it the oldest newspaper in the Middle East. Toeing the government line, its respect has steadily declined with the rise of independent dailies. Following it in circulation popularity are *al-Akhbar* (The News) and *al-Gumhuriyya* (The Republic) newspapers, which are also tied to the government. All these papers claim circulation figures of 900,000, but their real figures are probably much lower. These are not huge numbers in a country of nearly 80 million people, but then on the other hand, half of the population is illiterate.[33]

Overall, the Egyptian media has to function within the limitations of the Emergency Law, particularly since the Higher Press Council monitors and regulates the press. Its members are government sympathizers, who not only nominate the government press editors, but are also responsible for issuing permits for new publications. Up until now it has mainly refused applications, because in principle only political parties and professional unions are allowed to publish newspapers without a special permit.[34]

Journalists haven't taken these restrictions on their profession lying down. The draconian Press Law of 1995 was cancelled after 13 months, due to protests by journalists and the Press Syndicate. What they couldn't overturn was a section on different 'publication offences', and the prosecutor could still ban publication of materials considered too politically sensitive. Censorship was formally outlawed (most papers practise self-censorship), but deemed acceptable in certain circumstances, such as under the Emergency Law.

Then, despite his promises to the contrary, in 2006 President Mubarak approved amendments to the Press Law, which continued to allow the imprisonment of journalists – for up to five years.

These new amendments weren't just ink on paper: 2006 saw a peak (over the last ten years) in the number of journalists brought before court (26 individuals), coming down slightly in 2007 (22 journalists).[35] The Reporters Without Borders organization reports that in 2007 four editors were each sentenced to a year in prison for 'putting out false news harming the reputation and interests of the country' and for defamation. A reporter for *al-Jazeera* news channel was sentenced to six months imprisonment and fined €3500. She had been working on a story about torture in prisons. Two bloggers also received prison sentences.[36]

Often these charges are related to libel: editors or journalists accuse public officials of corruption. Yet it is often difficult to know whether corruption charges against someone are real, or whether it's just a political witch-hunt. For example, the independent *al-Dustur* (the Constitution) has been taken to court 2050 times since 2005 because of articles that appeared in the paper.[37] The President himself has scolded the press for 'going too far', which in his mind meant confusing freedom of expression with 'irresponsibility'.[38]

Although the constitution forbids censorship of the media and literature, the Emergency Law derogates from it: if publications deal with issues of 'national security', they have to go through censorship. Having a smaller readership, English and French language papers however have enjoyed greater freedom to tackle thorny issues. They circumvent censorship and restrictive press laws by registering themselves abroad, usually in Cyprus.

The first of the new papers was *Nahdit Misr* (Egyptian Renaissance), a weekly when established in 2003 although a year later it became a daily. The second was another daily, *al-Masry al-Youm* (Egyptian Today), a revamped version of *al-Dustur* and the latest addition, *al-Shuruq* (Oriental Affairs) in 2008. *Al-Masry al-Youm* is owned by a group of liberal, free-trade minded businessmen, and was first run by the publisher Hisham Kassem, the former publisher of the now defunct *The Cairo Times,* and the president of EOHR. On a hot summer day in 2004 in an office paralyzed by a power cut, he expounded the paper's philosophy:

> Previously, newspapers had a political agenda, and they weren't focused on plain news. This newspaper is fact oriented, and it doesn't have opinionated articles except in the op-ed pages. The idea is to help our society to integrate with the global community, because most of our press is nationalistic, you know, 'Arabs against the rest of the world'. This is not what we want, but it's hard because the press culture is what it is.

At first the paper was rumoured to be a propaganda tool paid for by the Americans, and Kassem had to defend the paper against these accusations. He thinks that the press is experiencing an opening.

> What is happening is clearly a political opening, not so much because the regime is committed to opening up, but more likely because of the international pressure towards the Middle East as a whole. And because of the realization, that the political clot that we had here made the region a threat to global security, and that we have to reverse this process.

Al-Masry al-Youm has since become a household name and a popular read. Yet the majority of Egyptians get their news feed from television – roughly one person in ten owns a TV set. Egyptian Television started broadcasting in 1960. At that time Egypt's film industry was the third largest in the world after Hollywood and Bollywood, and most of the technical expertise in TV came from the film industry.

During the second Gulf War in 1990, CNN announced that it would broadcast for free to Egyptian televisions. It became the first foreign satellite channel available. Subsequently, Egypt established its own satellite channel (*Nile TV*), which broadcasts in Arabic and English. The first NileSat101 satellite was launched in 1998, and NileSat102 followed in 2000. Nowadays it delivers over 400 TV and 100 audio channels.

In 2001, two private TV channels, *Dream* and *al-Mihwar* went on air. They are majority owned by successful entrepreneurs, but the Egyptian Radio and Television Union (ERTU) owns 20% of the shares. Although Cairo roof tops may resemble futuristic mushroom forests with their satellite dishes, the reality is that most Egyptians cannot afford a satellite box (or they get an illegal satellite line). They have to watch Egyptian Television, where the content hasn't changed much: it still toes the government line. A typical news broadcast starts with Mubarak's daily meetings – without audio.

Egyptian Television hasn't exactly been able to keep up with the times. The General Media Plan of 1999–2000 repeated again the state priorities: concentrate on state achievements and give information on state mega-projects, social development and effects of globalization and bring forth factors hindering development, such as illiteracy and environment. But according to surveys, Egyptians are not at all interested in educational programs, but rather Arab pop music, Qur'anic recitation programs, news, soap operas and sports.[39]

Radio broadcasting has also been riding on new, liberal waves lately. Egyptian radio broadcasts began in 1923 by radio amateurs, but it was nationalized early on, in 1934. In the

1970s, Egyptian radio was quite a prominent media machine: it broadcast in 34 languages which made it the 6th broadest radio station in the world. In 1971, the ERTU was established within the Ministry of Information; its role was to build a nationwide radio and television network. It obtained all the transmission rights, making it a state monopoly.

On August 2003, two independent radio stations, Arabic language *Nugum* (Stars) and English language *Nile FM* hit the radio waves in the Greater Cairo area. They were, and remain, music channels dedicated to the young, which play Arabic and international hits 24/7. *Nugum* is arguably the more popular radio station – the young audience is lured by competitions and phone-in shows, and the use of Cairene slang, unlike the other stations. The majority of Egypt's population is under 30, so the channel was hitting a nerve.

These popular stations were granted the first commercial radio licences for 70 years, and were launched by young media entrepreneurs, although ERTU is again a minority shareholder. The founders had to wait for three years for the licences, but the wait was worthwhile because the stations turned a profit after the first year, thanks to advertising revenues. The broadcasts are made from the Media Production City (MPC) in the middle of the desert on the outskirts of Cairo. It is the headquarters for many Arab satellite channels, such as the hugely popular *al-Jazeera* and *al-Arabiyya*.

Egypt has also been trying to lure foreign film-makers to MPC, after realizing that most historic films about Egypt were in fact filmed in Morocco. Since MPC is located in a 'free zone', it can circumvent red tape and hefty custom duties. MPC has quite a few different historical film sets, but let's just say that their Pyramids of Giza and the Sphinx didn't make an impression on us. And while the authorities are trying to market the place to foreign film companies, we stumbled upon an obstacle which proved that perhaps MPC wasn't quite yet ready for Hollywood producers.

It is normal when filming in the Cairo streets that everything is '*mamnu'a*' (forbidden), before you produce the right paper with the right stamp. But I didn't expect to face this bureaucratic hurdle in the middle of a 'free zone' dedicated to the media. On a press tour to MPC, we were filming the set for the 1973 war, the imaginary Bar Lev line, with barbed wire, a tank and dummy soldiers aiming their rifles at the enemy. "Don't go any closer!" an MPC worker warned us, as Dana filmed the set at a distance. It turned out that it was *mamnu'a* to film the scene close-up. Were the mannequins perhaps so badly finished that they couldn't stand a closer look? Or would filming them have revealed some kind of hidden military secret? We would have needed special filming permission to find out.

Notes

--

1 Human Rights Watch (HRW), 2004:3, 13–14.
2 Whitaker, 2006:10–11, 206–208.
3 The security forces have a tendency to overreact in murder cases involving gay men. They are followed by mass arrests of citizens who have nothing to do with the case itself. HRW, 2004:88.
4 See AP, 'Cyberspace-scouring cops accused of suppressing online expression', 16/5/2002.
5 HRW, 2004:11, 18.
6 HRW, 2004:16–17.
7 HRW, 2004:23–25. HRW lists the number of photos as 893; Ashraf al-Zanati claims that there had been as many as 47,000.
8 Egyptian human rights organisations were criticized throughout the case – almost all of the organizations had refused to defend the accused. The sole exception was the Hisham Mubarak (no relation to the president) Law Centre, which offered legal aid for some of the defendants.
9 HRW, 2004:6–7.
10 The judge read the new verdicts on 15th March 2003:21 of those convicted earlier received harsher penalties, some up to three years imprisonment. Four defendants appealed and the judge maintained the charges but reduced the sentences to a year, which they had already served. Ashraf al-Zanati moved to Canada after the trial.
11 *Egypt Almanac*, 2003:126–129.
12 Ordinary citizens are also against the Emergency Law. A survey in *al-Masry al-Youm* revealed that most of the participants rejected it. On the other hand, some had never even heard of it. *Al-Masry al-Youm*, Vol. 1, No. 26, 2/7/2004.
13 EOHR, 2002.
14 Kienle, 2001:95.
15 It took a year from that date for sentences to be passed: 43 were acquitted, while 51 got between 2 and 15 years imprisonment.
16 Kienle, 2001:93, Amnesty International, 'Egypt: Systematic abuses in the name of security', http://www.amnesty.org/en/library/asset/MDE12/001/2007/en/29f8281d-d3c5-11dd-8743-d305bea2b2c7/mde120012007en.html.
17 EOHR, an English summary of the 2007 report is available at http://en.eohr.org/?p=43.
18 See for example Amnesty International, 'Egypt: Systematic abuses in the name of security'.

19 HRCAP, 1999.
20 Hanaan Sarhan, 'Ministry denies torture reports', *The Cairo Times*, Issue 5, Vol. 8, 1–7/7/2004.
21 See HRW, 'Egypt: Police Officers Get Three Years for Beating, Raping Detainee', 6/11/2007.
22 http://freecopts.blogspot.com/2006/03/egyptian-blogger-expelled-from-al.html, the campaign to free him: www.freekareem.org.
23 http://www.freekareem.org/2007/03/07/kareem-amer-your-blessings-o-azhar/.
24 Kienle, 2001:90.
25 HRW, 2003:9, 24.
26 *Egypt Almanac*, 2003:128.
27 Nicola Pratt, 'Egypt Harasses Human Rights Activists', *Middle East Report*, 214, Spring 2000.
28 Lally Weymouth, 'It Is Out of Control', *Newsweek*, 31/3/2001.
29 Ibrahim's tribulations didn't quite end there. A string of lawsuits raised by individual lawyers is on-going against him, accusing him tarnishing Egypt's reputation – again. Out of fear for being arrested in Egypt, Ibrahim is mainly staying in the United States.
30 HRW, 2003.
31 Boutros Boutros-Ghali, 'Egypt's Path to Rights', *The Washington Post*, 7/4/2004.
32 Shaden Shehab, 'Terrible message, but who's the sender?' *al-Ahram Weekly*, 11–17/11/2004, no. 716; RSF, 'Opposition journalist abducted and beaten', 5/11/2004.
33 Oxford Business Group, 2004.
34 Kienle, 2001:40–41.
35 EOHR, 2007.
36 http://www.rsf.org/article.php3?id_article=25429.
37 Reporters Without Borders, 'Egypt. Internet: A weapon of mass revolution?' April 2009.
38 Kienle, 2001:100–102, 106.
39 *Egypt Almanac*, 2003:159–162.

7

Beauty is in the eye of the censor

— —

A six-member ensemble played entertaining tunes on the *Nile Maxim* cruise boat, warming up for the main attraction, who was preparing herself in the tiny dressing room below decks. A rodent-faced male singer tried to win the audience, but all eyes were focused on two newly-wed couples, celebrating their big day on the cruise-ship. One of the couples was noticeably young, and the teenage bride in the cream-cake dress clapped her hands to the melody.

Liza Laziza ('Lovely Liza') sailed in, dressed in a golden costume with a shimmering scarf stretched between her arms at the back; her pose was reminiscent of a Greek goddess's. A look-alike for Dallas's Pamela, Iranian-born Liza is one of the top professional Oriental dancers[1] in Cairo. Though she had danced for world leaders, tonight her audience mainly consisted of wealthy Egyptians. It was the end of the 'Arab season' – a reference to the Arabs from the Persian Gulf oil monarchies who were retuning home after a summer of entertainment in Cairene night clubs and casinos.

The *tabla* drummer – a new recruit to the ensemble – held the rhythm well, and Liza gave herself to the music. She swirled around with the music, her hips undulating, arms drawing sophisticated circles over her face, balancing on her toes, ankle chains jingling. Throughout her performance a satisfied smile lingered on her face, a sign of her love for the dance. This evening she really took her audience with her, as evidenced by their applause and singing along.

Her finale was her famous stick dance. At first, she balanced a sequined walking stick on her forehead, gesturing the audience to clap along. Even the veiled middle-aged ladies in the corner heeded her call. Then she dropped the cane onto her chest, tossing it on her bosom. Lastly, she let the stick drop to her belly, where it rolled downwards in a controlled manner. The audience didn't know it, but this was to be her last performance in the *Nile Maxim*.

In early 2003, the Egyptian authorities had suddenly announced that foreign dancers' permits wouldn't be renewed. This meant that they would all have to leave the country – including Liza, since her work contract was coming to an end.

She had become a dancer by chance. Having grown up in London, she moved to Paris in the 1980s, working as a personal assistant for a lawyer. One of her employer's clients was a Saudi sheikh, who invited them to an Arabic nightclub.

> This was my first touch with the dance; Arabic music was so catchy and it made an impression on me. A month later I went back to the club and just told them that I'm a dancer and that this is where I'll be working. I knew it was my calling. I just didn't know how to dance! But I had a good sense of rhythm and I imitated the other dancers.

Liza taught herself to dance, imitating the other stage stars, and slowly advancing in her career. Eventually she would perform on some of the main stages in the Middle East and North Africa. Her colleagues were mainly Lebanese, Syrian and Egyptian – and a few Russians. At the peak of her career she danced for Prince Charles in 1996 and 1999 at a private club in London.

> On the second time I got him to dance, he was a charming man. He noted that he was glad that I hadn't lost my talent. I replied: "And I'm glad that you're still trying to find yours!" We both laughed.

Liza also danced for George and Barbara Bush in 1996, at a private home in London. King Hussein of Jordan and Queen Nour invited her to dance for a birthday party in London 1997. Around the same time, Liza retired from cabaret performances and concentrated on private parties. In 1999 she got a phone call from a friend in Egypt, whose agent was looking for an Oriental-looking dancer for the five-star Marriott Hotel. Liza was familiar with Egypt because she used to shop there for costumes and music.

> That was it. As soon as I stepped on Egypt's soil, I knew I was home. Cairo is still the ultimate destination for the professional dancer, a touchstone where the road to stardom is sealed. There you perform to a critical audience.

She started her Egyptian career at the Marriott Hotel, and the following year began at the *Nile Maxim* cruise boat. Oriental dance is typically performed in these oblong Nile floaters, shaped like giant dragons, or Oriental night clubs in one of Cairo's luxury hotels. This high end is entertainment for the wealthy, an opportunity to show off shiny gowns and diamonds, cigars and expensive whisky.

Yet Liza was hardly happy with the situation. She felt that the night clubs were badly managed, that the business was rife with favouritism, and dominated by one particular 'impresario'. Whether the behind-the-scenes situation affects it or not, dance's appreciation has indeed declined lately, under the influence of the Islamist trend. Televised belly dance programs have been shelved due to Islamists' pressure (although old movies with the obligatory dance number are still shown), and a dancer is no longer a must at weddings.

Scandals, too, have added to the already dubious reputation of dancers. In December 2002 an Egyptian businessman named Hussam Abu al-Futuh, who held the coveted BMW import licence, was arrested for loan irregularities. He had allegedly been given loans without guarantees, and now had some €200,000 in unpaid loans.

But when the police searched Abu al-Futuh's home, they uncovered a stash of items that would have been more suitable for James Bond – hinting of an addiction to sex, booze and espionage. Police discovered unlicensed weapons, wiretapping devices and large amounts of smuggled alcohol. The hottest cache was secretly filmed videos, in which the thick-set Abu al-Futuh got intimate with various women in his bed. Perhaps the best-known of the unwitting video stars was the popular dancer Dina, known for her skimpy costumes and bountiful sex appeal.

The Egyptian tabloid press had a field day – for weeks. When the case first surfaced, Dina disappeared to the United States. The 'Dina video' circulated from hand to hand, and later was even sold in Cairo street markets. Dina's next move was to reveal that she was actually married to Abu al-Futuh, in that they had an *urfi* marriage (a financially non-binding, legal contract; see Chapter 2).[2] Dina returned to Egypt, performed the small pilgrimage and took the veil. Many believed that her career was over. She did indeed keep a low profile for a while, but it didn't take her long to get back on the stage.

Karin van Nieuwkerk, who has researched oriental dance, asserts that female artists who either dance or sing are regarded as shameless, yet both men and women want to watch it. She divides female performers into three categories: those who perform at weddings and popular feasts; night club artists; and dancers and singers who perform in concert halls, theatres and in the electronic media.

It is the night club performers who have the worse reputation of them all – they are often equated with greedy seductresses and prostitutes. The fact that night clubs serve alcohol adds to their seedy reputation. There is no denying that oriental dance is extremely erotic; voluptuous dancers gyrate in sexy costumes – in a culture where modesty rules.

What explains the dubious reputation, at least partially, are the early years: up until 1920s and '30s the dancers' main duty was to sit with customers and drink alcohol. Dancers received a commission on the drinks which customers ordered, and as a result sometimes they were too drunk to perform. Nieuwkerk argues that prostitution wasn't generally a part of their formal repertoire, although individual dancers may have practised it.[3]

It used to be obligatory at lower-class and lower-middle-class street and countryside weddings to have a dancer, who also sung and entertained the audience. Muhammad 'Ali Street in Cairo was famous for its musicians, singers and dancers. Its slow decline came in the 1980s, when other entrepreneurs entered the market, and the demand for live performers diminished in an era of cassettes and videotapes. The final blow fell when hard drugs were introduced – female performers left the street.

Theories abound on the origin of oriental dance. Some claim that it is a folk dance which combined different ethnic features and had been practised before Islam. It has been suggested that the dance, performed by women, might stem from the fertility cult of pre-Islamic gods. Others have searched for clues in Pharaonic wall inscriptions depicting dance scenes. Each Arab tribe had their own dance, but the origins of the so-called solo dance are murky. Romans, Bedouins and ancient Egyptians have all been suggested as the inventors of the dance.[4]

In the early days of Islam, music and singing wasn't regarded as sinful, but later jurists hardened the line. The principle is that if music or singing excites the listener, then it's bad. The place where the music was performed was also crucial, determining how immoral the dance or song was – the same applies today. Dance performed by women has been considered as the most pernicious form of entertainment. The shamefulness derives from the movement: a women's body is deemed seductive, while a man's is not. Male performers therefore don't share the reputational problem – an entertainer is a professional like anyone else. A man might be criticized for his (lack of) singing skill, but a woman would be scorned for her looks *and* performance.[5]

The appreciation of dance has also varied. During Nasser's time, folk music was favoured over oriental. This was the golden era for the Reda Troupe, which was established in 1959. The Reda Troupe was an East-European-style folk dance group, which performed Egyptian folk routines skilfully adapted by Mahmud Reda.

Although the group was formally independent, it was taken under the wing of the state. At home, it performed for visiting foreign dignitaries, while abroad it represented Egypt at dance festivals. The lead dancer, Farida Fahmi, was the opposite of sexy oriental dancers: she was a *bint al-balad*, a 'daughter of the country', a happy and decent rural girl from a good family. Everyone who had a television knew who she was. The fact that she performed as part of an ensemble also made her more respectable than the solo oriental dancers. The Reda Troupe continues to perform, albeit with new generation dancers.[6]

Around the same time, it became obligatory for oriental dancers to cover their abdomen with fabric, even if it was transparent nylon. In 1973, new laws were issued which required dancers to obtain a licence from the *munassafat* office, which regulates entertainers' and artists' work. Their ID card says *fannana*, artist, which facilitates going about at night-time, and signals to the police that they are not prostitutes. These new laws also forbade the previous custom of drinking and sitting down with the customers.[7]

Despite the facts both that dancing is strictly regulated, and that top dancers earn millions, few mothers hope that their daughters will become oriental dancers. Yet Egyptians still love to dance at weddings and parties; to a Westerner it seems as if both women and men get those smooth hip moves and rhythm with their mother's milk.

If interest towards dance is on the decline in Egypt, oriental dance has become a huge phenomenon in the West, and even as far afield as Japan. Abroad, most practitioners are amateurs, but in the Middle East (particularly in Egypt and the United Arab Emirates) a stage dancer can make a career. Foreign dancers have supplemented the local dancers who have become in short supply. Despite this, while they remain very few, the big divas have always been Egyptian. The Grand Old Dame of Dance, Fifi Abduh is semi-retired and Dina, now rehabilitated after the scandal and having cast off her veil, has returned to the scene – and is still the biggest star.

Lucy continues to attract a steady audience in Pyramids Street (a legendary entertainment district), while a younger performer – Randa Kamel – is on the way up.

The other popular dancers come from Brazil (Soraya), Argentina (Asmahan) and Russia (Nour). These foreigners have become household names, so no one could understand why the foreign dancers were shown the door. Liza believed that it was due mostly to the bad reputation of Eastern European 'Russian Show' dancers. These young women barely know how to dance, yet they perform wearing skimpy clothes in the Red Sea holiday resorts, and rumours of prostitution abound.

But even if these women wanted to, there is no facility in Egypt to study dance institutionally. So dance-enthusiasts have to take private lessons from former performers, such as Raqia Hassan. Middle-aged, short and dumpy, Hassan has tried actively to enhance the dance's reputation. She organizes an annual dance festival, attracting participants from all over the world. She teaches at her home-studio, in the Aguza district of Cairo, amusingly located between an Islamic bank on one side and a police station on the other. Her reception room's main attractions were an aquarium, and a group of super-feminine foreign dancers.

Hassan argued that the impetus for the expulsion law must have come from Egyptian stars such as Fifi and Lucy.

> They think that foreign dancers have taken their place, but this is not true. We have always had foreign dancers, together with Egyptians. Now it just feels as if there are more of them, because dance has become so popular abroad.
>
> But the greatest stars have always been Egyptian. Foreigners can learn how to dance well, but never as well as Egyptians, because they lack the feeling. If your mother taught you tango or Finnish folk dances, could I learn to dance like Finns? Of course I couldn't!

Hassan didn't think that the ban was motivated by moral concerns. She pointed out that in Egypt dancers' work is regulated by several decrees, right down to how revealing the performer's costumes can be. In her opinion, these regulations weren't created to impede dancers' work, but rather to improve the art form's reputation. "The law works: if a dancer performs in an overly-revealing costume, the police will catch her. The same applies if she does forbidden things, like selling sex," Hassan said.

But oriental dancers don't enjoy the same legal protection as musicians or actors. Moreover, only folk- and ballet-dancers can join the official Dancers' Syndicate. As a result, there was an initiative to establish a syndicate for oriental dancers, but it didn't receive a warm reception from the authorities. As for the decree banning foreign dancers, it was withdrawn in September 2004.[8]

Liza and the other dancers mentioned above represent the top of oriental dance, the professional elite. Yet there are dancers at all levels: there are about 300 registered dancers today, and maybe 200 unregistered.[9] One night, along with my Norwegian colleague Ib, I followed Lubna, a 20-year-old dancer, who performed solely in the somewhat dilapidated, seedy night clubs, favoured by locals and Arab tourists.

Ramadan was only days away, so Lubna toiled before the obligatory one-month break. Oriental dance isn't part of Ramadan festivities – one only hears folk music and religious songs during the holy month.

Before her performance, Lubna had powdered her face pale, and lined her eyes and lips with black liner. We met her at the Miami nightclub, in central Cairo's dying heart of entertainment. It is the realm of dim, tacky cabarets, where women are seldom seen in the audience. The Miami is a pitiful, dark cave, where lonely men sat on red velvet chairs, drinking beer.

The Miami's owner, Gamal Zikri, was dressed in a brown suit and sported a thick moustache. Perhaps for equality's sake – or to hedge his bets – he had hung pictures of King Faruq, and Presidents Nasser, Sadat and Mubarak on his shabby office's walls. He claimed that the Miami was a mid-level spot – not quite as fancy as the renowned Pyramid Street joints, but not the lowest level either.

Around 10 p.m., the singer fronting the house's quintet announced the obvious: "Good evening gentlemen! Tonight's performer is Lubna!" She stepped onto the stage wearing a two-piece blue-and-white dress with a plunging neckline, chewing gum and smiling lazily under the mirror ball. Her moves were routine-like, and her demeanour seemed to say: this is a job, just like any other. But the audience threw money on the stage nevertheless. In higher echelon clubs this is not part of the etiquette. Tips form about a third of Lubna's salary, so she stuffed the notes into her bra.

Samih, Lubna's husband, is a singer, and sometimes performs with his wife. Lubna embarked on her career after the wedding. "I always used to dance at weddings and other parties, but I learned my skills on Muhammed Ali Street," she joked (no one learns their skills on that street anymore). She had also danced in Oman, but quickly came home: "Egyptians are the best audience. I didn't like the Saudis there, because they only tried to get sex," Lubna told us.

Usually Lubna works from 10.30 p.m. until 8 a.m. Her last spot that night was in Helwan, a south Cairo suburb known for its cement factories. Vaguely resembling a saloon, the Happy Day night club greeted its guests with a 'Välkommen' doormat, although no one was able to tell us how this Swedish rug had ended up in a Cairene den of vice. It was almost 5 a.m., and the tired customers were drunk. Samih sung and Lubna danced, and only when she was accompanied by her husband's tunes did she seem to enjoy her performance.

* * *

Cairo is not only the centre for oriental dance, but a centre for Arabic culture more broadly. Most Arabic films, TV soap operas, music and literature are still produced in Egypt. Lebanese, Syrians and Tunisians have caught up with Egyptians in the entertainment business, particularly with their soap operas and saucy singers – but Egypt remains the number one. This spread of Egyptian entertainment means that the Egyptian dialect is known everywhere in the Middle East. Egyptians are very proud of this fact, and it is often their excuse as to why they don't bother to learn classical Arabic.

The most renowned Egyptian entertainment export was the singing legend Umm Kulthum (1904–1975), who recorded over 300 songs during her 50-year career. To this day, she is still undeniably the most appreciated artist in the Middle East. Nicknamed 'the Star of the Orient', Umm Kulthum's songs continue to be played and her tapes sold, while the older generation reminisces for the good old days when listening to her distinct voice from the radio was a favourite pastime.

Umm Kulthum's life was a classic rags-to-riches story. She was the youngest daughter of a village imam, who earned a few extra pounds from singing religious songs at weddings and other rural feasts. Umm Kulthum learnt to sing with her brother, and her strong voice caught the attention of the village chief. In no time, she became the star of the family in their village tours, and they moved to Cairo in 1923 so that she could pursue her music studies further.[10]

Sure enough, she was soon noticed for her extraordinarily strong and tuneful voice. Thanks to the teachers her father hired, the country bumpkin transformed into an elegant performer, resembling her elite audience. She started to add love songs to her repertoire of religious songs, and by 1928 she was one of Cairo's top singers, earning up to $80,000 a year.

Umm Kulthum also became a leading radio star. The first Thursday night of each month was dedicated to her singing, and these broadcasts could last all through the night, with the whole family glued to the wireless. Through radio, she reached not only the Egyptians, but also the mass audiences in other Arab countries, who couldn't afford to or didn't have the opportunity to attend her concerts. She also performed in the new art form – films – debuting in 1936 film *Widad*. In this, she was not alone: most actors and actresses of the time were primarily singers and dancers.

From early in her career, she made commercial recordings, which guaranteed her longevity and broad fan base. Recordings also allowed her to reap the financial rewards of her work. She was a shrewd businesswoman: in 1938, she got rid of her agents and thereafter managed all her business deals and contracts by herself.

The Star of the Orient's golden era was the 1940s and early 1950s. By then, her repertoire had become more folkloric, singing more popular ballads which appealed to an even wider audience. She had complete freedom to choose her work independently – and she was also the head of the influential Cairo Radio Committee and Egyptian Musicians Syndicate.

She has been characterized as a smart woman with a sarcastic sense of humour, but she kept quiet about her personal life. It is known that she married late in life, in 1954, to one of her doctors (she had a lot of health problems), and that she didn't have children. It was generally held that she had been disappointed in love as a young woman, and was thereafter unable to enter into long-term relationships.

Her improved health and the 1952 Free Officers revolution changed the direction of her career again. She gave more interviews, performed in other Arab countries and spoke in favour of Arab music. Her two trademarks were the handkerchief she liked to play with between her fingers, and the encompassing dark glasses she had to wear due to sensitivity to light.

Around the same time a new male star, Abdel Halim Hafez, a heart-throb also known as 'The Dark Nightingale', catapulted into stardom. Like Umm Kulthum, Hafez was born into a poor family. After graduating from a music institute, he made a living as a teacher and oboe player and went on to become a club singer. In 1951, he got the chance to sing songs by Muhammad 'Abd al-Wahhab, who was also Umm Kulthum's favourite composer.[11]

Hafez's first major concert performance was in 1953, right after the Revolution. If Umm Kulthum was alleged to be pro-Nasser, Hafez truly was that. He was harnessed as the voice of the Revolution – performing songs such as 'Long Live Socialism'. Nasser had control over radio broadcasts, and Hafez soon became the number one performer, on a level with Umm Kulthum. Although his talent is undisputed, it has been claimed that his rise to stardom was made smooth by Nasser.

Like Umm Kulthum, the melancholic, chocolate-eyed Hafez also appeared in many films. Yet the 1967 war, and the disappointment many felt towards Nasser's regime, affected the two stars very differently. Hafez's popularity went into a downward spiral, exacerbated as newcomers entered the market, introducing new styles. Young people especially deemed Hafez old-fashioned, but thanks to his own record label, Sawt al-Fann ('Sound of Art'), Hafez was financially secure.

But while Hafez's popularity declined, Umm Kulthum rose to greater stardom. After the war she became 'Egypt's voice and face' abroad, and embarked on a long concert tour to raise money for the losing side in the war, Egypt. The Star of the Orient received welcomes that are usually reserved only for heads of states. She even travelled on a diplomatic passport, which is on display at a museum dedicated to her in Cairo. But by 1971 her health had started to deteriorate, and she began to cancel concerts. During her last concert in 1972, she fainted in the middle of her performance – but recovered and carried on.

Finally, on 3rd February 1975, she passed away from chronic kidney problems. Her funeral was supposed to have been held at central Cairo's Umar Makram mosque, where all dignitaries receive their send-offs. But it became apparent that mourners from all over Egypt were going to attend, and the funeral was postponed for two days. Over two million mourners (more than at Nasser's funeral) processed their beloved singer's coffin around Cairo, ending at one of her favourite mosques, al-Sayyid Husayn. She was later buried in the al-Khalifa cemetery.[12]

So of the two rivals, only the sickly Hafez remained. As a child he had contracted bilharzia,[13] of which the symptoms had started to show some twenty years before. He struggled with cirrhosis of the liver caused by bilharzia, and had to stick to a strict diet. He never married, and died in 1977 at the age of 47. He definitely had a place in the hearts of the nation: half a dozen grieving teenage fans threw themselves from windows once they heard the death announcement.[14]

With Hafez mostly out of the game, the mid-1970s was the realm of an altogether different star, Ahmad Adawiyya. He launched a new *sha'abi* (popular) style, which combined catchy melodies with street slang. This proved to be a recipe for success: his cassettes sold better than anyone before – his first album in 1972 sold over a million copies.[15]

Hafez realized the challenge posed by this competitor, even though Adawiyya wasn't allowed to perform on TV or radio as his music was considered to be too low-class, and the print media shunned him as well. On the other hand, Hafez well understood the importance of cassette sales – radio was no longer the only medium for listening to music – and therefore took Adawiyya under his record label.[16]

Although no one could surpass the stardom of Umm Kulthum or Abdel Halim Hafez, Adawiyya became the Egyptian King of Pop. Appealing to a young urban audience, he continued to sell millions of cassettes into the 1980s. A plumber by profession, he too had learned his vocal skills on Muhammad Ali Street, escaping there from school. Eventually he dropped out of school altogether and moved to the famous street, studying under the *saltana* masters, learning the skill of fusing different music styles.

Like so many stars of the past and present, Adawiyya began his career by singing at weddings and saints' birthdays – huge popular feasts. Thickset, with a fondness for shiny suits, Adawiyya has remained loyal to his roots and has never tried to be stylish. Although cultured circles and the media frowned on him, he still has an enormous following. Even the late Nobel laureate Naguib Mahfouz named Adawiyya as his favourite singer. He has recorded over 200 songs (on his own record label Adawiyyat), sung at hundreds of parties and concerts all over the world, and like many singers, has appeared on the silver screen – in 18 films.

Contemporary popular music is divided into two branches: Arab pop and *sha'abi*. Probably the most successful Egyptian pop star is Amr Diab who, with his suave good looks, has been called the Ricky Martin of the Middle East.

He changes his look for each album, always appearing slightly younger and more muscular than on the previous. Following hard on his heels are the likes of Hany Shaker, and Kazem al-Saher, the Cairo-based Iraqi sex symbol.

But when it comes to female singers, the geographical focus has shifted away from Egypt to Lebanon. These sexy beauties have often smoothed their way to stardom with plastic surgery, giving them a distinct look with high cheekbones, miniscule nose, and full (if not duck-like) lips – and of course at least a C-cup bosom. And of course, they sing about love – or the lack of it. Their songs are accompanied by tacky music videos in which couples frolic in a forest or empty beach in slow motion. But lately Arab videos have started increasingly to resemble their Western counterparts – too much so for many.

Nancy Agram, a young Lebanese artist, started this trend of risqué videos. In her 2002 video for 'Akhashmak Ah' (I'll fall out with you, yes), she flirts in a bar wearing a figure-hugging red dress – and causes a fight. The video was banned from Egyptian state TV, but thanks to satellite channels, it beamed into private homes and middle-class coffee shops.

Egypt's gift to the daring videos market, Ruby, has also been subjected to heavy criticism. In her first video (2003), 'Inta 'arif leh' (You know why), she cavorts around a European city in a belly dance costume, and then writhes on a sofa. Her later videos were banned in Egypt, and in other Arab countries. She is rumoured to be married to her manager, Shirif Sabry.

Some see Ruby as the vanguard of a sexual revolution, others as the embodiment of immorality. In spring 2004, the Egyptian daily *Nahdit Misr* published a survey of young Egyptians' role-models. At the top of the list were singers, football players and actors. Social commentators lamented the state of the youth: they are lost, interested only in easy money; they idolize people of the same age, not scientists or politicians. How unusual indeed! Ruby appeared high on this list, even though by then she hadn't yet released an album.[17]

However, the moralist side seems to be in the ascendant. Around the time Ruby's first video was released, the Egyptian Musicians Syndicate decided to fight against the phenomenon it calls 'pornographic songs'. The syndicate sued Ruby, claiming that since she wasn't a member, she was singing without a permit. Her producer responded that she doesn't need an Egyptian permit because her songs are produced in the Dubai Free Zone. The debate about music videos spread to the Egyptian Parliament, prompting the culture committee to urge a boycott of these 'provocative songs'. But it is a lost cause, because neither the Musicians Syndicate nor the Parliament has control over the popular satellite channels.

Yet surprisingly, many young people agree with the politicians: such music videos are immoral – or so a survey conducted at the American University in Cairo (AUC) suggests. The result is surprising because the privileged AUC students are the ones who have access to satellite channels, are more likely to have contact with the West and (presumably) have more liberal values.

Rasha Abdallah, an assistant professor in AUC's Mass Media Department told me that almost 300 students were interviewed for the survey.[18] "The respondents argued that the videos only imitate the West, and that they don't represent Arab identity or cultural values in any way. The videos don't reflect their own thoughts or feelings, the Arab performer's creativity doesn't show – just the mimicking of the West."

Although video producers claim just to be responding to popular demand, the students disagree. Female students in particular found the videos demeaning to women, and they even wanted to censor the clips. The AUC students don't have anything against Western values, but they think that Arabs could do much better than blindly copy the West.

Around the corner from Professor Abdallah's study is the office of *Caravan*, the AUC student magazine. I asked Hani 'Abd al-Qawi, the editor, for his opinion of the video clip debate. "I think they are immoral and they don't fit into our conservative society. If children see these videos, they will think that this is the right kind of behaviour... I like Ruby's songs, but I don't like the idea that an Egyptian girl is doing this [acting provocatively]." The core of the debate is what is culturally acceptable. Everyone knows that, for example, Britney Spears represents Western pop culture (whether we like it or not), and there is nothing strange about that. But an Arab artist shouldn't perform in a similar fashion.

The music business itself has become more commercial and more centralized – and is now almost exclusively in Saudi-Arabian hands. The biggest record label in the Middle East, Rotana, has captured some 85% of the market for Arabic music. Egyptian companies regularly complained that Rotana wants to monopolize the whole regional music industry. It is owned by the Saudi billionaire Prince al-Walid bin Talal, who owns not only the rights to his artists' music, but also their videos and live performances. The Rotana label also owns several music and movie satellite channels, where videos are shown first, before wider distribution to other Arab channels.

In this cut-throat economic climate, local record labels have either gone under, or have shifted to producing only religious tracks because they cannot compete with this mega company. Nowadays a simple recording is not enough – a catchy promotional video is a must for success, which the small companies often can't afford to produce. Then there is the star's remuneration: rumour has it that bin Talal lures artists to his label by hosting parties where the artist is presented with his or her own BMW. However, Rotana's contracts are limited to contemporary stars – the rights to such timeless artists as Umm Kulthum and Abdel Halim Hafez are still in Egyptian hands.

Like young people all over the world, Arab youths dream of stardom. Glossy magazines depict the lives of stars in graphic detail, and the internet abounds with Arab entertainment sites. After a long break, foreign singers (Sting, Enrique Iglesias, Shakira, to name but a few) have returned to Cairo – thanks to the new private radio stations Nugum and Nile FM who have organized concerts and other events. This has boosted the local live music scene, and new bands emerge all the time.

Another innovation is the TV talent competition, in which a nobody becomes a star. The first Arab Big Brother, filmed in Bahrain in 2004, came to an abrupt end due to protests. The main point of contention was the fact that unmarried men and women lived under the same roof, albeit in different rooms. Critics also claimed that the female competitors were too flirty. Over a thousand Bahrainis gathered on the streets of Manama and demanded that the programme be shelved for being 'un-Islamic'.[19]

In the music business, the 'stairway to stars' has proved to be less scandalous. The first Star Academy (a French format, Idols-style song contest) was held in Beirut in 2004. The winner would receive $50,000 price and a record deal. The Lebanese LBC channel broadcast the preparations of 16 contestants 24/7: singing lessons, acting, dancing and physical training.

The audience could vote for their favourite singer by SMS messages or by email. By the end, only a Kuwaiti and an Egyptian contestant were left. This led to a massive campaign in Egypt to secure the latter's victory. His brother appealed to listeners of Nugum Radio to vote, and the mobile operator MobiNil promised one minute free talk for everyone who voted for the country's son. Many Egyptians had become totally addicted to Star Academy, and voted obsessively several times.

The Egyptian women's magazine *Enigma* interpreted this voting zeal as a new form of expression: because parents and Egypt's conservative culture constrain young people's lives, in voting for their favourite artists they were able to make their voices heard for the first time. They had the freedom to vote for people other than the "dinosaurs that rule Egypt", as one 24-year-old respondent put it.[20]

The national SMS campaign was indeed a success: Muhammad Atiya, 21, won the competition with 55.1% of the votes. Chaos awaited him on his return to Cairo, as thousands of screaming fans wanted to get a glimpse of Atiya, transformed overnight into a star. Fans had flocked to the airport from all over Egypt, and even from neighbouring Libya in busloads. The new idol was almost suffocated by the crowd.[21]

While not garnering any screams (except of fright, perhaps) the new king of *sha'abi* music, Sha'aban 'Abd al-Rahim, had his share of the limelight. An illiterate former laundry ironer and a father of five, he began his musical career by performing at neighbourhood weddings, and selling cheap cassettes to taxi and minibus drivers. By chance, a TV-presenter heard his music in one of these, and invited the hoarse-voiced man onto his show. This was the beginning of the man-of-the-street's success: "I never expected to eat meat every day, but Allah has blessed me," Abd al-Rahim has said.[22]

As someone representing the *sha'abi* style, 'Abd al-Rahim's fashion sense also leaves a lot to be desired. His trademark is the oily, curly mullet, and he sports golden chains resting on his hairy chest, framed by a floral pattern shirt. He has even admitted to having a penchant for suits made of material normally reserved for furniture. No wonder that cultured circles think of him as the epitome of bad taste.

His first hit, in 2001, was 'I hate Israel (And love Amr Musa)',[23] which captured the emotions of the nation, supporting the second Palestinian *Intifada* (Uprising). The lyrics are simple and catchy, sung in Egyptian slang. Like Adawiyya, there have been attempts to ban 'Abd al-Rahim's videos from TV because they are deemed too low-class. He doesn't in fact have a licence which would allow him to perform in TV or radio.

Yet he has been a popular guest on talk shows, where the hosts make fun of his boorishness: one presenter even asked his opinion of classical Arabic music. A product of the Cairo streets, 'Abd al-Rahim admitted that he didn't even know what the word classical meant.[24]

But the more people talked about him, the more his cassettes sold – he even got his own brand of potato crisps. And being a singer, he naturally had to make an appearance on the silver screen. His debut was in the film *Muwatin wa Mukhbir wa Harami* (Citizen, Detective and Criminal), in which he plays a small-time crook, fresh out of prison. There are of course the obligatory singing scenes, which he performs with a plump belly dancer. He ends up married to a vamp called Madiha.

Madiha was played by a new talent, Rola Mahmud, a petite, almond-eyed beauty. Having performed as a singer in five-star hotels in Cairo for years, this was also her first role in a feature film. Her career had taken off quickly, because the previous year she had made her debut in a very popular, but controversial, Ramadan drama series *Awan al-Ward* (Blossoming of the Rose).

265

Ramadan is the prime season for soap operas, because after finishing their fast-breaking meal, families often gather together in front of the telly. The star-studded *Awan al-Ward* raised a lot of comment, chiefly because the leading actors were Coptic Christians – a rare thing on Egyptian television (although Egypt's biggest star Omar Sharif is a Christian). The series' message was clear: different faiths should respect each other, in the name of national unity.[25]

The series' director encouraged Rola to continue acting, and she got some minor roles. But she could have never suspected what kind of reception her first starring role with 'Abd al-Rahim was about to get. "It was a scandal! I was labelled as the actress with the most seductive role," she told me. Undoubtedly there were some risqué scenes (at least by Egyptian standards): she is seen in sexy black underwear, lying in bed with the 'citizen'.

> When the press found out that I was married, they asked how my husband could allow me to appear on such a scene! As if I had no say! I changed my phone numbers and didn't want to speak to journalists. Because when I read the script, I didn't think it was a role of a seductress, but a role of a free, liberated woman. And if I had been a big star, my reputation wouldn't have been stained for a love scene!

Despite – or maybe because of – this, the film grabbed several awards in national film festivals. Madiha's role didn't stain her career in the end, but it made her more selective over the parts she auditioned for. When a seductive role in the film *Ma'ali al-Wazir* (His Highness the Minister) was offered to her, she declined. Instead, she took the role of the minister's daughter. After that she had a part in Muhammad Khan's digital film, *Klephty* (The Crook), aimed solely at foreign film festivals. In it, she played Hanan, a simple countrywoman – dressed in cheap clothes and hardly any make-up. This was unusual: normally the big divas wear thick make-up, even if they play beggars, or are seen waking up in the morning.

We chatted during Ramadan in Autumn 2004. By then she had started to make a name for herself: she was beginning to be recognized on the streets, and people would approach her for autographs. She was still singing and was finishing her first video to accompany '*al-Haqiqa*' (The Truth), a song she composed and wrote the lyrics for. She told me that she had to go through some tough times to reach her dream. Like Liza Laziza, Rola learnt that the path of a performing artist in Egypt is not easy:

> Working conditions are often inhumane: we work without food, and you cannot concentrate because everyone is talking to you all at the same time. What is lacking here is the kind of thinking that talent should be respected.
>
> Only the biggest stars have agents or managers, unlike in Lebanon, for example. Here, the newcomer often joins a 'gang' i.e. a group with certain producers, directors and actors. They then make films amongst themselves. I don't belong to these gangs, so it's more difficult to get roles. And acting really doesn't pay – I earn much more from my singing.
>
> On the other hand, a performing artist's reputation is bad, it is considered to be a shameful profession. When I tell people that I'm an actress, they pull a strange face. Religiosity is so strong these days. Actresses are deemed 'easy', even those who don't do love scenes. So nowadays I say at the beginning of the interview: I'm not married to a businessman, no one in the film industry, nor do I have a rich Sheikh boyfriend!

Although Egypt's film production is still the only real film industry in the Arab world, its quality has sunk and with it the respect. The Egyptian film industry began as early as 1923, when a local production *Fi Balad Tutankhamon* (In the Land of Tutankhamon) premiered.

During the early cinematic decades, Egypt produced over ten films annually, mostly relying on the talent of Levantine actors. The Golden Age of Egyptian cinema coincided with the peak of Umm Kulthum's career, and until the 1960s, the Egyptian film industry dominated the Middle Eastern market from Morocco to Iraq. Nasser's nationalization extended to cinema, which meant that the artistic level and quality slowly declined – the Hollywood on the Nile started to look more like Bollywood.[26]

By 2000, Egyptian Television was struggling with financial constraints. It decided to sell 800 film classics and over 3000 negatives from its archives to the Funun media company, as well as 200 newer films. Subsequently, the same Saudi media mogul, al-Walid bin Talal who owns Rotana, bought Funun. When the negatives were sold abroad, it quickly dawned that Egyptians didn't have other copies of them.

With the help of Professor Muhammad al-Kalyubi from Egypt's Higher Institute of Cinema, MP Fayda Kamil proposed a motion in the Parliament about a film rights law. According to the motion, original film negatives would remain the sole property of Egyptian Television. Kamil and al-Kayubi wanted to forbid selling original film stock abroad and to make destruction of negatives punishable in law.

The autumn semester hadn't yet begun, so when I met Professor al-Kalyubi at the Higher Institute of Cinema near the Pyramids, the school was sleepy and a bit dusty. He described the current situation as 'catastrophic', hence the proposed law. He added that the new law would also protect films from destructive actions by individuals.

"For example, a Saudi Sheikh can marry a former film star, and have any of her films which he deems immoral destroyed," al-Kalyubi said. His fear is not hypothetical: relatives of ex-actresses have destroyed films they considered 'dissolute'. Accidental fires have also ravaged film archives: al-Kalyubi maintains that the authorities don't seem to care much about modern Egypt's cultural heritage. "Films play a significant role as the interpreter of Egyptian national sentiment and culture. If you buy Egypt's culture, you buy the culture of the whole region – it all originates in Egypt."

The motion has since been buried in the back-log of parliamentary files. On the other hand, perhaps the Saudi owners are not the worst thing that could have happened to the negatives: the Egyptian classics are now broadcast 24/7 on satellite channels – for everyone to appreciate.

Because satellite dishes, videos and DVDs have become so common, going to the cinema is on the decline. While in 1970 some 65 million Egyptians visited a cinema, by 1998 it had gone down to a 'miserable' 21.7 million. Video piracy is another reason for the decline – for the price of a single cinema ticket, the whole family can watch a bootleg copy.

Piracy is indeed a major concern, although there isn't a huge effort to combat it. In Cairo, this phenomenon can be seen on every street, where vendors sell pirated tapes and videos. A slightly classier version is the travelling one-man video-rental.

A friend of mine always orders his videos from this middle-aged, heavy-set man for home delivery. He shows up with a 1970s faux leather suitcase, full of tapes recorded who-knows-where. Sometimes he has films that have not even been released in Egypt. But as a rule, the quality is terrible; often the crux remains a mystery because either the audio or the image is blurred just at that scene. The video-man's repertoire is as varied as the quality – he never forgets to mention to his male clients that porn films are also available.

This friend prefers to order films at home because he finds the cinema experience more nerve-wrecking than enjoyable. As a woman I can't go to the cinema alone (at least in Downtown or to shows in the evening), because I will immediately attract eager company, either beside me or in the seat behind. Some female friends' movie experience has even been interrupted by an intrusive pair of fingers prying between the seat.

Yet these days, the most annoying part of the experience is mobile phones, because *no one* turns them off. You often hear one side of a phone conversation: "Yeah, I'm here at the movies. Right now I can see a chase... no, it's ok, how are you doing?" As if that wasn't enough, the audience comments loudly on the plot and different scenes, while even small babies are brought to the cinema, which all makes concentrating on the plot rather challenging.

But after the slump of the 1980s and 1990s, movie production picked up steam – in 2001, 31 films were produced. The most popular films are commercial slap-stick films, usually with a rags-to-riches story. And they are genuinely popular: domestic production draws much bigger crowds than the mainstream Hollywood films on general release. In 2001 the Egyptian film industry netted LE1.7 million, whereas the best-selling foreign film took only about LE200,000.[27]

The Egyptian state and a few big production houses have a lot of power, which is why independent film-makers find it hard to get their products distributed, or to get funding. Yet it is usually the indie films that earn praise abroad. On the other hand, often the films shown abroad are not box office hits in Egypt. The films of the veteran director Youssef Chanine (1926–2008) may be known in Europe, but in Egypt it is light entertainment that sells better.

All films shown in Egypt have to go through censorship: excessively passionate kissing, and love-making are not allowed, nor is politically or religiously dubious content. In the 1990s, the Islamists managed to pressure the censors to ban the late Youssef Chahine's film *al-Muhagir* (The Emigrant). It depicts the story of Joseph, which was the reason for the uproar: according to certain religious opinion, portraying prophets is against Islam. The ban was eventually withheld in the Appeals Court. Violence, however, is seldom censored.

The Egyptian Censorship Committee monitors TV films and series, whereas the Censorship Committee for Artistic Works previews theatre plays and films. Although the censors are generally thought to be behind the times, the emergence of satellite channels has already made an impact and loosened the censorship.[28]

However, once a year, at the Cairo International film festival, uncensored films are shown. This is also a unique opportunity to see non-Hollywood foreign films on the silver screen. The longest running festival in the Middle East, Cairo is one of the so-called Class A festivals, which means that it premiers films in the competition category. Altogether there are 11 A-class festivals, such as Cannes, Venice and Berlin.

Although Cairo is formally listed in the same category as the most respected international film festivals, in practice Cairo's level is far from the top. Only a few world-class stars make an appearance, which is pretty much the only glamorous part of the festival. The practical arrangements leave a lot to be desired, and only in the last few years has the organization of the festival improved. Yet it is still difficult to get a programme, and often the shows mysteriously change venues.

The most alluring feature of the festival is the prospect of uncensored films. This aspect mobilizes lower-middle-class men in large numbers to invest in a cinematic experience at this one time of year. Few, however, are interested in the artistic content of these films, or even the plot. They come to the cinema simply for the promise of nudity.

Even if the organizers try to play down this unfortunate side of the festival, many factors encourage it. First of all, most of the films don't have Arabic subtitles, so these young men (who rarely speak English or French) don't get anything out of the films while they wait for the sex scenes. If the anticipated scenes are not there, they start loudly commenting on their absence and disturb other viewers' concentration.

Therefore those who want to get their pound of flesh ask beforehand at the ticket booth: "*Fi qissa walla manazir?*" (Does the movie have a story or scenes?). The box-office usually know the 'excitement guaranteed' films, while to read the unofficial festival magazines, you might think that Cairo had become the centre of the international porn industry for the next two weeks. These magazines overflow with juicy details from the most daring films, but usually omit any information about their storylines.

Often the best indicator of the film's likely content is the waiting audience: if the lobby is solely occupied by men, and the testosterone is approaching alarming levels, it is safe to assume that the film they are waiting for contains nudity. Because of this unfortunate side effect, often when I've been out movie-hopping with female friends, we have had to skip an otherwise interesting-sounding film. The best deterrent against unwanted buttock-squeezing is to bring along male Egyptian friends, but they feel embarrassed about this phenomenon. However, over the last couple of years the festival programme has become less revealing, and Egyptian women have also found the festival.

Every foreign festival-goer has a favourite story, which is linked without exception to reactions to the nude scenes. In the early 1990s, a Western female friend had seen *The Crying Game* in a Cairene cinema. In the seduction scene, a couple meet and retire to the woman's flat. The man waits while the woman changes into something a little skimpier. But when the woman returns and opens her silky number, the hero is faced with a little more than he was expecting: the woman is actually a man. The audience, which had expected to see something quite different than the penis between 'her' legs, became infuriated and started to throw things at the screen. Some of them mysteriously even produced tomatoes.

Sometimes the festival even shows Finnish films, such as *Ambush* (1999), a love story of a soldier and a nurse set during the Continuation War between Finland and Russia in 1941. The show was in the middle-class, Colonial-style Heliopolis suburb at midday, so the audience was only about 20 people – but all men. Who knows – maybe they had been lured there by the daring reputation of Scandinavian cinema, or by an interest in war films.

At the ticket booth, a straight-faced ticket inspector confiscated a newspaper from one of our four-member team – "for fire safety", was the bizarre explanation. Either we looked like hardened pyromaniacs, or the cinema had a history of fires, but the request was weird. The elements of an interesting movie experience were in the air.

The audience watched the film in silence, until it came to the main characters' love scene. To the disappointment of the local audience, the scene shows only the male character naked. As if that wasn't bad enough, he leaps out of the bed, and she says: "Do what you did before", to which he goes down on her.

This scene was something the audience hadn't expected at all – to show a man naked, and to hear a woman making sexual demands? *"La ilaha illa Allah! Oh my God!"* the audience shouted in disbelief. Some of them shook their heads and stood up, commenting on the crazy scene. In Arab culture, men are not supposed to be seen naked – it is an insult to their masculinity. Some of them calmed down a bit at the sight of the female protagonist's breasts.

But there was more to come. The film takes place during the summer, and one of the soldiers has to jump naked into the water to fix a burned-down bridge, naturally with his wedding tackle cheerfully on display. By now it had become obvious to the local cinema goers that it was futile to expect more female flesh. Some stood up to leave, cursing the ways of the world. Despite the concerns over fire risks, the doors remained closed – it is the rule of the festival that no one leaves before the curtain goes down. Our little Western cine club was secretly happy about their disappointment: we had come here to see stories, not scenes!

Censorship is also a problem in literature, which has seen its fair share of scandals. Literature dealing with religious and moral issues has been particularly controversial. Books and audiovisual products containing this kind of material have been subjected to a stricter censor since the 1980s. Publications Law 20/1936, the Emergency Law and decrees supplementing them in the criminal law all contain the principle of censorship: they mention the protection of the three revealed religions (Judaism, Christianity, Islam) by law. On the other hand, it also mentions punishment for disseminating extremist ideas.

Adding more teeth to censorship was the law of 103/1961, which granted al-Azhar Academy's Islamic Research Centre the right to monitor publications dealing with Islam and Islamic heritage. This vaguely defined right has been interpreted differently over the years, but the law *did not* give the Academy the right to confiscate publications it deemed forbidden. It can only recommend confiscation to the security officials. Often its recommendations have been classified as administrative decrees, so it has been possible to cancel them via administrative courts.[29]

In practice, however, the Academy has often exceeded the powers formally granted by the law. During the fight between the Islamists and the state, al-Azhar was able to use its power extensively, for example by confiscating books from the annual Cairo Book Fair. The Academy was allowed to function relatively independently, although it is under the authority of the state. The Grand Sheikh is nominated by the President, and al-Azhar gets its funding from the state budget.

Particularly since the 1990s, radical Islamists have listened carefully to al-Azhar's recommendations. The most dramatic example is the murder of secularist thinker and Islamist critic Farag Fuda in 1992. Fuda had specifically criticized the role of al-Azhar as the highest moral gatekeeper – a role that in Fuda's mind wasn't granted to it, because Islam doesn't have priesthood. He had asked why al-Azhar didn't merely refute the works it deemed anti-religion by offering differing opinions, counter-arguments and logic, as opposed to blind confiscations.[30]

Not surprisingly, al-Azhar ordered Fuda's critical book on the topic to be withdrawn from the market. Only a few weeks later, two masked men shot Fuda to death in front of his office in Nasr City. He had received death threats before, but had apparently refused a body guard. In a way, al-Azhar was directly responsible for his death: prior to his murder, the Academy had declared that everything Fuda did was against Islam. *Al-Gama'a al-Islamiyya* (The Islamic Group) claimed responsibility for the attack, and referred to al-Azhar's statement. "Yes, we killed him... al-Azhar gave the verdict and we executed it," their press release stated.[31]

Cairenes were deeply shocked by the murder. About a thousand intellectuals and artists mounted a demonstration in front of the Umar Makram mosque in Tahrir Square, shouting anti-Islamist slogans. At the trial of Fuda's killers, the prestigious al-Azhar theologian Sheikh Muhammad al-Ghazali testified. He stated that Fuda and people like him are apostates, who deserve to die. If the government failed to carry out the duty, individuals would be free to do so. [32]

Attacks against authors continued. In 1994, the icon of Egyptian literature, Nobel laureate Naguib Mahfouz, was stabbed in his shoulder, right outside his home. Again an al-Azhar edict had preceded the attack: his novel *Awlad Haritna* (Children of Gebelawi) had been banned in Egypt since 1959 on the basis that it insulted the Islamic prophets; the book, however, was smuggled in from Beirut. Then in 1988, when Mahfouz was awarded the Nobel Prize, the spiritual leader of *al-Gama'a al-Islamiyya*, Umar Abd al-Rahman, issued a *fatwa* declaring Mahfouz an apostate, referring to *Awlad Haritna*. The knifemen were indeed from *al-Gama'a*.

When Mahfouz was asked if he could recognize his attacker, he replied that he didn't. But he said he knew him: his face bore the marks of poverty and ignorance, and his spirit was crippled by the loss of opportunities. Mahfouz stated the belief that the stabber hadn't even read his book, but acted solely on the orders of his group elders. "Today's youth are all like my assassin: a whole generation that has been ignored and neglected." The attack was widely condemned; even Sheikh al-Ghazali (who had favoured banning his book) called it an attack against Islam.[33]

Naguib Mahfouz (1911–2006) was, and remains, the only Nobel laureate in the Arab world. His output amounted to 34 novels, 15 collections of short stories, as well as theatre plays some of which have been adapted for television. After the stabbing, as physiotherapy he started to write short philosophical stories for half an hour a day, with the working title *Dreams of Convalescence*. They were first published in *Nisf al-Dunya* magazine in 2003, with the first part translated into English in 2004, the second 2007.[34]

Up until his last days, Mahfouz attended a literary salon. Twice a week, he sat with a circle of literary friends, in discreet locations. I had the honour of attending these salons a few times, the last one in 2006 by which time he could no longer hear that well, but his mind was sharp as anyone else's. Fragile but alert, Mahfouz seemed to radiate happiness, and his entourage was clearly proud and pleased to be in his company, savouring his witty observations and ringing laughter.

His entourage was, for the most part, middle-aged, with a few thirty-something literature aficionados. People would come to sit beside him to read him newspapers, or tell him stories, shouting quite loud because he could only hear in his left ear, and that not well. The men of the group drank mint tea or Turkish coffee, and chain-smoked, in their eyes the far-away look of a creative person. Mahfouz would also smoke half a cigarette, which someone lit for him.

Mahfouz was not the only, or the last author, to be targeted, although the assaults were not always physical. Not only radical organizations, but some individuals, adopted the role of moralist. In the 1990s, Islamist lawyers re-introduced the concept of *hisba* (originally it meant guarding Islamic law, enjoining believers to strive for good and combat evil). According to this contemporary use of *hisba*, an individual may file a law suit if they think that someone has insulted Islam.

Perhaps the best-known *hisba* case is that of Nasr Hamid Abu Zayd, the former assistant professor of Arabic language and literature at Cairo University. In 1993, a group of Islamist lawyers sued him, accusing him of apostasy. Their 'proof' was Abu Zayd's writings – and in particular his argument that some Qur'anic texts can be understood metaphorically, not literally.

Because a Muslim woman cannot be married to a non-Muslim man, the Islamist lawyers then demanded that he divorce his wife. The Court of Appeal declared him an apostate in 1995 (which was confirmed in the Court of Cassation a year later), and ordered the divorce. The couple received death threats and went into exile in the Netherlands in 1995. Soon after the Cassation Court verdict, a new law was passed, which withdrew the right of individuals to initiate *hisba* cases – only the public prosecutor could decide whether a case could be taken to court.[35]

This new law didn't stop some eager lawyers to try *hisba* prosecutions anyway. In 2001, the populist attorney Nabil Wahsh sued Nawal el-Saadawi for apostasy. The case started with al-Saadawi's interview in *al-Midan* magazine – which according to el-Saadawi had distorted her words. In the interview she talked about several sensitive issues, such as the Muslim pilgrimage to Mecca. She was quoted as saying that kissing the Kaaba black stone was a remnant of a pre-Islamic rite. This prompted Egypt's Grand Mufti (the senior Islamic theologian, who issues *fatwas*, religious edicts) to state that el-Saadawi had "strayed from the path of Islam".

This time, however, the court ruled in el-Saadawi's favour. The court reminded the eager lawyer Mr Wahsh that the *hisba* law had changed – he had thus tried to take the law into his own hands. According to his logic, al-Saadawi was an apostate and therefore she should divorce her husband, however, the whole trial was absurd, and al-Saadawi continues to be happily married.[36]

Yet censorship can be found in some of Cairo's most liberal (at least in self-image) enclaves. In 1998, concerned parents and some influential alumni started a censorship campaign at the American University in Cairo (AUC) library. Among the books that disappeared from the shelves were Maxime Rodinson's *Muhammad*, Montgomery Watt's *Islamic Political Thought* and Charles Tripp & Roger Owen's *Egypt under Mubarak* – on the orders of the Minister of Higher Education. By the end of the following year, over 70 books dealing with different interpretations of Islam, with morals, or with the Mubarak regime had been purged from the reading lists.

The strange part was that the elite American University's board should have agreed so easily to withdraw these books, which continued to be displayed on the shelves of Cairo University library. But money talked – the American University depends on term fees, so it couldn't disagree with its donors and gave in.[37] A library search on the AUC website confirms that of the above mentioned works, only Watt's has resurfaced.

As one might expect, the Muslim Brotherhood has also tried to take on the mantle of nation's moral police. In January 2001, Brotherhood MP Gamal Hishmat demanded an inquiry into three books which were published by the state-owned Culture Palace series. These books are cheap because the government wants to encourage people to read more. To Hishmat's mind, the three books in question were obscene texts, if not outright porn, and certainly not the kind of material to be published with taxpayers' money, he argued.

Although this was a simple request for an inquiry, it led to unprecedented consequences. Faruq Husni, the Minister of Culture, fired the managing editor of Culture Palace, and

ordered the books to be reviewed. Critics accused the Minister
of trying to please Islamists – everyone still remembered the
student riots from the previous spring, which had called for
banning a novel *Walima al-Ahsab al-Bahr* (Banquet of the
Seaweed) by the Syrian author Haydar Haydar, which was
accused of bearing the hallmarks of blasphemy.

Then the Islamists had demanded the withdrawal of
Haydar's book, but Husni hadn't give in; indeed he had
rather allowed a re-printing. The Ministry of Culture (which
claims to support liberal values) and al-Azhar (representing
a conservative moralist view and protecting certain types
of Islamic interpretation) have collided many times over
what kinds of values literature may or may not represent.
In the Culture Palace case, it was generally thought that
Husni wanted to avoid another head-on collision with
the Islamists, who had demanded his dismissal during the
Seaweed riots.[38]

Al-Azhar's role as literature censor made the headlines
again in 2004. According to media reports, the Ministry of
Justice granted the Islamic Research Centre (subject to al-Azhar)
even broader authorization to ban and confiscate works which
it deemed anti-Islamic. But the law of 102/1985 had already
given al-Azhar and the Ministry of Justice the power to form a
committee, which had the right to confiscate material deemed
dubious from a religious point of view.

With their new authorization, the staff of the Islamic
Research Centre confiscated hundreds of publications, as well
as audio- and video-tapes, which they deemed un-Islamic.
They struck out unorthodox Qur'an editions, as well as works
of fiction.

Amongst the banned books was Nawal el-Saadawi's *Fall
of the Imam*, published some 20 years previously. The poetic
novel tackles both the oppression of women, and also the

double standards of the religious authorities. Thrown yet again into the firing line, el-Saadawi told me at the time that she believed that it was banned because its message remained relevant – there is still a lot violence committed in the name of religion. She blamed the state for the latest witch-hunt:

> We cannot make a distinction between the state and the fundamentalist movement – they are one and the same. They might quarrel sometimes, but their strategy is the same: to kill freedom of speech. Every decision against freedom of speech is a step backwards. If creative writing is banned, how can society advance? We must make a distinction between the state and religion if we really want to develop. Religion is something very personal, it should be practised at home – laws should be secular.

Al-Azhar has argued that it only opposes extreme groups' literature – yet anyone can buy this on the streets, although it doesn't have publication licence. It seems that the government wants to counter the Islamists by strengthening the position of al-Azhar as the voice of 'official Islam'. The Director of al-Azhar's Islamic Research Centre justified the confiscation policy by saying that they were merely civil servants. "The government is like our father. It does not have to flirt with us, it can fire us. They tell us do this, OK; don't do that, OK."[39]

Authors and human rights organizations argued that broader powers were a serious setback for freedom of expression. The fear was that al-Azhar inspectors would become a similar moral police force to Saudi Arabia's feared *mutawwa*. But the Egyptian inspectors have more limited powers, and they cannot detain those who possess forbidden materials.

The Director of the Library of Alexandria, Ismail Serageldin, participated in the freedom of speech debate in a column he wrote for the *al-Ahram Weekly* newspaper. He noted that every society discusses the parameters of the socially acceptable, and what kind of material can be published with public funds. Alexandria Library enjoys a special status in Egypt – it is directly under the presidency – and therefore it doesn't have to consider censorship when selecting materials.

> In Egypt feelings of anger and frustration at a world that appears to many Arabs and Muslims as hostile to their aspirations have led many to seek a lost purity and sense of security in a golden mythical past. This has produced a discourse where deviations from appearances of religiosity and adherence to the political views of the majority is severely sanctioned, both socially and in vehement political attacks—even, occasionally, in physical threats, abuse and even assassination. It takes courage to stand up for alternative views: all too frequently people give in to the tide of obscurantism and xenophobia and exercise self-censorship as draconian as anything imposed by the state.[40]

But an even bigger hindrance than censorship in the way of literature reaching its audience is illiteracy. In 2006, total adult (over 15-year-olds) literacy was 69.5%, but of this total, women's literacy was even lower: 57.3%.[41] But even those who *can* read, don't read works of fiction. Only a few Egyptians have read the domestic classics – most people prefer to watch the TV versions. In Egypt, the culture is overall more visual and interactive, collective. Television or plays can be watched together and commented upon, whereas reading a book is a solitary activity. This might be another reason for rare sightings of book-worms.

The most popular reads in Egypt are religious items or self-studying books. When you take the Cairo Metro, for example, this becomes evident: the very few who are reading something are either studying the Qur'an or the Bible – or other religious materials. Of all the printed books in the

Arab world, 17% are religious; globally the proportion of religious books is 5%. Alarmingly few foreign works are translated into Arabic: only 4.4 books per million people (1980–1985). By comparison, the corresponding figure in Spain was 920.[42]

On the other hand, official appreciation for literature increased during the 1990s – if it is measured by the number of literary prizes, literature conferences and published books. Still, an average book only sells a few thousand copies – not a big deal in a country of over 80 million. Publishers don't usually reveal print volumes, but it has been estimated that at least 500 new fictional items (including poetry and drama) are printed annually. Half of them are published by the state-controlled print sector, and the other half is usually self-published. Despite the low readership, literature thrives, mostly because it doesn't need huge monetary investments like music or the film industry.[43]

Writing alone isn't enough to make a living – even Naguib Mahfouz had to work as a civil servant to provide for his family, and eventually he made more money from translations into foreign languages than from domestic sales. Most authors finance their literary pursuits by working as script-writers for television, or by coining lyrics for the music industry.

But sometimes those who get recognized refuse to accept it, like Sonallah Ibrahim, who turned down a state literary award in 2003. I went to see him shortly after this cultural scandal, at his home in Heliopolis. The front door of the flat was decorated with a Palestinian solidarity movement's poster – he and his wife are active in the peace movement against Israeli actions and the Iraq war. This was the heyday of demonstrations and new citizens' activism. Ibrahim's apartment revealed the passion of its inhabitants: all the rooms overflowed with books in different languages.

Sonallah, bespectacled, with a shock of white curly hair, was still amused when he recalled the award event; how the audience cheered and some even kissed his hand! Sonallah Ibrahim had just announced that he didn't want to receive the LE100,000 Egyptian prize for Arab authors. His reason? Arab states' passiveness while Israel was killing Palestinians and Americans were occupying Iraq. Ibrahim felt that the time was ripe for a dramatic act. With this deed, he wanted to demonstrate that authors and intellectuals can also show resistance.

> It was my way of expressing myself about what is going on in the world. Palestinian children and Iraqis are being killed, and Egyptian children don't have milk or proper education or jobs after graduation. I felt that I couldn't celebrate something that is completely detached from what is going on around us.

Ibrahim says he didn't expect people to thank him for what he did: he was flabbergasted by the reaction. He took it as confirmation that there was indeed a demand for such deeds. Many praised it as a brave act, and a clarion call for authors' responsibility to comment on social evils. Yet some argued that he was a hypocrite, because in the past he had accepted awards from other Arab countries.

In any case, the refusal was a dramatic act, and all of a sudden Ibrahim was wanted everywhere: from the state media to small-town literary clubs. A Marxist writer who had spent five years in Nasser's dungeons, and who had always kept a safe distance from the state, Ibrahim was now the country's hottest author.

Although Ibrahim was sensing revival in literary circles, he pointed out that writers still need to take into consideration certain taboos: sex, religion and politics. Ibrahim felt that it is impossible to write psychological profiles without describing the person's sexuality. His first short story was banned for precisely this reason in the 1960s.

> I cannot just avoid talking about sex merely because our society doesn't know how to face itself, and doesn't know how to talk about those issues it suffers from, or feels for – the same goes with religion and politics. I would like to write a book about the republic's president, but I cannot!
>
> If I was a European reader, I would rather read American or Latin American books [than Arabic] because I can assume that the author is not trying to cheat me, and that he is telling me something about himself – freely and openly.

But it was an Egyptian author who did just that. Cairene dentist Alaa al-Aswany hit the jackpot with his novel *The Yacoubian Building*, which seemed to touch upon all those issues that were deemed taboos: homosexuality, Islamic fundamentalism and political corruption. Amazingly the book passed the censors and was a best-seller when it came out in Arabic, in 2002.

Since then, it has been translated into numerous languages, and adapted to the silver screen. Al-Aswany still keeps his dental office in Garden City, tucked in a non-descript apartment building. In his early 50s, al-Aswany is bearish and calm, although he keeps a very intense and engaging eye contact with his listener while he puffs away on his American cigarettes.

This is how he explained how the book and movie passed the censors:

> For the movie, we have an official censorship, but for books we don't But we have invisible censorship, which is very powerful. Meaning, for example, that there's no way you can publish a book without the draft being read by the state security, either directly or indirectly.

My novel had been refused by four publishers. And in the four cases I got almost the same response: it's a great book, but we cannot publish it. In the end I found a publisher who is an activist for democracy. He had already had trouble with the regime so it didn't make any difference to him.

The first edition was a run-away success: it was sold out in two months. And with very, very positive, exceptional responses for the movie, for the novel, so I think it is too late to ban it. And when you are known, here and abroad, they calculate before giving you trouble.

Al-Aswany has had his share of trouble, as has pretty much anyone who is politically active in Egypt. He is a member of the Writers for Change group, and he writes for the Nasserist daily *al-'Arabi,* which is very critical of the government.

This regime cannot at all be described as a democratic one. The regime makes (elections) every now and then; it likes to make a kind of decoration for its ugly face.

We cannot say we have democracy unless we have very specific requirements, like free elections, like the right of the people to choose their president in fair presidential elections, like the right of creating political parties without any kind of governmental interference, the human rights… We cannot say that we are a democratic country if we have torture of innocent people, like a routine practice.

There are millions of Egyptians who have been totally marginalized by the regime, they don't have the basic human rights, they don't have the right to have even future, the right to dream. And this poor, desperate Egypt is the raw material for terrorism.

The political message is that terrorism is a complication of the disease, dictatorship, not the disease, terrorism, corruption and poverty are just complications. And I think this is the point which was not at all comfortable for the regime. Because the regime was all time trying to convince us that the complication is the disease,

> that terrorism is the disease. The real bad image of Egypt is made by the dictatorship and not by writers.

Apart from el-Saadawi, women have been less active in political writing. Instead, they have revived older, more traditional forms of expression, such as story-telling. A group of Cairo University teachers set up the Women and Memory Forum in 1997 in order to revive the story-telling tradition and to challenge the traditional perception of gender roles. One of the group's activities is to re-write folk tales from a more egalitarian perspective.

The Forum has a cosy office in the Muhandisin district in Cairo; walls are decorated with portraits of well-known female figures, such as pioneer feminist Huda Sha'arawi. The idea for a forum rose from the desire to dig out important women from the depths of history, forum coordinator Sahar Subhi told me. "Arab women's history hasn't been documented a great deal. We're trying to find those voices and give them a place in history," she explained. The Forum seek out women's roles from court archives, history books, legal and commercial contracts, Islamic *hadith* (traditions) as well as old photographs.

The Women and Memory Forum also has a story-telling element to their activities. Because folk tales and fairytales preserve folklore in a dynamic way, the group wanted to enliven the stories. They would choose a particular story for treatment, and rewrite it giving women more space. These stories are then published for children and for adults, sometimes even as comic strips. The Forum also encourages others to rethink traditional gender roles, and whether their division remains justified today.[44]

Traditionally, story-tellers in market places and streets have been men: women tell stories at home. A young, modern story-teller Shirin al-Ansari is a pioneer in her field. A drama school graduate, she has made a living out of public story-telling for more than ten years. She began her career in Islamic Cairo, then different culture festivals and venues, particularly during Ramadan. Dressed in Oriental costumes à la *Thousand and One Nights*, she acts out the plot turns, bringing fairytales to life.

Story-telling is her calling, and the *Thousand and One Nights* stories are a natural choice. Although the stories are authentic, she rewrites Queen Shaherazade's stories so that they fit in her mouth, yet respecting the original plot and storyline. Another unusual aspect of her performances is the multilingual feature: she mixes Arabic, English and French. This is how one of her performances went:

> (In Arabic) Once upon a time was a land, without deserts or oases, without palm trees or mountains, a land lush of forests, high trees and fast streaming rivers. In this land lived an old king, who had an only son by the name of Amar al-Zaman…(changes into English) Amar al-Zaman – do I really need to say – was unbelievably handsome. His face was like the moon, his cheeks like two flowers and his lips like strawberries, teeth like shiny pearls…

Shirin is not alone in her trade anymore – other performance artists have found story-telling. Shirin thinks that this art form has been rediscovered because people have noticed that their cultural heritage is disappearing. "In the 1960s and '70s, there were attempts to revive story-telling. But now we are truly under attack [from the Western entertainment]. Story-telling is no longer an activity of the intellectuals, but purely a matter of cultural survival," Shirin told me as we sat in the artists' former hangout, the Café Riche downtown.

Nowadays, the majority of her performances take place abroad. She has noticed that in Europe and North America more and more performers choose this forum for expression. "An old, almost dead tradition is being revived there only now. In the Arab countries it might take a while longer," Shirin estimated.

In the final analysis, story-telling is something between literature and theatre. Most Egyptian theatre productions are governmental. State theatre actors are thus civil servants, and this mentality has meant that the quality has gone down (already since the 1960s). Commercial hits are therefore usually produced by the private sector, but even these leave a lot to be desired. They tend to choose scandalous themes, as their obsession with Monica Lewinsky testifies. When President Clinton's relationship with the intern hit the news, at least three comedies on this theme drew full houses in the Cairo theatres. Critics say that in the end, public and private sectors differ very little from each other content-wise.[45]

While critics lament the low quality of theatre, independent productions have enlivened the scene in the past few years. Even political theatre is still alive and kicking, as one of the best-selling numbers of 2004 – *Messing with the Mind* – demonstrated. It touched the anti-war nerve many Egyptians expressed at the time.

This anti-USA play was staged at the Hanagir theatre, tucked in the Cairo Opera House complex. If the Japanese-built Opera House offers high-brow culture, Hanagir represents the more experimental touch. Oozing creativity, leftie artists always like to hang out at its coffee shop.

I went to see this play with an Egyptian friend, who hardly ever goes to the theatre. When we reached the vestibule, gun-toting, camouflage-clad soldiers told us to move on, pushing us about, and guiding the audience to their seats: *Messing with the Mind* had already started.

Madame Nadia appeared on the stage, a mawkish talk-show hostess, who symbolized Egypt. She called the guest of honour to the stage: Tom Fox, Ruler of Iraq. This

General spoke in broken Arabic, explaining how much he loved the Arabs, and how he had come as a friend, swearing in the name of Islam and Christianity that he means well. The audience didn't take him seriously, commenting and hissing. My friend was in stitches.

It soon dawned that the general's motives weren't all that explicit. The talk-show hostess took calls from different Arab countries, and criticism towards him grew more intense. Clashes occur on the imaginary border between Israel and Morocco; the USA conquers new Arab capitals and tanks roll into Cairo's central square. The cordial relationship between the talk-show hostess and the general turns colder, and finally the general loses his temper. He curses all the Arabs: "If you don't shut up, I'll kill you all," he finally yells.

Messing with the Mind also laughed at the notorious Arab 'unity'. The audience was almost falling from their seats in laughter at the scene depicting different Arab TV channels' versions of the Umm el-Fahm capture. Madame Nadia (i.e. Egyptian TV) told the most polished version, whereas the Libyan television announced that Umm el-Fahm now belonged to Libya.

Eventually Tom Fox is rescued by George W. Bush himself, speaking Arabic on a TV screen. Bush swears that Arab oil belongs to Arabs, and that democracy belongs to Arabs. "Believe me, I love Arabs", Bush pleads. The play ends with Tom Fox's murder, a riot in Cairo and victory for the masses.

Messing with the Mind was directed by the actor who played Tom Fox, Khalid al-Sawi (who also played the role of the gay editor in *The Yacoubian Building*). He is well known as having a penchant for political plays, and he is a member of the independent *Haraka* (Movement) theatre group. *Messing with the Mind* was by no means the first anti-American play, but perhaps the most innovative. Al-Sawi thinks that the play's popularity might be explained by the overall anti-American sentiment, and Egyptians' antipathy towards American Middle East policy.

Hanagir's coffee shop seemed to be his second home – everyone knew him. As a waiter brought him Turkish coffee, he announced proactively that he describes himself as a radical socialist. He belongs to that small minority which refuses to accept the status quo in Egypt. Al-Sawi presented his rebellious view: "when the audience sees that all the players in society are connected and that they are all corrupt – they might think that it is time to get rid of them." His vision might be utopian, but his play's success is a telling sign that there is definitely still a demand for political theatre.

Yet too much politics can also ruin a playwright. 'Ali Salem is one the most renowned Egyptian playwrights, but his dramatic trip to Israel in 1994 rendered him a pariah in the eyes of the cultural establishment. He was expelled from the Writers' Union in 2001 in accordance with the union rules, which oppose normalization of ties with Israel. Only Naguib Mahfouz stood up for him.[46] Salem was effectively boycotted until 2004 when the independent al-Sawy Cultural Centre invited him to read his texts in front of an audience.

It was Ramadan in 2004, and Salem suggested meeting in a hotel coffee shop in Muhandiseen. It appeared that this place was his second office, also a place to meet with people. Salem, in his early 70s by then, was balding with a droopy, gentle face and gestured theatrically as he spoke. He didn't care about the Ramadan fast, but took long, satisfied drags from his American cigarettes and drank the obligatory accompaniment, Turkish coffee, as he prepared for his long-awaited al-Sawy performance. His longing for a live audience was finally going to be fulfilled.

Besides fiction, he often writes for local papers, as well as the London-based pan-Arabic *al-Hayat* newspaper. "But my job is on the stage. That distinct smell of dust, the dust heated by spotlights – it's a beautiful smell. I want to hear the audience's laughter, sense their breathing and smell them," Salem versed, sniffing the air for a dramatic effect.

He became famous with the theatrical comedy *School for Scoundrels* in 1971. After that he wrote some 25 plays and 15 books, but the last 10 years has been spent in enforced silence due to his decision to visit Israel after the Oslo peace agreement in 1993. His motive was to see what people there were doing, and who they were – and through this knowledge to get rid of hatred. He drove across the Sinai border with his Lada Niva and spent three weeks in Israel. When he returned, he wrote a book on his experience, *My Drive to Israel*. Although the cultural elite disowned him, against all odds the book became a huge success – it sold over 60,000 copies in Egypt, and it has been translated into English and Hebrew.

In the book, Salem reflects his own attitude towards the enemy. And also how difficult it is to differ in Egypt.

> We must focus on this point in raising our children. It is a person's right to hold differing views and ideas, as long as he doesn't espouse violence or aggression. Let ideas do combat with each other, theory against theory, for the benefit of the nation.[47]

After his trip, in 1996 he became the leader of Cairo Peace Movement (which promoted normalization with Israel). He visited and lectured in Israel – in the 'enemy' land – many times, and made appearances on Israeli television. He has tried to disperse fears of Israeli cultural invasion – surprisingly many respected Egyptian intellectuals believe that Israel is trying to wipe out the whole of Arab culture. In his book, he confronts the issue in his satirical style:

In all likelihood, Israel will launch Hebrew banners into the skies over Arab capitals and scald us by pouring ashes from them. They'll mount Hebrew novels on rockets so as to penetrate our minds and hearts and souls, from which they'll expel the works of not only Naguib Mahfouz, Taha Husayn and Ahmad Baha' ad-Din, but also al-Mutanabbi and al-Jahiz and even the complaints of the Eloquent Peasant.[48]

As for Hebrew melodies, Ariel Sharon himself will lead them in a swift pincer movement to encircle our hearts, destroying the melodies of as-Sunbati, al-Qassabgi, 'Abd al-Wahhab, and Baligh Hamdi. Israel will launch its short history inside a nuclear eraser, capable of wiping out your own history of creativity and wisdom.

Oh, what a wretched, helpless victim am I! How can I protect myself from this invasion? What should I do to confront these lethal weapons?

Don't speak with them, listen to them, or read them. Convince yourself that they don't exist. Imagine that Israel is the temptress of the folk tales, the voice of seduction luring you to desire and destruction, the siren of Greek mythology and of the Thousand and One Nights. She sings a captivating song, she possesses an enchanting voice that will lure you away and drag you to the bottom of the Nile. Plug your ears and become deaf. While you're at it, blind your eyes too, since a nuclear film or something like it could invade you ...

Young theatre enthusiasts and private theatre groups are the bright light in the otherwise somewhat faded theatre scene. One of the older groups is *Warsha* (Workshop), set up in 1987, which has enlivened puppet theatre and Upper Egyptian folk tales.

One of the most vocal young directors is the thirty-something, serious, and stern-faced Ahmed Al-Attar. With his courageous youth portrayals, he has opened up the debate about the role of theatre: young theatre performers don't get any kind of state funding, while governmental groups are favoured, for example at local festivals. Al-Attar's play on wife-husband power relations was staged on a bus parked in the Opera House courtyard. In itself, it was a manifesto against the fact that independent groups don't have proper rehearsal or performing facilities.

Yet these young groups stick together, thanks to strong directors – or to rebellious spirit. While al-Attar might be an insignificant name to the wider audience, his play *Mother, I want to be a millionaire* was sold out for weeks at the AUC Falaki theatre in spring 2004.

The play dealt with the star cult, still a relatively new phenomenon in the Arab world, the ordinary people's aspiration for stardom. Apart from media criticism, the play portrays young people's frustrations. The leading role is a young man, who complains that he doesn't have any goals, while he moves a video camera on his skin.

> I'm restless, I don't know what I want, I'm afraid that my decisions lead me astray, I'm lonely, shy... I'm always thinking a lot, I can't find answers... I'm weak, I do things I don't want to do... I have no goals, I'm stupid... sometimes I don't understand at all... I feel less than everyone else...

Actor Hasan al-Giridli argued that this figure is not necessarily specifically tied to the Arab world, but rather to the position of young people in general: young people everywhere dream of things they cannot achieve. As a member of an independent group, following his dreams sometimes means compromising with capitalism. "It's very difficult to find work if you don't want to participate in commercial productions. That's the actor's dilemma: to join or not? Sometimes you just need money!" he said laughing, shortly before his performance at the Falaki theatre. At the time he was supporting himself making by commercials and doing voice-overs.

Al-Attar divides his time between Egypt and France. He argues that independence is not appreciated in his native country.

> The idea of independence doesn't exist in Egypt or in the Arab world at a personal level. No one wants anyone to be independent: parents don't want children to be independent, mothers, friends... the state is just the picture of depressed society, the streets don't want you to be independent... so at a very young age, you are moulded into something. OK, I'm not saying that everyone has to be rebellious, but there isn't even the opportunity for a rebellion – all the time you are forced to be what others want you to be.

In his mind, the same applies to theatre: independent theatre means an independent voice, which might say things that people don't want to hear. In *Mother, I want to be a millionaire* the protagonists are looking for a hero, not necessarily from the world of entertainment. A caricature of a politician keeps on jumping onto the stage, performing nonsensical monologues.

> We are looking for a hero also in the political level, not just in Egypt but everywhere in the Arab world. We feel that our rulers are not our heroes... [laughs] They just play – or are forced to play games and they have nothing to say. [Today's] heroes are television heroes, those guys who just sing love songs and make a lot of money.

Al-Attar himself is not getting rich by making theatre: his group doesn't get any funding from Egypt, but rather from Europe. Most of his actors have outside jobs – one cannot make a living out of independent theatre, al-Attar arrests.

> As an artist you come to a stage where you really need support: both financial and artistic support in order to develop. If you can't

get that, you just stay in the same place and don't advance. And this has happened to a whole generation.

The young director thought that the Egyptian government might become interested in his troupe if they made a name abroad. This has previously happened to many young artists. The Egyptian fine arts scene has experienced an enormous change over the past ten years; the motor behind this renaissance is a private gallery called Townhouse, which opened its doors in 1998 in downtown Cairo. It has become the focal point for art lovers, a stepping stone for young artists, and a venue for cross-cultural soirées, seminars, concerts and film screenings.

The gallery space – which had been vacant for half a century – is located in the heart of Cairo, next to the majestic Champollion palace (named after the Frenchman who decoded the hieroglyphic text) which hosts a school, in the midst of garages and street cafes. The three-storey building has expanded to the other side of the alley, converting a massive warehouse into an exhibition and concert space. When the gallery owner, Canadian-born William Wells, an intense, ginger-haired man in his fifties, chose a derelict building in the un-cool neighbourhood of the city to be the gallery venue, everyone thought he was crazy.

> Everyone said that no one would venture in those stray alleys, they are so dangerous and dark, and the building will probably collapse and artists will refuse to come there… But this model – to establish a gallery in a working class area – is not a new concept and it was been used all over the world! And it works – so why not in Egypt?

The concept worked better that anyone would have believed. Artist friends Martin McInally and Kaare Troelsen told me about a new, fantastic gallery, which was a bit tricky to find for the first time. Their blue and pastel Cairo scenes were on display at the grand opening, signalling the appearance of young artists. Although the premiere hosted works of ex-pats, nowadays most of the works on display are by local artists.

Central Cairo's galleries and experimental modern art scene became known to a wider audience thanks to the Nitaq Festivals of 2000 and 2001. In addition to Townhouse, the Espace Karim Francis (its Lebanese curator) and Mashrabiyya (which has an Italian curator) galleries participated in the event, bringing art to Cairo's streets for the first time, in front of people who had never seen a work of art before. The festival coincided with the Cairo biennale and drew international attention. Cairo actually hosts several art events, not least because the Minister of Culture, Faruq Husni, is himself a well-known artist.

In the path forged by Townhouse, other small galleries sprang up in different parts of Cairo. Art can be seen in coffee shops, restaurants and even on local wine labels. But why did it take foreigners to awaken the Egyptian modern art scene? William Wells gave me the kind of look to suggest that this was not the first, or the last, time this question had been asked.

> Maybe you needed a foreigner to come here and say: Oh my God, you are sitting on all this! And because Cairo is by nature the kind of city where people walk on the streets looking down, then you need fresh eyes which say: let's look up! And that's how it in principle happened, it wasn't planned. When I came here in '98 I saw it so clearly everywhere: someone should do this work.

On the other hand, working in Egypt as a foreigner has its difficulties because people are suspicious. In the local press, Townhouse has been accused of being the headquarters of foreign interests. It has also been alleged that the sometimes provocative works are giving a bad name to Egypt – even if they are made by Egyptians.

> When you work in an area, which touches upon depicting Egypt, people only see the foreign face, although I'm the only foreigner working in this building. Some see it as a threat; all kinds of colonial references are taken along... on the other hand being a foreigner opened many doors because I didn't know exactly what was allowed and what wasn't... But in the end Townhouse should be an Egyptian institution.

Not so long ago, governmental galleries and the Ministry of Culture treated the private sector with suspicion. Wells says that now the state has realized that both sectors have their place, and there's therefore more co-operation. Traditionally, an artist's way to fame and fortune has been paved through governmental institutions: the Salon of Youth has been a particularly good stepping stone to stars.

Yet the independent galleries have taken more risks, and introduced young artists. They have also been more connected with foreign institutions and galleries and have organized cross-cultural work-shops and experiments. For example, artists Sabah Naim, Moataz Nasr and Wael Shawky have been sent to the Venice Biennale, by-passing government channels.[49]

As these visits attest, interest in Middle Eastern art has increased in Europe. Yet, some artists complain, abroad Egyptian artists are often categorized as a part of the Africa or Middle East section. So the works are not necessarily seen reflecting the artist's intrinsic skills, but merely his or her ethnic background. Curators, however, point out that for an up-and-coming artist it's sometimes better to become known as his area's representative – and make a name for himself later.

Although painting and sculpting are still the most popular art forms, lately we've seen local artists experimenting with photography, video art and installations. However, young artists are ambivalent towards foreign interest in their work, and about what others think that Egyptian art should be about.

Du'a Ali's installations mix modern elements with unsuspecting items such as children toys. In one exhibition, she stuffed inflatable beach toys into a plastic tube – they looked as though they were suffocating, yet they smiled inanely. In another work, a computer stands in a fresh grave, surrounded by green grass. The screen says: *It is now safe to turn off the computer*. Perhaps it was a reflection of her frustration when we worked together in the culture section of an internet magazine, which went bankrupt before it went online. After that work experience, Du'a became a full-time artist.

A diplomat's daughter, Du'a grew up both in Egypt and abroad, but got her art education in Egypt. Because foreign influences are everywhere, in commercials, films and the night-life scene, she thinks that many Egyptian artists reflect this intermediate space between the two cultures in their works. "I see this confusion in all the good artists' works, this vacillation between the different worlds. I think it depicts the state of the whole country, its identity crisis," Du'a told me.

Like many of her colleagues, Du'a thinks that the difference between Egyptian and Western artists can be explained by education; or the lack thereof. In Egypt, the quality of art education is weak, it doesn't encourage critical analysis nor provide tools for research. "If you want to look for information, you can find it in Western books. That's why Egyptian art is more emotional and spontaneous than Western art," Du'a argues. She thinks that this might be the key to understanding Egyptian art's appeal.

Egypt's first Fine Arts Institute was established in 1908, until then painting had been the hobby of the aristocracy.

The Institute's tuition was based on Western art styles and techniques. As early as the 1920s, art education was integrated into the national school curriculum and into the new Higher Institute of Fine Arts for Female Teachers (which men could join from 1947 onwards).

Nationalist sentiments characterized the Egyptian art scene in the 1930s; mixing Pharaonic symbols with rural life using Western techniques. Surrealism also had a strong presence. The 1952 Revolution undoubtedly left a mark on the fine arts: symbols of Arab unity replaced hieroglyphs; art became more politicized, reflecting Egypt's place in history with a sense of triumph. But by the 1980s political art had made way for a more abstract trend, incorporating motifs from Islamic calligraphy.[50]

The trend to more religiosity also made itself felt in the tuition: live models were banned in the 1970s. Du'a confirms that religiosity among students is also on the rise. Some students have started wearing the full-veil *niqab,* and some Salafi-influenced male students have refused to shake hands or even speak with female students. Du'a thinks that this kind of intolerance doesn't advance creativity, quite the contrary. "How can you paint reality if you are looking at it behind a veil?" she asks. That would actually be interesting – as far as I know an exhibition by a *munaqqaba,* a fully veiled artist, hasn't been shown in Cairo yet.

Notes

—

1 The practitioners of the dance and Egyptians in general use the term 'Oriental Dance' (*raqs sharqi*); the term 'belly dance' is in fact a foreign invention. I use both terms without added value.

2 See for example *The Middle East Times*, 28/2/2003; *Maydan*, 23/1/2003; *Al-Ahram Weekly*, 19–25/12/2002, Issue No. 617.

3 Nieuwkerk, 1991:121–132.

4 Zuhur, 1998:6.

5 Nieuwkerk, 1991:10–14.

6 Franken, 1998.

7 Nieuwkerk, 1991:48–49, 58.

8 'Egypt allows foreigners to belly dance', *United Press International (UPI)*, 5/9/2004.

9 Hammond, 2007:196.

10 See Danielson, 1991.

11 Saeed Okasha, 'Ode to the "Dusky Nightingale"', *Cairo Times*, 6–12/4/2000, Vol. 4, issue 5.

12 Danielson, 1991; Rodenbeck, 1998:328–331. See also Danielson, 1998.

13 Bilharzia is a common condition in Egypt, in which a parasite from the snails living mainly in Nile irrigation channels is transmitted to humans.

14 Saeed Okasha, 'Ode to the "Dusky Nightingale"', *Cairo Times*, 6–12/4/2000, Vol. 4, issue 5; Rodenbeck, 1998:334.

15 Hammond, 2007:170.

16 Injy el-Kassef, 'Ahmed Adawiya: the king is in the house', *Al-Ahram Weekly*, 8–14/2/2001, Issue No. 520. See also Armbrust, 1996.

17 *Nahdit Misr*, 5/5/2004.

18 Abdallah referred me to the survey in an interview at her office in AUC: *Youth attitudes towards Arabic video clips in Egypt*. Presented to the American Research Center in Egypt Conference on Music and Television, Cairo, Egypt.

19 Adam Sherwin, 'Would the Big Brother please leave the Arab house', *The Times*, 2/3/2004.

20 Amy Mowafy, 'Celebrity Culture, The New Arab Obsession,' *Enigma*, 7/2004.

21 Yasmine Fathi, 'Attia mania', *al-Ahram Weekly*, 15–21/4/2004, Issue No. 686.

22 Nicole Veash, 'Pop crooner hits sour note with Egyptian elite', *Christian Science Monitor*, 18/1/2002.

23 Amr Musa is Egypt's former Minister of Foreign Affairs, who was known for his anti-Israel statements. He is currently the Chairman of the Arab League.

24 Egypt Almanac, 2003:83.

25 Amira Howeidy, 'This rose has thorns', *Al-Ahram Weekly*, 14–20/12/2000 Issue No. 512.

26 *Egypt Almanac*, 2003:73–74.

27 *Egypt Almanac*, 2003:74–77.

28 Magid Fayez, 'For the good of the people', *The Cairo Times*, 11–17/3/2004, Vol. 8, issue 2.

29 Hossam Bahgat, 'Al-Azhar is wrong, but the state is the real culprit', *The Daily Star*, 23/9/2004.

30 EOHR, 1994.

31 EOHR, 1994; Amnesty International, 1998.

32 Alexander Flores, 'Secularism, Integralism, and Political Islam: The Egyptian Debate', in Beinin & Stork, 1997; Kienle, 2001:91; Elst, 1998.

33 Baker, 2003:53–59. Two men were sentenced to death and 11 got prison terms.

34 *Nisf al-Dunya*, 21/12/2003, special supplement.

35 Kienle, 2001:108–111. See also Benin & Stork, 1997:327–338, Nasr Hamid Abu Zayd interview.

36 Hossam Bahgat, 'The political gets personal,' *The Cairo Times*, Volume 5, Issue 2 – 8/2/2001.

37 Kienle, 2001:111–112.

38 Hossam Bahgat, 'Cultural house of cards', *The Cairo Times*, 18–24/1/2001, Vol. 4, Issue 44.

39 Manal el-Jesri, 'The Last Say', *Egypt Today*, 8/2004.

40 Ismail Serageldin, 'Shifting boundaries', *Al-Ahram Weekly*, 28/10–3/11/2004, no. 714.

41 UNDP: *Egypt Human Development Report*, 2008.

42 AHDR, 2002; UNDP, 2004.

43 *Egypt Almanac*, 2003:86–89; Rodenbeck, 1998:324.

44 See Elsadda, 2003.

45 *Egypt Almanac*, 2003:78–81.

46 'Spot the dinosaur', *Al-Ahram weekly*, 31/5–6/6/2001, Issue No. 536.

47 Salem, 2002.

48 The first three are renowned Egyptian authors, the latter two are Medieval Arab poets, and the Eloquent Peasant is a story preserved in ancient papyrus.

49 See *Egypt Almanac*, 2003:89–91, See, Negar Azimi, 'Aperto Cairo', *Flash Art*, 10/2004, issue no. 238.

50 Mikdadi Nashashibi, 1998.

8

Egyptian Eden

——

A German, a Frenchman, a Brit and an Egyptian went to an art museum. They stopped in front of a painting depicting Adam and Eve in the Garden of Eden. Having studied the painting, they started to argue about Adam's and Eve's nationality.

The German said: "Look at the perfection of their bodies. Eve's slender and graceful figure, and Adam's athletic, muscular body – there's no doubt that they are German."

The Frenchman intervened: "C'est impossible! Anyone can see clearly the sexuality radiating from them... the woman, so feminine, the man, so masculine... and them both so blissfully unaware of the awaiting temptation... They must be French!"

The Brit shook his head and stated: "It is not like that at all. Pay attention to the sternness of their faces, calm posture and moderation of their gestures. They can only be British."

After a quiet moment, the Egyptian protested: "I don't agree with any these theories. Look closer: they have no clothes, no

shoes, and not even a roof over their heads. The ONLY thing they
have is ONE lousy apple to eat, and even that is forbidden! They
don't protest and they STILL believe that they are in paradise! It is
obvious that those idiots can only be Egyptian!!!"

This joke, circulated via e-mail in Cairo, is telling for
Egyptians' ability to laugh at themselves – but it also sheds
light on Egypt's contemporary reality. Financial constraints,
how to acquire the daily bread is the number one issue and
headache for most Egyptians. One quarter of Egyptians live
below the poverty line, and another quarter just barely make
ends meet. This means that there are around 40 million
poor Egyptians, but who are not willing to protest. It is not
the downtrodden masses, but doctors, textile workers and
pharmacists who protest for better pay – something that was
unimaginable even as late as 2000.

The lives of the poor took a turn for the worse in 2003,
after the devaluation of the Egyptian pound. The government
wanted to take control of the black market currency exchange,
and to ease exports. On the macro-economic side, these
measures seemed to have given the hoped-for boost, but for
ordinary Egyptians, the masses, it meant dire straits. The cost
of basic goods went up by 40%, but already marginal salaries
remained the same.

The deepening economic distress prompted the government to issue ration cards in spring 2004. Even today, some
50–60 million people are eligible to receive them and buy
basic foods (cooking oil, rice, tea, macaroni, beans and pulses)
cheaper in government-run co-operative shops.[1] But people
complained that the co-op foods' quality is much worse than
in regular shops.

The Egyptian government spends about 2.5–3% of its
GDP on food subsidies, mainly bread, 'aish, which also means

'life'. This is not a co-incidence – for many, bread is the only staple they can afford, keeping them alive. On average, Egyptians eat three loaves of *baladi* bread (whole wheat pita bread about 15 cm in diameter) per day. It is usually cut in two half moons and stuffed with the basic Egyptian food: *fuul*, a thick broad bean stew, spiced with cumin and lemon.

If Egypt was the bread basket of the Roman Empire, today it produces only half of the wheat its huge population needs. Egyptians are the world's biggest consumers of wheat: they eat 183 kilograms per person every year. This makes Egypt the world's second largest wheat importer after China: it imports around 7 million tonnes, mainly from the United States, Russia and Australia.

But no one starves in Egypt as the government has an interest in keeping the citizens' bellies full. In order to maintain social stability, the government keeps the price of bread artificially low. Ever since the bread riots of 1977 (which were sparked after doubling the price of bread) the price increases have been extremely cautious and subtle. The masses may not respect the government, but they trust that it will keep prices affordable, so that even the poorest may eat. Subsidies which guarantee social complacency are not questioned, nor is the government going to stop them completely.

But the global food crisis at the beginning of 2008 had a particular effect on Egypt. After a dramatic increase of over 40% in the price of basic commodities, and a general inflation rate of at least 15%, the demand for bread went up. Queues at the government-sponsored bread kiosks started to grow and grow as a result of which people got frustrated and angry – at least ten people were killed in the scuffles.' Yet the real reason for the bread shortages was corruption. The government sells subsidized wheat flour to bakeries, but it doesn't properly control what happens to the flour after that:

officials can be bribed to turn a blind eye, and the subsidized wheat was often sold to the private sector – for a hefty profit. The queues started to shrink only after Mubarak ordered army bakeries to serve the nation.

The foreign currency Egypt needs to buy this wheat comes from four main sources: tourism, oil, the Suez Canal and remittances from Egyptians working in the Persian Gulf oil states.[3] Tourism is the most important of these sectors, and at the same time the most vulnerable. When the Middle East goes through times of unrest, Egyptian tourism officials hold their breaths. They still remember what the attack of 1997 in the Hatshepsut temple at Luxor meant: tourism collapsed completely. This led to increased security measures, and armed guards can be seen now in the main tourist attractions.

Egypt's tourism sector has changed its image: instead of the Valley of Kings or the Pyramids, Egypt is now advertised as the Red Sea Riviera. This advertising strategy has its benefits: when the Middle East makes unwanted headlines (such as the war on Iraq), the Red Sea is not necessarily associated with Egypt, and tourists keep on coming. Indeed, Egypt faired well despite the invasion of Iraq in 2003 – and several attacks on Sinai resorts. In 2008, Egypt received over 11 million tourists and $9.5 billion in revenue. When you add the sectors which benefit indirectly from tourism (transportation, the food and beverage industry, real estate and entertainment services) tourism revenues exceed 10% of GDP.[4]

The Iraq war didn't affect Suez Canal revenues – quite the contrary. Despite criticism from the opposition, Egypt allowed US warships to use the Canal en route to the Persian Gulf. The government's response to criticism was that the Suez Canal is an international waterway, which is required to be open. In 2003, 15,634 vessels passed through the Canal, and it made a record profit: $2.6 billion dollars.[5] By 2008, revenues hit another record of $4,5 billion, but subsequently piracy in Somali waters had an adverse impact, bringing revenues down by over 20% in early 2009.[6]

Most of Egypt's oil fields are in the Gulf of Suez, south of the Suez canal. The rest are scattered around the vast Western desert. Oil exports comprise around 8% of Egypt's GDP and 40% of export revenues. Current oil reserves stand at over 4 billion barrels. The reserves are, however, being rapidly exhausted and Egypt already imports most of its refined oil products, such as diesel. Egyptians use gas, oil and its derivatives wastefully because the government keeps their prices artificially low through subsidies: a litre of gasoline costs ten times less in Egypt than in the neighbouring Arab countries.[7]

The government spends about 6.5% of GDP on fuel subsidies. The system needs revamping because the same cheap fuel is available to everyone, regardless of their financial means. In a way subsidies have become entitlements for the people, so it will be very difficult to reverse them.

Were the government to remove these subsidies, riots would erupt again. Raising the price of diesel by 50% in 2004, and the subsequent price rise in bus tickets, led to fights between bus-drivers and passengers.[8] Natural gas might therefore be the answer to future energy problems – not to mention how it would reduce Cairo's notorious pollution levels. Notable gas discoveries have been made in Egypt, and production is on the rise. Compressed natural gas has been converted into car fuel, and currently some 100,000 cars run on natural gas.[9]

While the poor struggle for their daily bread, the expanding middle class demands a better quality and broader range of products. As late as the 1990s, it was difficult to find cornflakes, clothes not made of polyester, or tampons. As students in Cairo in the mid-1990s, we would make bi-monthly pilgrimages to Sunny supermarket in Zamalek, just about the only outlet with imported goods such as instant noodles, Swiss chocolate and smoked cheese.

Nowadays everything from Paul Newman salad dressing to Harley Davidson motorbikes is available. Like everywhere around the world, shopping malls have become the meeting and mating places of the youth, who like hanging out in the cafes and cinemas. Supermarkets of various types and sizes serve the middle class. But the entry of some foreign franchises wasn't so smooth. The British chain Sainsbury's stormed the scene in the late 1990s; to the dismay of small shop owners, it bought the best locales in the city with such efficiency that in two short years it had over 100 outlets.

In the beginning, it sold goods below market price in order to lure customers. This angered local merchants, and soon rumours started to circulate that the chain was Jewish-owned (which is not the case). This coincided with the second Palestinian *Intifada* and the heightened anti-Israel mood. Demonstrators attacked Sainsbury's outlets and a popular boycott against the British chain was initiated: Sainsbury's had to withdraw from the Egyptian market in 2001.[10]

Despite such events, Egyptians actually prefer imported goods to domestic ones. People still carry memories of the socialist era, and so are suspicious of the quality of domestic goods. A few years ago, I used to try buying Egyptian as much as I could, in an impromptu effort to support the local economy. The cleaning lady I had at the time protested when I tried to offer her the local *Savo* washing powder: "It will destroy your clothes!" she exclaimed. The next week she showed up with a bag of Ariel.

While my maid might buy the same washing powder as the people she works for, the gap between the poor masses and the small elite is widening. The gap is now so wide that it is sometimes difficult to conceptualize. One day, I was doing a story on the garbage collectors of the miserable Muqattam Hill in the morning, and filming a top Cairo hair stylist in his fancy salon in the evening. Those two extremes never meet.

The increasing impoverishment of the middle class puts them in a cleft stick: they are afraid of falling into the lower class, but at the same time, they cannot realistically aspire to get any higher than their financial standing. Economist Galal Amin has noted that up until 1975 the income distribution between rich and poor was much less stark than today. "Egyptian society may have come to deserve to be called a society of two nation, (*sic*) now more than any other time since, and perhaps even before, the revolution."[11]

So how does this grey mass, fully one half of the Egyptian population, make a living when there are no welfare offices around?[12] They run the unofficial economy, the so-called grey sector, which is said to comprise a third of Egypt's economy. It is the biggest employer: over 80% of Egypt's entrepreneurs are unofficial, as well as their well-over 8 million workers. Most of these companies are small, service sector companies with fewer than five employees. Their lifespan is about 10 years, and they rely upon manpower rather than technology.[13]

They are doormen, street hawkers, shoe-shiners and maids. They are the young boys and girls who will try to sell you napkins or small lemons when your taxi stops at traffic lights. Or street vendors downtown, selling clothes on the pavement, who quickly disappear when someone shouts "Police!" Many companies which look legal don't actually exist officially: entrepreneurs will tell you that working in the unofficial sector offers better chances, although they then lose many legal benefits, such as pensions. They say that the shift to the official sector is simply too expensive and difficult, which it undoubtedly is.

According to a study by The Egyptian Centre for Economic Studies, to register an Egyptian company requires 91 different transactions in 43 different instances, and it takes on average 232 days. The procedure costs LE8039, which is simply unaffordable for many start-ups. On top of these expenses, the prospective employer has to pay social security contributions, taxes and lawyer's fees. In addition, they have to cater to officials' inspections. No wonder so many of them would rather stay 'outlaw'.[14]

Yet everyone loses from such a system. According to the same study, incorporation would benefit the state, companies, and employees as well. Employers would benefit from the fact that a registered company can reach a higher market value – something few entrepreneurs are aware of. Employees stand to gain from higher salaries and better social security, while the state would receive more tax revenue. To top it all off, consumers would benefit from a better quality of products.

Overall, Egypt's economy is in transition. Nasser's socialist, state-run structures are being dismantled, slowly but surely. President Sadat initiated this trend with his 'Open Door' policy in the 1970s, when he tried to lure foreign investors to Egypt. Back then, with high oil prices, Egyptian migrant workers' remittances and foreign aid streaming into Egypt's 'liberal economy', the local economy got its much needed boost. Import-export businesses flourished, but only a few genuinely benefited from the economic recovery: nepotism, corruption and insider dealing abounded.

Coming to the 1980s, this changed – oil prices slumped and Egyptian workers in the Gulf weren't in as high demand as they had been; tourism was on a roller-coaster, and domestic economic growth slumped. Egypt had to ask for foreign assistance. This meant that it had to adopt the structural adjustment program as a condition for securing loans from the International Monetary Fund (IMF) and the World Bank (WB). After the Gulf War of 1991, the Paris Club wrote off a $10 billion loan as thanks for Egypt's support for the anti-Iraq coalition. Egypt signed up to the IMF's structural adjustment programme, which required the dismemberment and privatization of the state-run, inefficient economical structures.[15]

One of the reasons for this inefficiency is over-employment: government establishments just have too many employees. This is a remnant of Nasser's era, when the government promised to employ all new graduates. By the late 1980s, the guarantee had been abolished, but the public sector is still an attractive employer for many: salaries are twice as big as in the private sector and jobs are more secure and offer benefits like maternity leave.[16]

Public sector salaries are not based on productivity, and the sector is plagued with needless bureaucracy – as is obvious to anyone who has ever paid a visit to one of these workplaces. One illuminating example is the central post office in Ramses square, opposite the railway station. The post office is an enormous, monstrous warehouse, with dusty, long-expired conveyer belts criss-crossing below the ceiling; shelves, desks and lines and lines of filing cabinets jumbled together. I approached the first desk with my parcel slip. The employee brought the package, and I thought: "Wow, this is easy!" I spoke an hour and a half too soon.

The clerk wrote me a note and told me to go to another desk. There, another clerk wrote something on the note, and directed me to another desk. I zigzagged between these desks until my 11th transaction: payment. This desk was hidden underneath one of the conveyer belts, with a man and a woman sitting behind it. I sat down on a chair next to it, and must have sighed because the female clerk told me that I looked upset. "Well, I've been here over an hour by now, and I still don't have my parcel," I told her. "Oh yes, this place is crazy. People don't really do anything; they just pretend that they're working!" she said, laughing heartily. I've never heard a government employee admit this before.

But the state cannot just kick out the workers – a government job had been as good as winning the lottery jackpot: it's for life. Or at least that is how the thinking went until recently. Part of the economic reform programme has been the privatization of public companies. The privatization programme gained speed in 2004 after the formation of the revamped, pro-business government, which is close to the President's son, Gamal Mubarak. Companies are often sold to foreign investors, which increased fears that the new owners might not be so loyal to the Nasserist ideal. This has led to an unprecedented wave of strikes. Although, according to the Unified Labour Law of 2003, striking is theoretically legal, it needs the approval of the (ruling party NDP-dominated) General Federation of Egyptian Trade Unions. In practice, all strikes since 2003 have been illegal.[17]

The protests first started among textile sector workers of the Nile Delta city of Mahalla al-Kubra in 2006, a major textile industry centre, known for its working-class militancy since the 1930s. The strike, at the massive Misr Spinning and Weaving Company (which has 24,000 workers), was sparked by false promises of raising the workers' annual bonuses from LE100 to two months' salary. When the workers discovered that they had only been paid LE89 (after tax), thousands of workers assembled in the square across from the mill. Production lines were shut down, some of the workers staged a sit-in protest inside the factory, while thousands of other workers protested outside. State security did not intervene. On the fourth day of the protest, government officials offered a 45-day bonus, and the strike ended.[18]

The Mahalla al-Kubra strike paved the way for other protests: railway engineers, truck and microbus drivers, tax collectors, poultry farmers and circus workers. *Al-Masry al-Youm* newspaper reported 222 protests from sit-ins to hunger strikes in the year 2006 alone. Not only did the workers protest over pay, but some of the Mahalla al-Kubra strikers also demanded the establishment of an independent trade union federation. Although the government has responded to workers' monetary demands, it has made it known that it will not tolerate political requests. In 2007, an independent NGO Centre for Trade Union and Workers' Services was shut down and the government started to clamp down on protests.[19]

The situation escalated in April 2008, again in Mahalla al-Kubra. Protesters demanded more bonuses, but also protested against the general increase in prices, and so began calling for a general strike. They eventually called off the local strike, but the police (who had been gathering in the town before the strike was called) clashed with the demonstrators and a youth was shot by police. Elsewhere, a young woman called Isra' 'Abd al-Fatah set up a Facebook group calling for a general strike on 6th April. Some 60,000 Egyptians signed up to stay at home that day. 'Abd al-Fatah was subsequently seized by State Security and detained for over two weeks.

Joel Beinin, a visiting professor at AUC in 2008, is a specialist in the Egyptian labour movement and we spoke soon after the calls to strike. He assessed that the political process started by *Kifaya* in 2004 broke a whole range of taboos in Egyptian politics, and paved the way for other forms of protest.

Since the current government of Prime Minister Ahmed Nazif was installed in July 2004, there have been over 1000 strikes, sit-ins, protests of various sorts of workers. This is a number and intensity which is absolutely unprecedented. It's probably the largest mass movement in the modern history of Egypt, involving maybe half a million people. And the government's response to it for the most part has been to meet the demands. I guess they are thinking that it is better to buy people off than to try to crush them and risk having uprisings. And they have the money because the price of oil is up, and the Nazif government has increased the pace of selling the public sector.

He sees the subsequent Facebook campaign as a potentially powerful tool for change.

The Facebook protest call was an expression of youth culture, similar to what brought Muhammad Khatami of Iran to power. Egyptian society and the Egyptian state are structured to totally suppress young people. There is no public space to express themselves, there is no privacy for young people, they are compelled to show deference to older people. Facebook is a youth mechanism, (where they) found a way to express themselves – this hasn't happened before. Will it become more public than that, will there be other ways of expressing this youthful discontent? I don't know. If that does happen, then I think the combination of that and the workers' movement means the regime is in big trouble.

What started the parallel political street protests by *Kifaya* was essentially a demand to change Egypt's political system by curbing the vast executive powers of the President.[20] The constitution doesn't put a ceiling on presidential terms: indeed, President Husni Mubarak has been serving the nation continuously since 1981, and is now in his fifth 6-year-term. He is one of the longest serving heads of state in the Middle

East, and shows no sign of wanting to retire to his holiday home in Sharm el-Sheikh. He has never nominated a vice-president – he doesn't have to because the constitution doesn't require it.

The President appoints (and can dismiss) the Prime Minister and the Cabinet, all 29 Governors, the senior army and security directors, all 15 university principals and a number of other key officials. The President maintains his dominance by overseeing foreign policy, as well as all the Higher Councils (of Culture, Antiquities, Human Rights etc.), the Intelligence Services, and the Religious Affairs Department, all of which are grouped directly under the Presidency. The Prime Minister also has substantial, although subordinate, powers. By contrast, the legislative organs (Parliament and the *Shura* Council) are weak, which in practice centralizes governance in a very few hands.[21]

According to the constitution, if the President dies or is otherwise unable to fulfil his duties, the Speaker of Parliament takes over, pending elections which have to be held within 60 days. Now everyone in Egypt speculates that the President's younger son Gamal will be his successor.

Gamal Mubarak is a tall and handsome man in his forties (his hair is receding from his temples) who recently married. A former investment banker with a career in London, his entry into politics was in 2002 by nomination to the influential Policy Committee of his father's party, the omnipresent National Democratic Party (NDP). This party represented the political centre under Sadat's multiparty system of the 1970s. If one can talk about such a thing as party ideology in Egypt, then NDP is a centrist liberal party, which claims to promote a liberal economy, an element of wealth re-distribution, and guaranteeing a basic livelihood for the poorest. In reality, it is a party based on patronage and a system of favouritism, which claims to have the support of 2.5 million adherents.[22] More importantly, the NDP has become synonymous with the Egyptian state.

As well as the Parliament and the Upper House, the NDP also controls municipal politics through Popular Councils. Their composition (46,000 seats altogether) is chosen by municipal elections. The Popular Councils are overseen by Executive Councils, whose members are appointed by the central government. The Popular Councils don't actually have a lot of power, since they mainly make decisions regarding local infrastructure and social services. They have been accused of rampant corruption and not without reason: most of their budgets are re-allocated to secondary purposes such as advertisements congratulating state officials in official papers. The Councils' main purpose has been to act as the bottom rung on the ladder of the party hierarchy.[23]

Gamal Mubarak is trying – somehow – to burnish the NDP's reputation, and has been branded as the party's reformer, under the 'New Thinking' slogan. The NDP's leadership has begun talking about human rights and democracy and the need to bring in young people. About a third of Egypt's population is under 15, and the NDP would like to recruit them into party politics once they come of age. Yet these NDP reforms were little more than cosmetic, created for the sole purpose of looking good to the outside world (read: to the United States).

Although President Mubarak has denied preparing the throne for his son – by saying that Egypt is not Syria – Egyptians are not entirely convinced. The Cabinet's inner circle is close to Gamal, particularly the financial portfolios. However, while Gamal's profile is emblazoned across the state media, his supporters can't get away with everything.

When the five gold medallists from the Athens Olympics returned to Egypt, they were received by the heir apparent.

An enormous four-sided hoarding was erected on Tahrir Square, and in one of the pictures Gamal was seen shaking hands with the victorious wrestlers and boxers. NGOs and opposition papers voiced their disapproval at his picture being on view, since he has no official position, only the party committee. His picture was removed silently one night.

But the party, the NDP, has reigned supreme for over 30 years. This monopolization of politics and the myriad laws hampering other parties from functioning properly paralysed the political atmosphere – at least this was the case until the 2005 elections. Internal politics is dominated by 'stability first' thinking, few changes are allowed, or they are painstakingly slow. Egypt simply doesn't have the same vibrant political culture as in the West. The ordinary citizen has probably never even thought of joining a political party, because politics is deemed a dirty game. Most people consider elections to be fraudulent (usually with justification) and believe that money talks: you can buy yourself a seat in Parliament.

Egyptian author Alaa al-Aswany describes in his novel *The Yacobian Building* how a seat in Parliament is secured. Businessman Hagg Azzam aspires to be a candidate and goes to speak to the governing Patriotic Party's corrupt Secretary Kamal el Fouli, who registers applications. In his office, the Secretary draws a large rabbit on a piece of paper.

> "I don't understand what you mean, Your Excellency."
>
> El Fouli answered quickly, "You want to guarantee your success in the elections, and you are asking what is needed. I've drawn you a picture of what's needed."
>
> "A whole 'rabbit'? A million pounds, Kamal Bey? That's a huge amount!"

El Fouli then explains to Hagg Azzam that the sum in question is the deposit in the electoral district where he wishes to stand as a candidate.

> "You mean, if I pay that sum, Kamal Bey, I'll be sure of winning the elections, God willing?"
>
> "Shame on you, Hagg! You're talking to Kamal el Fouli! Thirty years' experience in parliament! There's not a candidate in Egypt can win without our say-so, God willing!"[24]

In the celebrated novel, the candidate does indeed make it, after a few tricks. In real life those few who do vote, vote for a person, not a party. In return, the candidate is expected to deliver concrete services to his electors, such as smoothing a business deal or getting a child into a better school – i.e. using his position to bypass bureaucracy. The legal age for voting is 18 (a candidate has to be 30 years old), but it also requires prior registration, something few are willing to do. Voter turn-out percentages have been alarmingly low, only 3–25% depending on the region. Government employees are obliged to vote – they are actually driven to polling stations in state buses during working hours.[25]

In principle, any 50-member group can set up a party, but in practice, registering it is extremely difficult. With the introduction of the multiparty system in 1977, the Committee for Political Party Affairs was established. It consists of six NDP members, and either accepts or refuses party applications. It has mainly dismissed applications – indeed, since its inception it has rejected over 60 applications and accepted only four.

Usually the reason given for rejection is that the applicant's program doesn't differ enough from the existing parties. With the Muslim Brotherhood, the official reason for rejection is that Egypt's electoral law doesn't allow parties based on religion. The real reason, of course, is that the government is afraid of its popular appeal.

In the early 2000s, nine parties managed to obtain one of those much coveted licenses, bringing the total number of official parties to 24. But most of these newcomers are now lost in political obscurity: the National Harmony Party and the Democratic Generation Party got licences in 2000 and 2001 respectively. No one's heard of them since.[26] Then, in 2004, the Committee accepted the liberal *al-Ghad* (Tomorrow), whose Chairman Ayman Nur turned out to be a serious contender for the Presidency itself.

Like the NDP, the larger and more established opposition parties are also hide-bound and run by time-honoured troikas. Despite their slogans, which are all about democracy and reforms, there is no respect for democratic principles within the parties. In general, very little information is available about party manifestos (beyond their slogans), and even less so about their membership numbers. Apart from the Muslim Brotherhood (which is not an official party) these parties don't enjoy wide popular support – they tend to be run by a small group of activists, whose main task is to publish party mouthpiece newspapers.

These groups come out of hibernation just before elections, wipe the dust off old slogans, and perhaps polish them up a bit for the sake of appearances. Since they cannot implement their programs in reality, elections become merely exercises in which the real questions are avoided, as are the real needs of the citizens. Still, whatever the parties' message may be, it is difficult to disseminate it outside the party offices due to restrictive laws and decrees, or even to hold campaign rallies or political meetings.[27]

Imad Shahin, Professor of Political Science at AUC, compares the opposition's room to manoeuvre with a football match: you have 22 players, certain agreed upon rules and a referee. Players can play all they want, but they cannot score goals. If someone does score a goal, he'll be shown a red card immediately and sent off the pitch.[28] But most of the players are in a sad state: their team captains are in their 70s, and they play against each other, as well as the other teams.

The New *Wafd* (Delegation) party is heir to Egypt's oldest party. The name and heritage are derived from the Egyptian delegation which went to the United Kingdom in 1918 to demand Egypt's independence. The delegation members also demanded social and economic reforms in their later electoral platform. In the first elected parliament of 1924 they gained a majority, and the party played a leading role in Egyptian politics until it was abolished under Nasser. It was, however, a markedly elitist, upper-class voice.

The New *Wafd* was established as a result of Sadat's multi-party experiment. It emphasizes secularism, private enterprise and good relations with the West. The secular approach has been particularly appealing to Copts, which are prominent among the party supporters. Although the party claims to have 2 million members, it doesn't really enjoy grass roots support. The party lives too much in the past and doesn't address, let alone answer, today's challenges or the needs of the younger generation.[29]

When Sadat started his multiparty experiment, *Tagammu'* (i.e. the Progressive National Unionist Party) represented the Left. It is a Marxist communist party, which was in favour of Nasser's centralized economy and social program. Nowadays it also opposes dialogue with the Muslim Brotherhood, although it has allied with it in previous elections. *Tagammu's* slogans are very close to those of the ruling party, particularly in its anti-Brotherhood stance. Yet after the collapse of Soviet Union, and the general retreat of the Left from party politics, *Tagammu'* has found it increasingly difficult to attract new members, nor has it been able to co-operate with the striking workers. Its following is allegedly only in a small circle of intellectuals. Perhaps more honestly than others, it claims to have 30,000 members.[30]

The Nasserist Party (established in 1992) lost its only seat at the last elections, but it is still one of the main players in opposition politics, particularly through its anti-establishment *al-'Arabi* newspaper. As the newspaper's name suggest, the party supports Arab socialism, sovereignty and social justice. In an age of privatization, the party is unfashionably in favour of a state-led economy, which shows that the party doesn't exactly live in this day and age. The party is wracked by internal disputes, and it doesn't enjoy grass roots support, although it claims to have 400,000 members.[31]

The newest entry into parliament is *al-Ghad* (Tomorrow) Party – with one representative in the Parliament. It finally got the much-coveted licence after three rejections. The party's first convention was held in a packed Cairo Conference Centre in 2004. The party Chairman was Ayman Nur, then only 39 years old, a former journalist and lawyer. Like many in the party, he's a former member of New *Wafd* and had previously held a seat in the Parliament as an independent. Coptic politician Mona Makram-Ebeid was elected as the party Secretary – the first and only female party secretary.

Al-Ghad calls itself a liberal party, which promotes improvements in the situation of women – 37% of its founding members were women (and 22% were Copts). It stands for a free market economy, respect for the law, good governance and good relations with the West. It also announced that it refused to take the state's party subsidies, but rather would fund the party with donations from members and supporters.[32] This suggests that many of the party members are wealthy.

It's difficult to assess whether the granting of a licence to *al-Ghad* was a sign of political opening, or simply the state's willingness to divide the opposition field even more. Critics argued that the licensing was yet another cosmetic procedure to please the US administration, and that the new party would further weaken the opposition, particularly the New *Wafd* party, because it lost members to *al-Ghad*. Mona Makram-Ebeid said that in March 2004 they had 5000 supporters, but their aim was to reach a million in time for the 2005 parliamentary elections.[33]

But there is one party above the others, and that is why it is illegal: the Muslim Brotherhood. It tries to participate in societal activities through legal means, and has participated in the Parliamentary elections since 1984 (standing as independent candidates), or by forging alliances with other parties. Egypt's political system has been termed 'restricted pluralism' – echoed in the words of the President. In 1992, Mubarak stated that neither the parties not the people are ready for a truly multiparty system. An ignorant nation might be manipulated towards dangerous thoughts – meaning Islamism.[34]

It took 13 years for Mubarak to decide that Egyptians were mature enough. Both the *al-Ghad* party and *Kifaya*, as well as the general protest movement on the streets had stated that their goal was to change the constitution so that the President wouldn't be elected by referendum on a single, parliament-nominated candidate, but rather by direct popular vote on a list of several candidates. Whether it was due to the opposition's insistence or simply Mubarak's change of mind, this is indeed what happened in 2005.

In February 2005, at the University of Menufiyya (close to Mubarak's home town) the President made a surprise announcement that Egypt would be holding historic, multi-party presidential elections in September 2005. The core of the announcement was a revision of Article 76 of the constitution, which defines how the president is elected. Previously, Egyptians could only vote 'Yes' or 'No', to a candidate approved by two thirds of the Parliament. Now the President suggested that the people could directly choose their President from several candidates – so long as they approved this fundamental change in a referendum. Egyptians were mesmerized.

But it soon dawned on everyone that this was too good to be true. The 'small print' required that independent candidates were endorsed by at least 65 Members of Parliament, 25 Members of the Shura Council (Upper House) and ten members of local councils; in addition they had to find a further 20 endorsements from any of the above. These rules wouldn't apply to legal parties, but the parties could only participate under strict conditions: they had to have been active for five years, hold at least 5% of seats in the Parliament and the Shura Council, and the party's candidate must have held a senior position for at least five years. However, these rules would apply only after the 2005 elections.[35]

The picture started to look clearer: none of the legal opposition parties had anywhere near 5% presence in the legislative bodies, so the game would remain the same. Since the Muslim Brotherhood is illegal, and it would never gain those endorsements, it, too, would be out of the presidential game for good. The NDP would keep hold of its two thirds majority, and thus continue dictating policy in the future. Once the opposition understood that this 'reform' was all hogwash, they called for a boycott of the May 25th referendum. At the same time, the Grand Mufti had declared voting in it as a religious duty.

The mood was restless on Election Day and, soon enough, news of NDP-hired thugs harassing voters began to emerge. We watched a typical example of this drama in front of the Journalist Syndicate, where a peaceful *Kifaya* demonstration was disrupted by a group of thugs. The really unnerving aspect was that the thugs seemed to target women in particular, trying to tear off their clothes. Similar incidents were reported elsewhere.[36]

But there were also some quiet pro-referendum demonstrators who were made to look like protest movement supporters, wearing orange T-shirts, *al-Ghad* party's colour of choice. We followed two of these young men and asked them how they ended up there. They looked a bit embarrassed and said someone had given them a meal consisting of half a chicken and a soft drink, and LE20 in cash.[37]

Under these circumstances, all the opposition could do was to prepare for the upcoming presidential election in September. Eventually ten contenders announced their candidacy (initially including independents such as the feminist Nawal el-Saadawi), the most prominent being *al-Ghad* party's charismatic and young Chairman, Ayman Nur. He had been stripped of his parliamentary immunity and imprisoned a month before Mubarak's surprise announcement, accused of forging party registration cards. Thanks to Western pressure, Nur was released two months later, in time to launch his presidential campaign. A talented orator, Nur was truly able to inspire people and make them believe that change was possible.

But of course it was all make-believe – everyone knew who was going to win. The NDP re-branded the incumbent as The Reformer, who was pictured relaxed, with almost a humble look in his eyes, his shirt collar slightly open, without a tie. Half way through the campaign, in July, he announced his reform package. Again, it looked too good to be true. He promised to strengthen the role of the Parliament and local administration, and create checks on the powers of the President. While the manifesto omitted proposals to guarantee the independence of the judiciary, none of the other candidates could match this kind of agenda. It was widely believed that US pressure was behind this grand gesture.[38]

According to official figures, Mubarak won 88.6% of votes, leaving Nur way behind him with 7.3% and New *Wafd's* Nu'man Gum'a with 2.8%. After being successfully defeated in the elections, on Christmas Eve 2005, Ayman Nur was sentenced to five years in prison. Nur made several appeals on health grounds (he is diabetic) and the Americans demanded his release. In February 2009 he was suddenly released, a few months before his sentence would have finished. During his incarceration, his party split in two, further fragmenting the opposition.

In the September 2005 Presidential elections, the cash-strapped opposition parties barely had the funds to run a campaign, but immediately afterwards they had to start preparing for another contest, the parliamentary elections in November and December. This time the stakes were higher than before, because of the 5% seat (which translates to a minimum of 25 seats) requirement for Presidential candidacy. Yet all eyes were on the organization which in the future wouldn't be able to field any presidential candidates: the Muslim Brotherhood.

Arguably the strongest opposition force in Egypt, the Muslim Brotherhood had 'only' 17 seats in the previous Parliament, making it the largest opposition group. But the number of seats doesn't directly relate to its power – or at least what used to be its power bases: university campuses and professional syndicates.

During the Mubarak era, the political weight of these syndicates has increased, at least until recently; the lawyers', journalists' and doctors' syndicates in particular used to be the most independent and active of them. University campus Islamist activists shifted easily into syndicate activism and leadership after graduation. For many fresh graduates, joining a syndicate was the first step in getting organized, because in most fields union membership is a prerequisite for employment.[39]

Through the unions, the Brotherhood – or the 'Islamist Trend' as it is often called – has been able to reach the educated, disregarded middle class, for whom the state has neither been able to provide jobs, nor political freedom of expression. The youngish Brothers were popular on the syndicate boards because they spoke the same language as those they helped, having gone through the same difficulties after graduation. By working in the syndicates, the Brotherhood has been able to bridge the gap between the political elite and the ordinary citizens. In other words, politics got a humane face.

Since the early 1980s, the Brotherhood has dominated the doctors', engineers' and pharmacists' unions. Although, as in other elections, the turnout has been small, the Brotherhood has been able to mobilize its supporters by offering them jobs at Brotherhood hospitals or schools – neither the state nor the other political parties have been able to match this. What also makes representatives of the Islamist trend more popular is the fact that they are considered to have genuinely higher morals than rank-and-file secular politicians.

In 1992, the Brotherhood gained a majority in the influential Lawyers' syndicate, which had until then been an island of secularism and liberalism. Their victory surprised – and shocked – many, but their victory came through only 10% of the syndicate members, those who had bothered to vote. The new syndicate Chairman was none other than Sayf al-Islam al-Banna, son of the Brotherhood founder Hasan al-Banna.[40]

At this point, the government started to wake up to the Islamist challenge, particularly when the Brotherhood showed up on another stage, demonstrating that its backbone was a wide social assistance network. In 1992, Cairo was struck by a devastating earthquake. Before the government emergency aid teams could do anything, the Brotherhood medical assistance volunteers were already erecting tents, and delivering food and medicine. The Brotherhood's scout-like efficiency prompted the Minister of Interior to say: "What is this becoming, a state within a state?"[41] This is the same line officials had used on the Brotherhood during its heyday in the 1940s. Soon enough, a new law was drafted which forbade NGOs from giving emergency aid.

While the government was able to keep the radical Islamists (*al-Jihad, al-Gama'a al-Islamiyya*) somewhat at bay, it was more difficult to extinguish the Brotherhood's grassroots appeal. So the state tried again to stem the Islamist tide with legislation. In 1993, a new law was passed which made a syndicate board election valid only if at least half the syndicate members voted in the first round, and at least a third in the second round. If these conditions were not met, the government would appoint a panel of judges to oversee the running of the syndicate. Islamist-governed unions staged demonstrations and sit-ins, but this law is still in place.[42]

Just before the 1995 elections, the government made the Brotherhood pay. A month before the elections, the Brotherhood headquarters were closed, and 136 leading members were arrested. They were accused – in military tribunals – of membership of an illegal organization, as well as supporting underground terrorist groups.

Soon after the elections, the Brotherhood's internal difficulties surfaced. The organization had been hit hard, and its activities ground to a halt, when its leading members were sent to jail. The government froze the Brotherhood-led lawyers' and engineers' syndicates, citing 'financial irregularities'. Around the same time Abu al-Ila al-Madi and some other 'younger generation' members left the Brotherhood and established *al-Wasat* (Centre) Party.

Al-Madi is from Upper Egypt, Minya, a former student union leader and Chairman of the Engineers' Syndicate. He passed my handshake test – which I regard as a measure of his emancipation – with flying colours: he grabbed my extended hand, looked me in the eye, smiled, and politely asked me to sit down in his simple office. Al-Madi bears the typical hallmarks of the educated Islamist: trimmed salt-and-pepper beard and well-fitting suit. He speaks with the literary Arabic that Islamists favour as a sign of their high education, interspersed with bursts of laughter. This is what he told me about establishing al-Wasat:

> Until 1995 we were able to control the Brotherhood's problems internally, but then came the arrests. The Old Guard refused to take concrete steps to obtain legal status for the organization. They control the whole leadership.[43]
>
> We resigned in January 1996 to establish a new organization, *al-Wasat*. We had realized that when you bring politics and religion together there is a danger. *Al-Wasat* is a pure political party. Politics without any religion is dangerous and politics with too much religion is also dangerous.

Al-Wasat has also Coptic members in its ranks – the party's ideology states that Arab-Islamic culture is also Christian culture. Yet the ideology sounds similar to what many Islamists advocate: developing voluntary institutions (such as charities), and reducing the presence of governmental institutions (strong state). In other words, the community (*umma*) and state should be separated, and the role of civil society should be strengthened. The state would reign over foreign policy, defence, police and the judiciary. The society, which would consist of voluntary associations, would take care of the rest. The state's leadership would be elected but it wouldn't have the right to rule over religious values. Women would have more rights than now: they could serve in the military or as judges.

Despite these moderate assurances, the government sees *al-Wasat* as an Islamist project and its attempts to register have been turned down. Al-Madi sees the situation like this:

> The government attitude is two-sided: on one side we don't have democracy, it's very narrow, serious parties are not accepted. On the more specific side, our background is a factor: we are from an Islamic group. But the government should make a distinction between peaceful groups and those who support violence.

The government still sees the Brotherhood as the ideological *eminence grise*, which gives it a convenient excuse to restrict its activities (particularly in the light of fighting terrorism). Usually these restrictions come to the fore before elections. Just before the 2000 parliamentary elections, a new law was adopted whereby the monitoring of polling stations was taken from the Ministry of Interior and given to judges. This reform was supposed to curb electoral fraud, which had been quite visible in the previous elections. It was believed that the Brotherhood would gain more seats – so over 200 members were arrested before the elections.

For the first time in its history, the Brotherhood nominated a female candidate, Jihan al-Halafawi from Alexandria. Although she was inexperienced in politics, her husband, Ibrahim Za'farani, is no novice. He had been the Chairman of Alexandria Doctors' Syndicate, and a three-time candidate on the Brotherhood list. He had, however, been among those arrested in the previous elections, and served a three-year prison term. As a result, in 2000 he wasn't eligible to stand, because according to electoral law, a candidate has to have enjoyed full civil rights for five years before the elections – his conviction by the military court annulled these rights.

A little before the elections, I went to see al-Halafawi in her home. She has a BA in finance and MA in theology, but she's been a homemaker for two decades. Wearing a cream-colored *khimar* veil, al-Halafawi resembled more the housewife that she is than the politician she aspired to be. We sat in the simply decorated reception room, a fan humming in the corner, moving her daughters' wedding gowns that were hung from hooks on the wall, clouds of pink lace. Shyly, al-Halafawi served Coca Cola in gold-decorated stemmed glasses, smiling incessantly.

She denied that she was participating in the elections instead of her husband, but she emphasized that she had his support. "Muslim women's role hasn't been clear-cut. Although women have all kinds of jobs, they haven't had a role in politics or in the Parliament," al-Halafawi said. Indeed, Egyptian women gained the right to vote in 1956, but only a few have been elected.

Like many Muslim feminists, al-Halafawi argues that Islam gave women political rights. "In the time of Prophet Muhammad, women participated in war, issued *fatwas*... they had an important role. I'd like to see this role expanding," she added. Yet her ideas of women's role in society follow the line of the Muslim Brotherhood: "Primarily God created women to take care of the family. But now [in the modern age] women's role has changed," she acknowledged, smiling. After her wedding she left her work at a bank and stayed at home to take care of her children. They are now adults, so she felt she could participate in societal activity.

During the campaign, her campaign manager and PR representative were arrested. She chose to go on with her programme, accompanied by her husband. On one of those evenings, Steve and I followed her campaign in the Qala'a neighbourhood of Alexandria. It is one of the countless slums of Egypt -- a poor, miserable area, beyond the reach of basic services. Unpaved roads were crowded with barefooted children running about; many buildings looked unfinished. Colourful laundry hung from racks, lit by pale street lights. Cow carcasses hung in a butcher's shop, their tails intact. He had no customers.

Although all political meetings are effectively illegal, dozens of supporters had gathered in a small square. During her speech, the crowd shouted pro-Brotherhood slogans: "Islam is our light and the Qur'an is our constitution!" After this impromptu gathering, she continued touring the neighbourhood on foot, talking with locals. Many of the faces revealed surprise and interest: the Brotherhood had a female candidate who was dressed simply and modestly, not in Western clothes like the other candidates, and more importantly, she had bothered to come to their neighbourhood. A few days later al-Halafawi's husband was arrested.

Because judges were monitoring the elections, voting inside the polling stations was reportedly fair. Yet the situation outside was completely different: according to many reports, small-time thugs (popularly known as *baltagiyya*) had been released from prisons to scare off opposition voters. In these elections, local and international media were also subjected to violence, and cameras and recorders were broken.

We met some Brotherhood members on Election Day, who promised to take us see al-Halafawi voting. First they took us to Mina al-Basal neighbourhood, where violence had been reported. Locals told us that the men agitating outside the polling station were known thugs from the neighbourhood, and that they had just been released from prison. A group of anxious Brotherhood supporters told us that they hadn't been allowed inside the polling station at all. This depiction is very typical of the kind of fraud and interference that unfortunately takes place during Egyptian elections.

One woman, dressed in jeans with her hair uncovered, told us that she was actually an NDP supporter, but even she hadn't been allowed in. Then suddenly a group of Brotherhood female supporters made a rush towards the polling station gate, but they didn't reach it because the thugs blocked their way, and beat at them. Some received a bloody lip or a torn veil. When I tried to take a picture of the scene, three men tried to grab my camera – the riot police just stood and watched, a few metres away. This is what is usually referred to as 'passive neutrality' on the part of security forces. Only when someone said the magic words 'foreign press', did the thugs then let go.

We toured some other polling stations, where fraud was visible. In one spot a veiled woman tried to vote twice. In front of another place, a truck-load of voters from Upper Egypt had shown up – they weren't allowed to vote in Alexandria, because voters are either registered in their home town or where they work. And they have to register in advance – in 2000, Egypt had almost 25 million registered potential voters.[44]

The Brotherhood supporters were so eager to show the press the worst violations that my wish to see al-Halafawi vote was dismissed. Was this an example of the Brotherhood's much-advertised emancipation? Supporting a female candidate didn't seem to be as high a priority as showing the oppression the Brotherhood suffers from. I was disappointed, and now even less convinced about their talk of equality and the importance of women's position.

To prove sceptics like me wrong, the Brotherhood fielded another female candidate, Makarim al-Dayri, Professor of Arabic literature at al-Azhar University, in the much-awaited 2005 elections. In light of the political opening and high stakes, the atmosphere was upbeat. The Brotherhood fielded 160 candidates (running as independents) – three times more than in the previous elections. Again, hundreds of Brotherhood members were arrested, but this time they were all released by the first day of voting. They formed an electoral alliance with 10 other opposition entities, agreeing for example not to run against each other. Other novelties in this election included improved judicial monitoring, transparent ballot boxes, and the use of phosphorus ink to mark voters.

During the first round, I went to see a prominent Brother, Isam al-Aryan, at the Doctor's Syndicate. He admitted that so far the voting had gone smoothly, in a new and positive atmosphere, but he wanted to wait and see if it continued until the last round. "Our goal in these elections is to revive the life in streets, encourage people to vote and restore Egypt's political and constitutional rights. Secondly, we aim to get more representatives into the Parliament, and finally, to co-operate with the rest of the opposition in order to form a Parliament which is capable of hammering out reforms." He said that if they managed to get half their candidates in, it would be an excellent result. "But if the state interferes, and we get fewer seats, we have to settle for that. If we get 50–60 seats, I'd consider it a good result."

That's exactly what happened – and more. After the first round, it became clear that the Brotherhood had already doubled its previous Parliamentary presence. Not only the government, but the Coptic minority and secularists were alarmed by their electoral landslide. The Brotherhood responded with a PR campaign to dispel fears, reassuring

Egyptian and foreign audiences that they were a moderate, democratic force.

The government wasn't convinced, and resorted to the same old trickery: polling stations were closed abruptly, hired *baltagiyya* attacked voters and the state press launched an anti-Brotherhood campaign, accusing it of orchestrating the violence. Altogether, 11 people died in election-related violence, and most of the population stayed away from the polling stations – the official turnout was about 25% of registered voters, although in reality it was probably much lower.[45] Despite this, the Brotherhood amassed a large number of seats: a historic 88 Members of Parliament.[46]

As expected, there was a price to be paid. In their victorious mood, the Muslim Brotherhood General Guide Mahdi Akif declared that the organization would participate in all upcoming elections: Municipal Councils, Shura Council, trade unions and Cairo social clubs. The government would have none of this. Municipal elections, due to be held mid-2006, were postponed for two years. Soon after, the security forces unleashed the worst crackdown on the Brotherhood since the 1960s: hundreds of members were subsequently arrested, they were blocked from entering trade union elections, travel bans were imposed on the leadership, and contacts with other opposition curtailed.[47]

In the Parliament, the Brotherhood was really under a microscope. Speculation ran wild as to what the Islamist legislators would do: would they resort to populist tactics, and ban books, beauty contests and alcohol? Did the Brothers take their votes as a mandate to further Islamize Egypt? After the initial alarm, the audience was reminded that the Brotherhood's slice of the pie was not big enough to change the policy.

While the Parliament is still largely a rubber stamp, the Brotherhood has revived the parliamentary routine. It has a pool of professionals from different backgrounds who form a so-called 'kitchen', a group of MPs specialized in different fields, who share information on the parliamentary issues at hand.[48] While the previous Parliament had become known for raising sensational moralist issues, the new one more resembles a proper political party: keeping a close watch on the NDP.

Four months after the swearing in of the new Parliament, I went to see Muhammad Sa'ad al-Katatini, the head of the Muslim Brotherhood parliamentary bloc. He admitted that the Brotherhood hadn't managed to get through any legislative proposals, so instead they have mainly requested clarifications and asked questions. "But the Parliament is not the only venue for decision-making. We have a lot of activities in our constituencies," he said, lamenting the fact that municipal elections were postponed "because the NDP wasn't ready", as he put it.

Researcher Amr Shubaki from al-Ahram Centre for Political and Strategic and Studies was positively surprised by their performance:

> Their numbers allow them to act as a kind of motor for balanced politics. They have put pressure on the government on issues such as the spread of bird flu, issues dealing with freedom of expression – and have not said a word about shari'a. This is a bloc which is against corruption, wants to solve the financial problems, the problem of transparency... They have understood that the main issue is political and financial reform, not laying down punishments suggested by its members in the past. They have indeed been good politicians.

Then the Brotherhood did something very stupid – although it is not known how much the leadership knew about the event beforehand. A group of al-Azhar university students staged a martial arts show, wearing Hamas-style black ninja costumes, complete with hoods. It was meant to be a show of defiance to the security forces, present to prevent students from rioting, after they were blocked from the student union elections.

The media had a field day, and speculations about a reactivated armed wing, the Secret Section (*al-jihaz al-sirri*) ran wild – also in the independent media. This 'al-Azhar militia' case led not only to the arrest of the students, but also of several prominent Brotherhood politburo members, including prime financier and Brotherhood-government go-between, Khayrat al-Shatir. Mubarak ordered him – and several others – to be tried in a military tribunal. They were eventually sentenced to seven years in prison. But there was no outcry from the West: with the violent Hamas takeover in Gaza and Hizbollah's war with Israel fresh in their minds, the global mood wasn't favourable towards Islamist pursuits.

These arrests and, crucially, cutting the cash flow was a heavy blow to the Brotherhood. Soon after the arrests, I paid a visit to the Brotherhood parliamentary bloc's office, not too far from their main headquarters. Once the elevator doors closed, Qur'anic recitation escorted the lone passenger. As the doors opened, the familiar sight of carpets greeted me, and the polite request to remove my shoes. Two MPs, Sa'ad al-Husayni and Mahmud Amir were waiting, both wearing grey suits, looking like any Egyptian MP.

Al-Husayni noted that the latest crackdown was different from previous occasions, because of the financial aspect. "Many people are suffering now because companies cannot pay their employees, they have had to close and the workers' families are in anguish." Several publishing houses, import-export firms and others were closed, and merchandise was confiscated. These losses were estimated at tens of millions of pounds.[49]

The al-Azhar incident had prompted the President to call the Brotherhood "a threat to the nation". He warned that if the Brotherhood ruled Egypt, foreign investors would flee and Egypt would become isolated from the rest of the world. "The al-Azhar events were a sports performance and the security officials know this very well. It has been used as a tool to strike back at us," Mahmud Amir pitched in. "But is it true that the Brotherhood still has a secret paramilitary wing?" I asked. "No, it's not true. If we had one, the security forces would know about it. There isn't anything in Egypt that the security doesn't know about!" he exclaimed.

The MPs – and many analysts – believe that the real reason for the crackdown was the President's urge to push through a package of constitutional amendments in a referendum, set for March 2007. The government didn't want the Brothers – or the opposition as a whole – to make noise or to demonstrate. The amendments were supposed to be the fulfilment of Mubarak's electoral promises of reform, but instead they further cemented one-party authoritarian rule in Egypt. While it was already written in the electoral law, it is now *unconstitutional* to have a political party based on religion – a tool clearly aimed at further curbing the Brotherhood's ability to participate in political life. For, in January, the Brotherhood had declared that it would seek a licence to establish itself as a political party.

"But surely there's no hope of getting the party registered?" I prompted the Brothers-in-suits. Al-Husayni laughed and asked his colleague to answer. "We will present the application to the party committee and it is up to them to decide," Amir stated the obvious. "But they have rejected all the applications until now," I said. They both laughed. Obviously they knew it was a lost cause from the start. It seemed more like a move from the Brotherhood, publicly challenging Mubarak to make good on his promises. But the al-Azhar incident had damaged the Brotherhood's media image, so no one at first seemed to take the party pledge seriously.

The other constitutional amendments included the formation of an 'electoral commission' instead of judicial supervision for voting. This was another setback to the judiciary, which had previously confronted the government on electoral fraud. The two prominent judges who had presented these charges had been taken before a disciplinary court in mid-2006. Because of their prestige, this measure prompted an unprecedented show of popular support and weeks of protests. Eventually they were just reprimanded, but the new amendment curtailed the judiciary's authority and independence. In 2009, a pro-government candidate was elected to lead the Lawyers' syndicate.

Yet perhaps the most controversial amendment was Article Number 179, the new Anti-Terror Law. It gives the security apparatus even wider powers to arrest, confiscate, wiretap and search terrorist suspects without warrants. Now the President's power – under the Emergency Law – to refer civilian cases to military courts, is written into the permanent constitution. Human rights organizations noted that the amendments basically annulled the right to privacy, to a fair trial, and it grants impunity to human rights violators. At the time of writing, this law hasn't yet been approved.

These measures marked the end of the Cairo Spring. There was less tolerance of street demonstrations, and the *Kifaya* movement slowly disintegrated. It had focused too much on one issue, Mubarak's re-election, and didn't manage to formulate a positive, constructive reform initiative. Thanks to the government's divide and rule strategy, opposition forces are not used to co-operating, so the momentum was lost. But the struggle has largely moved from the streets into cyberspace, which the state cannot control as much – a fact that didn't go unnoticed within the Brotherhood.

Despite the realization that the current regime would never allow the Brotherhood to register as a party, they went ahead with publishing their first party platform in summer 2007. It was first presented for internal debate, and to select journalists and analysts, but soon enough causing uproar not only from outside critics, but also inside the Brotherhood. The most controversial issues were the notions that women or Copts wouldn't be allowed to be the President of Egypt, and the formation of an 'ulama (religious scholars) council. It would advise the legislative and executive branches in matters touching upon shari'a, and its rulings would be binding.[50]

These ideas reveal that not much of substance has changed in the Brotherhood's thinking since the days of Hasan al-Banna. Their claims of emancipation for women come alive only in the run up to elections, in order to win some brownie points by appointing female candidates. Their high-handed treatment of religious minorities raised further fears among the Copts, who were already experiencing an upsurge in sectarian violence. I wanted to know what the Coptic thinker, Rafiq Habib (who often rubs shoulders with the Brothers), thought about the platform. Unlike the majority of Copts, he was very understanding:

> The Muslim Brotherhood thinks that the state will be responsible for organizing the Islamic field, to protect Islam in the society. They think that the responsibility will not be on the state, but on the one person who is the head of the country's administration: the President. So they think that it's logical that no Christian can handle this kind of responsibility. Anyone can handle the political responsibilities of the President, but for this Islamic responsibility he must be a Muslim because it will contradict with your doctrine.

These same points sparked a debate inside the Brotherhood, among the different generations.[51] Particularly the young Brotherhood bloggers criticized the organization's decision to seek party licence and complained that the platform didn't reflect their worldview. One of them was thirty-year-old 'Abd al-Munaym Mahmud, who blogs under the name *Ana Ikhwan* (I'm a Brother). He is also a journalist at the opposition paper *al-Dustur* (The Constitution).

We met in early spring 2009 at a popular middle-class coffee shop in Zamalek. He was wearing a denim shirt, jeans and white sneakers and he apologized profusely for being late. He looked like any other guy in the coffee shop, except he was more serious, yet relaxed and polite. He ordered an orange juice while I sucked my guava juice through a straw, like a teenager.

Altogether, there are at least 160 Brother (and Sister) bloggers entering the space which was, until very recently, the sole domain of Leftist activists. Mahmud has been a Brother since an 'early age', as he put it. Like the other Brotherhood bloggers, he wants to stay within the organization, and try to reform it from within rather than to repeat the *al-Wasat* party mistake by seceding.

He started his blog in 2006 – prior to that he had been detained twice, for several months each time. "The third time was in 2007. I had been in this very coffee shop, talking with people from Amnesty International, and then the state security came to my house and arrested me the same evening!" he told me and laughed. He spent the following two months in detention – a much shorter period than the previous incarcerations. I can never get over the ease with which political activists speak of their ordeals – perhaps looking back on it helps. His blogging during the party platform debate put him into the limelight again.

They might change the *'ulama* council, it wasn't a good idea. What they won't change is the eligibility to the Presidency of a Copt or a woman. My opinion is that anyone can run, and Egyptians can choose who they want.

What differs between us and the older generation are the inventions of our time. The previous generation didn't have internet or blogs where you can talk. But there has been criticism inside the Brotherhood before, for example [General Guide] Hasan al-Hudaybi's critique of Sayyid Qutb [in the 1960s]. But our criticism is more visible because anyone can see it on the net, whereas before the criticism was inside the organization.

The differences of opinion are not based on age, on the contrary. There are some young Brothers who are very radical, and the same can be said about some older members. So it doesn't depend on age, it depends on upbringing and openness to the society. We joined the Brothers in order to work with the rest of the society, not so that we can stay in a room and read the Qur'an and listen to speeches – no, we want to go out. This is the main difference.

Yet he says that the Brotherhood bloggers have the endorsement of the General Guide – the latest crackdown had a lot to do with it. "Akif sees blogging as something positive because it breaks the security confinement of the Brothers. My relationship with the leadership has improved lately," Mahmud said. A month after we spoke, the Supreme Guide had a surprise, something his age-sake, Mr President, would never dare to declare: he would step down from his life-time position.

In 2004, Muhammad Mahdi Akif, a former gymnastics teacher, was 75-years old when he was appointed to the post on the death of his predecessor. Akif has been a Brother since the 1940s, and like many of his fellow Brothers has spent his prime years in prison, 20 years in all. I've met him only once, soon after his swearing in. The atmosphere was like being in the Headmaster's office, as if I had been playing truant. With stoic posture, Akif gave impatient answers, accusing the United States of interfering. At the time, the Brotherhood was lying low, the defensive mood of post 9/11 still very much present.

To this day, the Brotherhood engages a great deal in charitable work, it runs its own schools and hospitals. Akif didn't want to talk about the charities in detail, because after 9/11 Islamic charities got a bad name. "Ask about this from Bush, because he wants to stop the work of charities and calls them terrorist groups. They call those who oppose American and Zionist terror, the friends of truth, as terrorists, although America herself is the cradle of terrorism!" Akif exclaimed, his voice getting louder.

No one knows for sure what their membership base is exactly. Estimates run from 20,000–30,000 full members, to 200,000 supporters, mostly concentrated in northern Egypt. During the 2006 elections, the prominent Brother Isam al-Aryan (who is known for giving independent statements) confronted the governmental daily al-Ahram's figure of half a million members. "We don't keep a register. But one day, if we get a legal status, we will give those numbers. And the figure will be higher." The blogger Mahmud was more in line with the academic estimates. "The Brothers don't want to reveal membership numbers for security reasons, but also they would find out that the numbers are not big, they are maximum 200,000–300,000 in all of Egypt." He reminded me that it takes a long time and several steps to become a full member.

Despite these numbers, the government still sees the Brotherhood as a threat. Now the government has more leverage to deal with them and Western pressure is not there anymore. But the situation was very different in the not too distant past, in the post 9/11 world and Bush's grandiose Greater Middle East plan.

At onset of the Iraq war, Egypt was afraid of not only its economic but its political effects. What if Iraq became the cradle of Middle East democracy – would Egypt lose its leading role in the region? Would the US take Iraq as its new partner? Would Americans occupy other Arab countries? These fears have turned out to be premature and the region's dictators have slowly drifted back to their Sleeping Beauty dreams. Compared to the Iraq of today, the other Arab countries are havens of calm, stability and security. Why then idly rock the boat with too many reforms? It would just confuse the masses. It would be better to administer the medicine one drop at the time, these leaders seem to think. Yet it was the foreign pressure that made Egypt change the rules of the game – for a little while.

In the aftermath of the Gaza war in 2009 and Egypt's failed attempts to work out a prisoner exchange deal with Hamas and Israel, I went to see Hussam Zaki, the spokesman at the Ministry of Foreign Affairs. He expressed optimism about the new American administration's approach to the Middle East. I asked him how he saw the dark Bush years' effect on the region and Egypt.

> Some people in the previous American administration thought that regime change was the order of the day. Egypt was very cautious from the beginning – it was not clear to us where the Americans want to take the region. It seemed like a trip to the unknown, really. Naturally, if you talk about the need to open up societies and to introduce more changes – this is not the right way to do it. These processes are supposed to grow from within, not imposed from the outside.
>
> Obviously the approach that the previous American administration adopted was not the optimal one. It didn't address

> the root causes of the problems, it coerced rather than convinced,
> it was not about dialogue. Egypt is a different story – at least in
> regional issues there was a dialogue, but on those internal matters
> we were very clear that there is no dialogue that we are going to
> sustain with the administration because we refused the way they
> looked at issues. And it continued… the collision sometimes.

Despite the criticism, Egypt cherishes its strategic partnership
with the United States, and Egypt has been a solid partner
in the tumultuous Middle East. Launched in 2002, the US
Middle East Partnership Initiative is based on the theory that
by liberalizing the economy and strengthening civil society,
reasons leading to terrorism will be dispelled. The United
States calls for democratization, pluralism and educational
reform. Although the situation hasn't been quite as alarming
as in, for example Saudi Arabia, some schools in Egypt have
also preached extremist thoughts, and some text books contain
old-fashioned information and harmful stereotypes.[52]

Yet the reasons and definitions of terrorism are seen quite
differently. Arab countries argue that the conflict between the
Palestinians and Israel is the root cause for resistance; local
NGOs say it is the dictatorial regimes. For example, not all
Arab countries like Hamas, but they do not think that it is
a terrorist organization, rather it has the legitimate right to
fight illegal occupation. By comparison, the United States and
the European Union have both listed Hamas as a terrorist
organization. The Egyptian regime does not like it, mainly
because it is a branch of its nemesis, the Muslim Brotherhood.

The EU initiative, the Barcelona Process – started in
1995. It emphasizes peace and stability, the importance of
dialogue in political and security questions. The EU initiative
seems to stem from the idea that once neighbouring areas
are developed, security threats diminish. In other words,
the European Union wants to open borders for free trade, but

at the same time build a barrier against immigrants coming from outside EU borders.

These reform initiatives have also referred to the UNDP *Arab Human Development Report*, which was first published in 2002. The report team consisted of top researchers from different Arab countries, and the results were alarming, although not entirely unexpected: the region lags behind the rest of the world in various fields. Economic growth is slow, and corruption rampant. Arab countries don't participate in world economy or international financial institutions. Education is merely learning by rote. Women are shut off from society, and half of them are illiterate, more often unemployed than men, and they are not represented in decision-making bodies.[53]

There have been attempts to explain the weakness of the Arab world as a result of superpower politics, and particularly the Israeli-Palestinian conflict. Because, throughout their independence, Arab countries have been in virtual readiness for war with Israel, reforms have been delayed. Most resources have been used for the arms race, at the expense of education and developing civil society. This scenario has served the authoritarian regimes well: the nation has been forced to form a unified front against the external enemy.

The main difference between the initiatives is that the United States was looking for fast, strong solutions and it did not really tackle cultural dialogue. It wanted to change the Arab world's societies, not the regimes. The European Union, on the other hand, favours a slower, softer approach and co-operation in the fields of economy, education and culture. The European Union would also be more willing to include moderate Islamists in dialogue, because they are undoubtedly one of the main political forces in the Arab world, and they cannot be ignored in the future either. Yet there is still a debate over what kind of groups can be included – most likely only groups who deny violence and adhere to democratic principles.[54]

But where are the Arab leaders? Critics have pointed out that they don't really want change, but instead they prefer to talk about reforms while keeping the status quo – this is certainly the case for Egypt. The Arab League objected to these initiatives at first, but then decided to answer the challenge by proposing their own reform program.

Toothless and weak, the Arab League went through a facelift when Egypt's former Minister of Foreign Affairs, the veteran politician Amr Musa was elected as its chairman in spring 2001. Some speculated that Musa had been too articulate in his criticism of US support for Israel, so he was sent to 'cool off' in the 22-member Arab League. Yet, the organization's profile has greatly improved with Musa at its helm. After Musa took over, the central Cairo headquarters were painted, and its long-stuck clock started working again. Yet inside, the League is still bureaucratically rigid, over-crowded, and its member states owe it some $100 million.[55]

In its declarations, the Arab League has stated that the Arab states are committed to respecting human rights and the freedom of expression. The pan-Arab organization confirms that the Arab states are expanding political and public participation, strengthening all components of civil society and widening women's participation in all fields. The catch-phrase here is also cross-cultural dialogue, with the emphasis on the human side of Islam, of tolerance and peaceful coexistence. Islam should not be confused with terrorism, the Arab League states.[56]

It is, of course, altogether a different issue how individual Arab countries implement these lofty principles. What difference do politicians' word-mongering and declarations make to the life of an ordinary Arab? Not a whole lot. These reform initiatives don't include the needs of ordinary people – to them it is more important to have food on their tables than to have a political reforms. This gives the regimes another excuse not to lift their fingers.

Egyptians love to complain, and to rant about their miserable fate, but they love their country. Despite human rights violations and lack of real reforms, Egypt is still a relatively free and liberal country. And it still hasn't lost its crucial, if not central, role on the Arab stage, particularly as a mediator between the Palestinians and Israel. Nasser tried to bring the Arabs together with pan-Arabism and Arab socialism; but Sadat pushed other Arabs away after Egypt signed the peace treaty with Israel. In hindsight, Sadat's mistake was that the treaty remained only between the two countries (Jordan signed its own peace agreement in 1994), and that the Palestinian state still doesn't exist.

After the Yom Kippur war, Sadat badly wanted the Sinai Peninsula back, which was occupied by Israel. The peace treaty with Israel was supposed to bring an end to Israel's occupation in all areas it took over in 1967 and to solve the Palestinian issue. In his historical speech at the Knesset on 29 November 1977, Sadat said:

> An interim peace between Egypt and Israel, or between any Arab confrontation state and Israel, will not bring permanent peace based on justice in the entire region.
>
> Rather, even if peace between all the confrontation states and Israel were achieved in the absence of a just solution of the Palestinian problem, never will there be that durable and just peace upon which the entire world insists.[57]

The Arab world's harsh response came a week later: the Arab League condemned Sadat's visit as a "great betrayal of the sacrifices and struggle of our Arab people in Egypt and their armed forces" and demanded that the member states should freeze their contacts with Egypt and with companies and individuals who do business with the Zionists.[58]

Despite the Arab boycott, President Sadat and Israeli Prime Minister Menachem Begin signed the Camp David Treaty, hosted by President Jimmy Carter on 17 September 1978. This brave and historical deed won Sadat and Begin Nobel Peace Prizes the same year. A year later, the two parties formally signed a peace treaty in the White House. According to the Treaty, Israel promised to withdraw from the Sinai and the countries restored diplomatic relations. Negotiations on the West Bank and Gaza and Palestinian autonomy were supposed to start a month after the signing. This didn't happen.[59]

Sadat's successor Husni Mubarak was left with trying to patch up the bad relations with Egypt's fellow Arab states. He eventually succeeded in this mission, and in 1989 the Arab League Headquarters returned to Cairo from Tunis. Egypt's relationship with Israel has not been warm, to say the least. During the optimism surrounding the Oslo Process, relations got warmer, but now they are so chilly that the peace treaty is called the 'Cold Peace'. The depths of this Cold Peace came in 2000 when Egypt recalled its ambassador in the wake of the second Palestinian *Intifada*. President Mubarak has visited Israel only twice, once for the funeral of the assassinated Prime Minister Yitzhak Rabin in 1995 – and once before while he was still the Vice President.

I asked the Foreign Ministry spokesman Hussam Zaki how he would define the peace between Egypt and Israel.

It is a correct peace. It is peace that is at the service of both countries, and of the question of stability in the region. We are engaging with the Israelis in ways that serve bilateral interests and also our role in the Palestinian question. We have to be very careful not to do anything that would either harm bilateral relations or harm our role in the region in general or with the Palestinian question in particular. In the end, peace is an outcome of popular interaction as well. Not only is it an agreement signed between two governments. If you go around in Egypt and ask if they want to engage in peace with Israel, I think you would find a lot of people that are reluctant to do that, primarily because of the issue of Palestine.

Zaki is correct about the mood of the people. The Egyptian press is often openly anti-Israel (and anti-Jewish in general): in daily cartoons, Israelis are compared to Nazis and the now comatose Ariel Sharon has been depicted as a pig with a swastika on his forehead. The neighbours have modest trade relations (about $44 million/year), even though co-produced products from Qualified Industrial Zones (QIZ) enjoy reduced custom duties when sold to the US market.[60] Despite terror attacks in the Sinai, Israeli tourists bring some income to the Sinai.

In its foreign policy, Egypt has played the role of moderator, the messenger of peace. At least one signpost artist has been inspired by Egypt's role. Near the Pyramids, next to a dirty Nile canal where women wash their laundry and clean their dishes in brown water, is a signpost resembling a traffic sign. In white letters on a blue background, is printed – in English – the phrase "Egypt is the leader of peace." The Foreign Ministry spokesman Hussam Zaki had a similar message. "Egypt holds the monopoly of the middle ground in the region. People have to realize that this is a country that pursues peace, stability and prosperity for the region."

Stability, indeed. In the pursuit of 'stability', the Egyptian regime has grossly violated human rights and curbed the opposition. People don't trust the government and they always expect the worse. The Cairo Spring ended in 2006, leaving activists depressed, and all hopes for reform buried. EIPR's Hussam Bahgat is one of them. He captures the prevailing mood perfectly:

> The only reason that the political forces, the reformists are not completely in despair is that there is at least the tenuous hope of the post-Mubarak era. That's the one thing keeping people at least remotely interested or intrigued, or wondering what will happen next. Had it not been for Mubarak's old age in these last years in power, it would have been really depressing, like what happened in Syria with their crackdown of the Damascus spring.

The publisher, Hisham Kassem, was a bit more optimistic. He has left *al-Masry al-Youm* and was finalizing the business plan for a new newspaper, his true brainchild.

> There was a momentum created, there was space gained. In lots of cases this whole movement for reform predates the Bush years. While the government pushed back a little, it did not push back all the way. It's becoming clear that the regime in doing so has acquired itself a very bad name internationally. And of course while there are things like this Gaza thing [Israel's three-week attack in 2009] – it was very good for Mubarak. He's the corner stone of stability in the region!
>
> There is no doubt that Mubarak is successfully blocking things, or as much as possible – he's a genius I have to say. But the next person will have to make a decision quickly: does he try to sustain a legacy that's very difficult to sustain?

We were sitting in his living-room, and BBC Arabic was on. There was a live broadcast from Khartoum after the International Criminal Court announced the arrest warrant for Sudan's President Omar al-Bashir. Kassem said that he had just watched how a Sudanese ambassador had tried to defend the Sudanese position. "What a job!" Kassem exclaimed, shaking his head and laughing.

> The case is behind closed doors with anybody on the Mubarak team now. They're just working to sustain this man. Mubarak has a reason: 27 years of economic mismanagement, human rights abuses and corruption – perfect Pinochet [scenario] if things go wrong. The next guy has five years before he raises the personal enmity of media, politics etc. So if things go wrong for him when he does an opening up – which is much easier than sustaining the Mubarak regime – I think he would try and open up the system. He's smart enough – considering that I think it's Omar Suleiman.

Kassem is referring to Omar Suleiman, the Egyptian chief negotiator and the head of intelligence. He is only five years younger than Mubarak, and the majority of Egyptians believe that the President is looking for younger blood – his son. Gamal Mubarak's friends and colleagues swear that he only wants to work within the party, and doesn't seek the presidency. Gamal himself has repeated this several times. No one really knows what the big post-Mubarak plan is, but the armed forces will have their say in it. Since 1952 all Presidents have been from the military, so key officers might not accept a civilian and someone so young.

So uncertainty prevails, and Egyptians are a nation in waiting. Some think that Egypt is a pressure cooker, waiting to explode. Others say that Egyptians prefer to wait and see, rather than raise hell. The former Israeli Minister of Defence with the trademark eye patch, Moshe Dayan, once said that he wouldn't be afraid of Egyptians if they acquired nuclear weapons, but he would get nervous if Egyptians stopped telling jokes about themselves and others.[61] This joke making rounds in Cairo perfectly sums up the Egyptian mood:

Bush, Putin and Mubarak were holding a three-way summit in an undisclosed location when God appeared to them. "I came here to warn you: Doomsday will come the day after tomorrow," God said. All three leaders hurried home.

Bush addressed his nation on television, broadcast from the Oval Office. "My Fellow Americans, I have good news and bad news. The good news is that God really exists, just like I've been telling you all along. The bad news is that Doomsday will fall upon us tomorrow."

Putin also appeared on television from the Kremlin. "Comrade Russians, I have two pieces of bad news for you. First, God exists, unlike what we've been telling you since the Soviet times. The other bad news is that we will all die tomorrow."

Finally it was time for Mubarak's appearance, broadcast from the confines of his holiday house in Sharm el-Sheikh. "Ladies and Gentlemen, Honoured viewers, I have two pieces of good news to deliver you. The first one is that God truly exists and we had a consultation together. The other good news is that I will be Your President until The End."

Notes

——

1 Summer Said, 'Govt. to issue ration cards', *Business Monthly*, 4/2004.

2 Vodafone Egypt admitted that, at the government's request, they had provided communication data to identify rioters. http://news.zdnet.co.uk/itmanagement/0,1000000308,39614610,00.htm.

3 In the fiscal year 2003/4, Egyptians living abroad sent home $2.999 billion. Most of it was sent from the US ($1.111 billion), Saudi Arabia coming second ($951 million), 'Ex-pat remittances surpass $2.9 billion', *Business Monthly*, 12/2004.

4 Egyptian Center for Economic Studies, quoted in OBG, 2004; *Egypt Almanac*, 2003:238; http://www.eturbonews.com/3710/egypt-tourism-continues-winning-streak-releases-2008-projections.

5 OBG, 2004.

6 http://www.zawya.com/Story.cfm/sidKUN0014090320083026/Suez%20Canal%20Posts%20Highest%20Revenues%20In%20'08.

7 Daliah Merzaban, 'Fossil Fuel', *Business Monthly*, 5/2003.

8 Yasmine El-Rashidi, 'Cheap cars, costly buses', *al-Ahram Weekly*, 16–22/9/2004, issue no. 708.

9 http://www.egas.com.eg/Egyptian_Natural_Gas/Expanding_gas_print.htm.

10 'Age of the hypermarket', *Business Middle East, Economist Intelligence Unit*, 1–31/12/2004, vol. XII, no. 22.

11 Amin, 2004:131.

12 Egypt doesn't have a welfare system, but various laws govern retirement and disability pensions. The amount depends on the fees paid into the pension fund, the minimum being LE50–100. In the fiscal year 2001/2 7–8 million citizens received a pension.

13 Galal, 2004. By comparison, at the time of the study, the private sector employed 6.8 million, and the public sector 5.9 million.

14 Galal, 2004.

15 Amin, 2004:140–144; Kienle, 2001:155–156.

16 Hassan & Sassanpour, 2008.

17 Joel Beinin and Hossam al-Hamalawy, 'Egyptian Textile Workers Confront the New Economic Order', *Middle East Report Online*, March 25, 2007.

18 Ibid.

19 Joel Beinin & Hossam el Hamalawy, 'Strikes in Egypt Spread from Center of Gravity', *Middle East Report Online,* May 9, 2007.

20 Egypt's constitution is a mixture of Islamic, French and British legislation. Islamic law is enforced within the framework of family law (see Chapter 2), while other areas of law adhere to secular principles.

21 *Egypt Almanac*, 2003:137–138.
22 AUC political science professor Imad Shahin's lecture at a seminar by Finnish Institute in the Middle East (FIME), Cairo, 27/11/2004.
23 *Egypt Almanac*, 2003:142.
24 Al Aswany, 2004:82–84.
25 Only sports club elections have a high voter turnout, but only members are eligible to vote.
26 *Egypt Almanac*, 2003:154.
27 Wickham, 2002:68–92.
28 AUC political science professor Imad Shahin's lecture at a seminar by FIME, Cairo, 27/11/2004.
29 Mustafa el-Sayyed, 'Honorable past', *al-Ahram Weekly*, 19–25/10/1995, issue no. 243; also Imad Shahin's lecture.
30 'Seeking a new style', *al-Ahram Weekly*, 2–8/11/1995, issue no. 245; also Imad Shahin's lecture; Beinin & el-Hamalawy, MERIP May 9, 2007.
31 Several authors, *al-Ahram Weekly* 9–15/11/1995, issue no. 246; also Imad Shahin's lecture.
32 See for example Mona el-Nahhas, 'Younger politics', *al-Ahram Weekly*, 11–17/11/2004, issue no. 716.
33 Mona Makram-Ebeid's lecture at the FIME seminar, Cairo 28/11/2004.
34 For previous Brotherhood elections, see Abed-Kotob, 1995:328; Azzam, 1996:110–111; Wickham, 2002:66–67.
35 See for example International Crisis Group (ICG): *Reforming Egypt: In Search of a Strategy*. Middle East/North Africa No.46 – 4 October 2005.
36 This prompted some women to establish a movement called The Street is Ours, arguing that women have a right to be visible in the streets.
37 According to official figures, the referendum passed by 82.8% of votes cast, with 53.6% of registered voters showing up. These figures were criticized by the political opposition and the respected Judges Club.
38 ICG, 2005:23–24.
39 Wickham, 2002:180–181.
40 Wickham, 1997:120–123; Wickham, 2002:199.
41 Chris Hedges, 'Cairo Journal, After the Earthquake, a Rumbling of Discontent', *The New York Times*, 21/10/1992; Wickham, 1997:130.
42 Wickham, 1997:130–133; Abed-Kotob, 1995:329.
43 We spoke in 2001, when the General Guide was Mustafa Mashur, who had belonged to the secret apparatus, and al-Madi said Mashur's clique still had a militant mentality.
44 International Institute for Democracy and Electoral Assistance, http://www.idea.int/vt/region_view.cfm?CountryCode=EG.
45 Issandr El Amrani: 'Controlled Reform in Egypt: Neither Reformist nor Controlled', *Middle East Report Online*, December 15, 2005.
46 The other opposition seats went to: New *Wafd*, 6, *Tagammu'*, 2, and *al-Ghad*, 1 seat.

47 ICG (2008): 8–11.

48 Samer Shehata and Joshua Stacher, 'The Brotherhood Goes to Parliament', *Middle East Report,* Issue no. 240, Fall 2006.

49 Samer Shehata and Joshua Stacher: 'Boxing In the Brothers', *Middle East Report Online,* August 8, 2007.

50 See Nathan J. Brown, Amr Hamzawy, 'The Draft Platform of the Egyptian Muslim Brotherhood: Foray Into Political Integration of Retreat Into Old Positions?', *Carnegie Papers,* Middle East Series No. 89, January 2008.

51 The Brothers are often said to belong to four generations: First, the oldest and most conservative, General Guide Mahdi Akif's generation; the second is the conservative element of the 1970s generation, such as Deputy General Guide Muhammad Habib; third is the reformists like Isam al-Aryan, and the fourth generation are the young tech-savvy Brothers. See Joshua Stacher, 'The Brothers and the Wars', *Middle East Report,* Issue no. 250, Spring 2009.

52 http://mepi.state.gov/.

53 *Arab Human Development Report,* 2003.

54 Finnish Institute of International Affairs, 2004.

55 *Egypt Almanac,* 2003:148.

56 Tunis declaration 2004, http://www.arabsummit.tn/en/tunis-declaration. htm.

57 Sadat's speech, Laquer & Rubin, 2001:209.

58 Laquer & Rubin, 2001:215–218.

59 See for example Heikal, 1996:245–289; Shlaim, 2001:352–383. Egypt receives about $2 billion in financial and military aid from the United States as part of the Camp David peace agreement with Israel.

60 'US, Israel and Egypt to set up free-trade link', *Agence France Presse (AFP),* 7/12/2004.

61 Saeed Okasha, 'That's not funny', *The Cairo Times,* 31/8–6/9/2000, issue 25, vol. 4.

Acknowledgements

——

This book was first published in Finnish in March 2005. I would like to thank Lawrence Wright, who encouraged me to write a book. As for the English version, I want to thank my publishing editor Dan Nunn for taking up the project. And I'm grateful to James Spencer who proofread the English translations and made valuable comments.

For names appearing in the book, mostly I have used the guidelines specified by the Finnish standardization union, but used well-known forms (e.g. Gamal Abdel Nasser), or the spelling the person concerned uses in print (e.g. Saad Eddin Ibrahim, Nawal el-Saadawi). I use "g" to represent the Arabic "j" (pron: "dz"), as this is the way it is pronounced in Egypt (e.g. *higab*, not *hijab*).

In addition I would like to thank the following: Marja-Liisa Aarnio, Nanna Ahlmark, Negar Azimi, Hussam

Bahgat, Gry Ballestad, Katherine Bray, John Edwards, Issandr El Amrani, Mandi Fahmy, Helen Gambold, Pascale Ghazaleh, Hisham and Hadil Ghunaim, Maria Golia, Guissa Gray, Hussam al-Hamalawi, Heidi Huuhtanen, Andreas Indregard, Falastin Ismail, Ferida Jawad, Kirsti Kaasinen, Aleksi Kalliomäki, Hisham Kassem, Anna-Leena Lohiniva, Philip Luther, Neil MacDonald, Kate Massey, Adil 'Abd al-Munaim, Steve Negus, Louise Nissen-Stigsgaard, Heli Oksanen, Päivi Paappanen, Irmeli Perho, Leena Reikko, Minna Saarnivaara, Mohamed H. Samy, Paul Schemm, Yasmeen Siddiqui, Dana Smillie, Lubna al-Tabai, Rauli Virtanen, Elijah Zarwan.

Bibliography

— ·—

Literature

Abed-Kotob, Sana (1995). 'The Accommodationists Speak: Goals and Strategies of the Muslim Brotherhood of Egypt', *International Journal of Middle East Studies*, Vol. 27, No. 3.

Abu-Lughod, Lila (1998). 'The Marriage of Feminism and Islamism in Egypt: Selective Repudiation as a Dynamic of Postcolonial Cultural Politics', in Abu-Lughod, Lila (ed.), *Remaking Women. Feminism and Modernity in the Middle East*. Cairo: American University in Cairo Press.

Ahmed, Leila (1992). *Women and Gender in Islam. Historical Roots of Modern Debate*. New Haven & London: Yale University Press.

Amin, Galal (2002). *Whatever Happened to the Egyptians? Changes in Egyptian Society from 1950 to the Present*. Cairo: American University in Cairo Press.

Amin, Galal (2004). *Whatever Else Happened to the Egyptians? From the Revolution to the Age of Globalization.* Cairo: American University in Cairo Press.

Armbrust, Walter (1996). 'Popular Culture and the Decline of the Egyptian Middle Class', *The Journal of the International Institute*, Vol. 3, No. 3, Summer 1996, University of Michigan.

Al-Aswany, Alaa (2004). *The Yacoubian Building.* Cairo: American University in Cairo Press.

Atiya, Nayra (1984). *Khul-Khaal. Five Egyptian Women Tell Their Stories.* Cairo: American University in Cairo Press.

Ayubi, Nazih (1991). *Political Islam. Religion and Politics in the Arab World.* London and New York: Routledge.

Azzam, Maha (1996). 'Egypt: The Islamists and the State Under Mubarak', in Sidahmen, Abdel Salah and Ehteshami, Anoushiravan (eds.), *Islamic Fundamentalism.* Colorado: Westview Press.

Badran, Margot (1993). 'More than a Century of Feminism in Egypt', in Tucker, Judith (ed.), *Arab Women. Old Boundaries, New Frontiers.* Bloomington: Indiana University Press.

Badran, Margot (1996). *Feminists, Islam and Nation. Gender and the Making of Modern Egypt.* Cairo: American University in Cairo Press.

Badran, Margot and Cooke, Miriam (1990). *Opening the Gates. A Century of Arab Feminist Writing.* Bloomington: Indiana University Press.

Baker, Raymond William (2003). *Islam Without Fear. Egypt and the New Islamists.* Cambridge, Massachusetts and London: Harward University Press.

Al-Banna, Hasan (1990). *al-Mar'a al-Muslima.* Cairo.

Baraka, Iqbal (2004). *al-Hijab. Al-Ru'iya 'asriyya.* Cairo: Dar al-Hilal.

Basyouny, Iman Farid (1997). ' "Just a Gaze." Female Clientele of Diet Clinics in Cairo: An Ethnomedical Study', *Cairo Papers in Social Science*, Vol. 20, No. 4, Winter. Cairo: American University in Cairo Press.

Beinin, Joel & Stork, Joe (eds.) (1997). *Political Islam. Essays from the Middle East Report*. New York: I.B. Tauris.

Carré, Olivier and Michaud, Gérard (1983). *Les Frères Musulmans: Egypte et Syrie, 1928–1982*. Paris: Julliard.

Commins, David (1994). 'Hasan al-Banna (1906–1949)', in Rahnema, Ali (ed.), *Pioneers of Islamic Revival*. London and New Jersey: Zed Books.

Cooper, Artemis (1989). *Cairo in the War 1939–1945*. London: Penguin Books.

Dalrymple, William (1998). *From the Holy Mountain. A Journey in the Shadow of Byzantium*. London: Flamingo.

Danielson, Virginia (1991). *Shaping tradition in Arabic song: The career and repertory of Umm Kulthum*. University of Illinois, PhD thesis, quoted at http://almashriq.hiof.no/egypt/700/780/umKoulthoum/biography.html.

Danielson, Virginia (1998). 'Performance, Political Identity, and Memory' in Zuhur, Sherifa (ed.) *Images of Enchantment. Visual and Performing Arts of the Middle East*. Cairo: The American University in Cairo Press.

Dekmejian, Hrair R. (1985). *Islam in Revolution. Fundamentalism in the Arab World*. New York: Syracuse University Press.

Egypt Almanac. The Encyclopedia of Modern Egypt. (2003). Cairo: Egypto-file Ltd.

Elsadda, Hoda (2003). 'Revisiting Popular Memory and the Construction of Gendered Identity: The Story of a Project', *Middle East Women's Studies Review*, Vol. Xvii, Nos. 1 & 2, Spring/Summer 2003.

Elst, Koenraad (1998). 'The Rushdie Rules', *Middle East Quarterly*, 7/1998, Volume V, No. 2.

Esposito, John L. (1994). *Islam. The Straight Path*. Oxford and New York: Oxford University Press.

Esposito, John L. (2002). *Unholy War. Terror in the Name of Islam*. Oxford and New York: Oxford University Press.

Faraj, Muhammad Abd al-Salam (1991). 'Al-Farida al-Gha'iba', in Ahmed, Rifa'at Sayyid, *Al-Rafidun*. London: Riad al-Rayyis Books Ltd.

Franken, Marjorie (1998). 'Farida Fahmy and the Dancer's Image in Egyptian Film', in Zuhur, Sherifa (ed.), *Images of Enchantment. Visual and Performing Arts of the Middle East*. Cairo: The American University in Cairo Press.

Galal, Ahmed (2004). *The Economics of Formalization: Potential Winners and Losers from Formalization in Egypt*. Egyptian Center for Economic Studies, Working Paper No. 95, March 2004, Cairo.

Ghannam, Farha (2004). 'Quest for Beauty. Globalization, Identity, and the Production of Gendered Bodies in Low-income Cairo', in Sholkamy, Hania and Ghannam, Farha (eds.), *Health and Identity in Egypt*. Cairo: The American University in Cairo Press.

Al-Ghazali, Zainab (1994). *Return of the Pharaoh. Memoir in Nasir's Prison*. Translated by Mokrane Guezzou. Wiltshire: The Cromwell Press.

Ghoussoub, Mai (2000). 'Chewing Gum, Insatiable Women and Foreign Enemies: Male Fears and the Arab Media', in Ghoussoub, Mai and Sinclair-Webb, Emma (eds.), *Imagined Masculinities. Male Identity and Culture in the Modern Middle East*. London: Saqi Books.

El-Gibaly, Omaima; Ibrahim, Barbara; Mensch, Barbara S.; and Clark, Wesley H. (1999). *The Decline of Female*

Circumcision in Egypt: Evidence and Interpretation. Population Council Working Papers.

Golia, Maria (2004). *Cairo, City of Sand.* Cairo: American University in Cairo Press.

Gordon, Joel (1996). *Nasser's Blessed Movement. Egypt's Free Officers and the July Revolution.* Cairo: American University in Cairo Press.

Hafez, Sherine (2001). 'The Terms of Empowerment: Islamic Women Activists in Egypt', *Cairo Papers in Social Science,* Vol. 24, No. 4, Winter 2001. Cairo: The American University in Cairo Press.

Hämeen-Anttila, Jaakko (translation) (1997). *Koraani.* Jyväskylä: Gummerus Kirjapaino Oy.

Hämeen-Anttila, Jaakko (2001). *Koraanin selitysteos.* 2nd edition. Helsinki: Basam Books.

Hammond, Andrew (2007). *Popular Culture in the Arab World. Arts, Politics and the Media.* Cairo: The American University in Cairo Press.

Hassan, Mohamed and Sassanpour, Cyrus (2008). 'Labor Market Pressured in Egypt: Why is the Unemployment Rate Stubbornly High?', *Journal of Development and Economic Policies,* July 2008.

Heikal, Mohamed (1973). *Nasser the Cairo Documents.* London: New English Library.

Heikal, Mohamed (1983). *Autumn of Fury: the Assassination of Sadat.* London: Deutsch.

Heikal, Mohamed (1996). *Secret Channels. The Inside Story of Arab-Israeli Peace Negotiations.* London: HarperCollins Publishers.

Hiro, Dilip (1989). *Holy Wars. The Rise of Islamic Fundamentalism.* New York: Routledge.

Hoffman, Valerie (1985). 'An Islamist Activist: Zaynab al-Ghazali', in Fernea, Elizabeth Warnock, *Women and the Family in the Middle East. New Voices of Change.* Austin: University of Texas Press.

Hoffman-Ladd, Valerie J. (1987). 'Polemics on the Modesty and Segregation of Women', *International Journal of Middle East Studies*, Vol. 19, No. 1. Cambridge: Cambridge University Press.

Ibrahim, Saad Eddin (1980). 'Anatomy of Egypt's Militant Islamic Groups: Methodological Note and Preliminary Findings', *International Journal of Middle East Studies*, No. 12, 1980. New York: Cambridge University Press.

Ibrahim, Saad Eddin and Lethem Ibrahim, Barbara (1998). 'Egypt's Population Policy: The Long March of State and Civil Society', in Jain, Anrudh (ed.), *Do Population Policies Matter? Fertility and Politics in Egypt, India, Kenya and Mexico.* New York: Population Council.

Ibrahim, Sonallah (2002). *The Committee.* First published in Arabic in 1981 as *al-Lajna.* Cairo: American University in Cairo Press.

Karmi, Ghada (1996). 'Women, Islam and Patriarchalism', in Yamani, Mai (ed.), *Feminism and Islam. Legal and Literary Perspectives.* Reading: Ithaca Press.

Kent, Carolie and Franken, Marjorie (1998). 'A procession through time. The zaffat al-'arusa in three views', in Zuhur, Sherifa (ed.), *Images of Enchantment. Visual and Performing Arts of the Middle East.* Cairo: The American University in Cairo Press.

Kepel, Gilles (1993). *Muslim Extremism in Egypt. The Prophet and Pharaoh.* Berkeley: University of California Press.

Kienle, Eberhard (2001). *A Grand Delusion. Democracy and Economic Reform in Egypt.* London and New York: I.B. Tauris.

Laqueur, Walter and Rubin, Barry (eds.) (2001). *The Israel-Arab Reader. A Documentary History of the Middle East Conflict.* New York: Penguin Books.

Lewis, Bernard (2002). *What Went Wrong? Western Impact and Middle Eastern Response.* London: Phoenix.

Mahfouz, Naguib (2001). *Adrift on the Nile.* Cairo: American University in Cairo Press.

Meinardus, Otto F.A. (1999). *Two Thousand Years of Coptic Christianity.* Cairo: American University in Cairo Press.

Mikdadi Nashashibi, Salwa (1998). 'Gender and Politics in Contemporary Art', in Zuhur, Sherifa (ed.), *Images of Enchantment. Visual and Performing Arts of the Middle East.* Cairo: The American University in Cairo Press.

Mitchell, Richard P. (1969). *The Society of the Muslim Brothers.* London: Oxford University Press.

Moghadam, Valerie M. (1993). *Modernizing Women. Gender and Social Change in the Middle East.* Boulder and London: Lynne Rienner Publishers.

Mubarak, Hisham (1997). 'What Does the Gama'a Islamiyya Want?', in Beinin, Joel and Stork, Joe (eds.). *Political Islam. Essays from the Middle East Report.* New York: I.B. Tauris.

Muhammad Ahmad, Makram (2003). *Mu'amara am Muraja'a. Hiwar ma'a qada la-tatarruf fi sijn al-'aqrab.* Cairo: Dar al-Shorouq.

Negus, Sanna (2002). 'Egyptin maltillinen Muslimiveljeskunta ja radikaalit taistelijat', in Juusola, Hannu and Huuhtanen, Heidi (eds.), *Uskonto ja Politiikka Lähi-idässä.* Helsinki: Gaudeamus Kirja.

Nelson, Cynthia (1996). *Doria Shafik, Egyptian Feminist. A Woman Apart.* Cairo: American University in Cairo Press.

Nieuwkerk, Karin van (1996). *"A Trade Like Any Other".* *Female Singers and Dancers in Egypt.* Cairo: The American University in Cairo Press.

Palva, Heikki (2002). 'Islam ja kuningasvalta Saudi-Arabiassa', in Juusola, Hannu and Huuhtanen, Heidi (eds.), *Uskonto ja Politiikka Lähi-idässä.* Helsinki: Gaudeamus Kirja.

Perho, Irmeli (1998). 'Mamelukit, osmanit, mogulit ja safavidit', in Palva, Heikki and Perho, Irmeli (eds.), *Islamilainen kulttuuri.* Helsinki: Otava.

Qutb, Sayyid (1993). *Ma'alim fi al-Tariq.* 16th edition, Cairo.

Qutb, Sayyid (1995). *al-Adala al-Ijtima'iyya fi al-Islam.* 14th edition. Cairo.

Ramadan, Abdel Azim (1993). 'Fundamentalist Influence in Egypt: The Strategies of the Muslim Brotherhood and the Takfir Groups', in Marty, M. and Appleby, A. (eds.), *Fundamentalisms and the State: Remaking Polities, Economies, and Militance.* Chicago: University of Chicago Press.

Rodenbeck, Max (1998). *Cairo the City Victorious.* London: Picador.

El-Saadawi, Nawal (1997). *The Nawal el-Saadawi Reader.* London: Zed Books.

El-Saadawi, Nawal (1999). *A Daughter of Isis.* London: Zed Books.

Salem, Ali (2002). 'My Drive to Israel', *Middle East Quarterly*, Vol. IX, No. 1, Winter 2002.

Sayyid Ahmed, Rifa'at (1991). *Al-Rafidun.* London: Riad al-Rayyis Books Ltd.

Al-Sayyid Marsot, Afaf Lutfi (1985). *A Short History of Modern Egypt.* Cambridge: Cambridge University Press.

Shaarawi, Huda (1986). *Harem Years. The Memoirs of an Egyptian Feminist (1879–1924).* English translation, editing and foreword by Margot Badran. New York: Virago Press.

Shaarawi, Huda (1990). 'Pan-Arab Feminism (1944)', in Badran, Margot and Cooke, Miriam, *Opening the Gates. A Century of Arab Feminist Writing.* Bloomington: Indiana University Press.

Shahd, Laila S. 'An Investigation of the Phenomenon of Polygyny in Rural Egypt', *Cairo Papers in Social Science*, Vol. 24, No. 3, Fall 2001. Cairo: The American University in Cairo Press.

Shlaim, Avi (2000). *The Iron Wall, Israel and the Arab World.* London: Penguin Books.

Solihin, Sohirin Mohammad (1991). *Copts and Muslims in Egypt. A Study on Harmony and Hostility.* Broughton Gifford, Wiltshire: The Islamic Foundation and Cromwell Press Ltd.

Sullivan, Earl. L. (1986). *Women in Egyptian Public Life.* Cairo: The American University in Cairo Press.

Tripp, Charles (1994). 'Sayyid Qutb: The Political Vision', in Rahnema, Ali (ed.), *Pioneers of Islamic Revival.* London and New Jersey: Zed Books.

Trofimov, Yaroslav (2007). *The Siege of Mecca.* New York: Doubleday.

Wakin, Edward (2000). *A Lonely Minority: The Modern Story of Egypt's Copts.* Lincoln: iUniverse.com.

Weaver, Mary Anne (2000). *A Portrait of Egypt. A Journey Through the World of Militant Islam.* New York: Farrar, Straus and Giroux.

Wendell, Charles (transl.) (1978). *Five Tracts of Hasan al-Banna (1906–1949): A selection from the Majmuat Rasail al-Imam al-Shahid Hasan al-Banna.* Berkley: University of California Press.

Whitaker, Brian (2006). *Unspeakable Love. Gay and Lesbian Life in the Middle East.* Berkeley and Los Angeles: University of California Press.

Wickham, Carrie Rosefsky (1997). 'Islamic Mobilization and Political Change: The Islamist Trend in Egypt's Professional Associations', in Beinin, Joel and Stork, Joe (eds.), *Political Islam. Essays from the Middle East Report*. London and New York: I.B. Tauris.

Wickham, Carrie Rosefsky (2002). *Mobilizing Islam. Religion, Activism, and Political Change in Egypt*. New York: Columbia University Press.

Wright, Lawrence (2002). 'The Man Behind Bin Laden. How an Egyptian doctor became a master of terror', *The New Yorker*, Issue 16/9/2002.

Wright, Lawrence (2006). *The Looming Tower. Al-Qaeda and the Road to 9/11*. New York: Alfred A. Knopf.

El-Zanaty, Fatma & Way, Ann (2001). 'Egypt Demographic and Health Survey (DHS) 2000'. Calverton, MD: Ministry of Health and Population [Egypt], National Population Council, and ORC Macro.

Zuhur, Sherifa (1992). *Revealing Reveiling*. Albany: State University of New York Press.

Zuhur, Sherifa (ed.) (1998). *Images of Enchantment. Visual and Performing Arts of the Middle East*. Cairo: The American University in Cairo Press.

Newspapers and magazines
Al-Ahram Weekly
Business Middle East, Economist Intelligence Unit
Business Monthly
The Cairo Times
Christian Science Monitor
The Daily Star
Daily Telegraph
Egypt Today

Enigma
Flash Art
The Guardian
Al-Hayat
Al-Masry al-Youm
The Middle East Times
Nahdit Misr
New York Times
The New Yorker
Newsweek
Nisf al-Dunya
The Observer
Al-Sharq al-Awsat
Washington Post

Other sources

Amnesty International (AI). *Egypt: Human rights abuses by armed groups.* AI Index: MDE 12/22/98.

Amnesty International. *Torture remains rife as cries for justice go unheeded*, 28/2/2001.

Amnesty International. *Country Report Egypt*, 2004, 2008.

Arab Human Development Report (AHDR), 2003.

CEWLA (2002). *Garai'm al-Sharaf. Nazra tahliliyya wa ru'i mustaqbaliyya.* Magmu'a Bahithin.

CIA, *Factbook Egypt* 2003, 2004.

EIPR (2004). *Freedom of Belief and the Arrests of Shi'a Muslims in Egypt.*

Egyptian Organization for Human Rights (EOHR) (1994). *Freedom of opinion and belief: restrictions and dilemmas. Proceedings of the workshop on the Azhar's censorship of audio and audiovisual productions, organized by EOHR.*

EOHR (2002, 2007). *The Situation of Human Rights in Egypt, Annual Report* (English summary).

Finnish Institute of International Affairs. *Arab reforms and the challenges for EU policies,* conference report 16–17/9/2004. Espoo: Otamedia OY.

Human Rights Center for the Assistance of Prisoners (HRCAP) (2001). *Torture in Egypt. A Judicial Reality.*

HRCAP (1999). *The Price of dignity! Torture in Egypt is a judicial reality.*

HRCAP (2001). *Torture in Egypt. A Judicial Reality.*

Human Rights Watch (HRW) (1995). *Middle East, Egypt.*

Human Rights Watch (HRW). *Egypt, Security Forces Abuse of Anti-War Demonstrators.* Vol. 15, No. 10, November 2003.

Human Rights Watch (HRW) (2004). *In a Time of Torture. The Assault on Justice In Egypt's Crackdown on Homosexual Conduct.*

Human Rights Watch (HRW). *Divorced from Justice. Women's Unequal Access to Divorce in Egypt.* Dec. 2004, Vol. 16, No. 8 (E).

Human Rights Watch (HRW). *Mass Arrests and Torture in Sinai.* February 2005, Vol. 17, No. 3 (E).

Human Rights Watch (HRW). *Black Hole: The Fate of Islamists Rendered to Egypt.* May 2005, Vol. 17, No. 5 (E).

International Crisis Group (ICG). *Islamism in North Africa II: Egypt's opportunity.* Middle East and North Africa Briefing, 20 April 2004.

International Crisis Group (ICG). *Reforming Egypt: In Search of a Strategy.* Middle East/North Africa No. 46, 4 October 2005.

International Crisis Group (ICG). *Egypt's Sinai Question.* Middle East/North Africa Report No. 61, 30 January 2007.

International Crisis Group (ICG). *Egypt's Muslim Brothers: Confrontation or Integration?* Middle East/North Africa Report No. 76, 18 June 2008. *Middle East Report*

Oxford Business Group (OBG). *Emerging Egypt 2004, The annual business, economic and political review.*

Reporters Sans Frontières. *Egypt Annual Reports.*

Suomen kehitysyhteistyö (2003). *Ulkoasiainministeriö.* Porvoo: Uusimaa OY, 2004.

UNDP and the Institute of National Planning (2004). *Egypt Human Development Report. Choosing Decentralization and Good Governance.*

UNDP and the Ministry of Planning (2004). Millennium Development Goals Second Country Report, Egypt.

UNDP (2004). *Development Cooperation Report Egypt.*

UNDP (2008). *The Millennium Development Goals. A midpoint assessment.*

UNDP (2008). *Egypt Human Development Report. The role of civil society.*

United Nations Human Development Report 2003.